W9-AGQ-129

Learn
VBScript

Learn VBScript

In a Weekend

Jerry Lee Ford, Jr.

Premier
Press

© 2002 by Premier Press, Inc. All rights reserved. No part of this book may be reproduced or transmitted in any form or by any means, electronic or mechanical, including photocopying, recording, or by any information storage or retrieval system without written permission from Premier Press, except for the inclusion of brief quotations in a review.

Premier

P

Press

The Premier Press logo, top edge printing, related trade dress, and In a Weekend, are trademarks of Premier Press, Inc. and may not be used without written permission. All other trademarks are the property of their respective owners.

Publisher: Stacy L. Hiquet

Marketing Manager: Heather Buzzingham

Managing Editor: Sandy Doell

Acquisitions Editor: Todd Jensen

Project Editor: Elizabeth A. Agostinelli

Editorial Assistant: Margaret Bauer

Technical Reviewer: Zac Hester

Copy Editor: Linda Seifert

Interior Layout: Bill Hartman

Cover Design: Christy Pierce

Indexer: Johnna Dinse

Proofreader: Suzannah Walker

Microsoft, Windows, Internet Explorer, WordPad, Microsoft Word, Calculator, Notepad, VBScript, ActiveX, and FrontPage are trademarks or registered trademarks of Microsoft Corporation. Netscape is a registered trademark of Netscape Communications Corporation.

Important: Premier Press cannot provide software support. Please contact the appropriate software manufacturer's technical support line or Web site for assistance.

Premier Press and the author have attempted throughout this book to distinguish proprietary trademarks from descriptive terms by following the capitalization style used by the manufacturer.

Information contained in this book has been obtained by Premier Press from sources believed to be reliable. However, because of the possibility of human or mechanical error by our sources, Premier Press, or others, the Publisher does not guarantee the accuracy, adequacy, or completeness of any information and is not responsible for any errors or omissions or the results obtained from use of such information. Readers should be particularly aware of the fact that the Internet is an ever-changing entity. Some facts may have changed since this book went to press.

ISBN: 1-931841-70-5

Library of Congress Catalog Card Number: 2001099845

Printed in the United States of America

02 03 04 05 RI 10 9 8 7 6 5 4 3 2 1

To Mary, Alexander,
William and Molly

Acknowledgments

There are a number of individuals who deserve credit for their work on this book. I especially want to thank Todd Jensen, who served as the book's Acquisitions Editor, and the book's Project Editor Elizabeth Agostinelli. I also want to acknowledge the book's Copy Editor, Linda Seifert and its Technical Editor, Zac Hester and everyone else at Premier Press for all their hard work.

About the Author

Jerry Lee Ford, Jr. is an author, educator, and an IT professional with 14 years experience in information technology, including roles as an automation analyst, technical manager, technical support analyst, automation engineer, and security analyst. Jerry is a MCSE and has also earned Microsoft's MCP and MCP + Internet certifications. In addition, he has a Masters in Business Administration from Virginia Commonwealth University in Richmond, Virginia. Jerry is also the author of seven other books, including *Learn JavaScript in a Weekend* and *Microsoft Windows Shell Scripting and WSH*. He has over five years experience as an adjunct instructor teaching networking courses in Information Technology. Jerry lives in Richmond, Virginia with his wife, Mary, and their children William, Alexander, and Molly.

CONTENTS AT A GLANCE

CONTENTS

INTRODUCTION

Congratulations on the purchase of this book and on your decision to learn how to program using VBScript. *VBScript* is a powerful but easy-to-learn scripting language that you can use to perform a number of useful activities, including enhancing your web pages and automating repetitive or complex desktop and system tasks.

You may be wondering if you can really learn how to program using VBScript in a single weekend. The answer is yes. Now I am not saying that you will be a VBScript programming expert come Monday morning, but if you sit down on Friday evening and dedicate yourself to this task for the rest of the weekend, you'll come away with all the basics and be well on your way.

In addition to teaching the VBScript programming language, this book will show you how to integrate your VBScripts into HTML pages so that you can jazz up and add interactivity to your web site. You'll also learn about the Windows Script Host (WSH) and how you can write VBScripts that work with the WSH to automate any number of Windows tasks. Not only will you have a lot of fun but you'll also find that you can become more productive and efficient.

What This Book Is About

This book is about VBScript. I have written it to teach you how to write your own VBScripts. Whether you are an experienced programmer or a first timer, you will find everything that you'll need to know to begin using VBScript to improve your web pages and automate the chores you regularly perform on your own computer.

This book will provide you with all the information and background that you'll need to get started. By the time Monday morning rolls around you will have learned.

- ✿ The basic syntax and programming statements that make up the VBScript language
- ✿ How to add interactivity to your web pages with VBScripts using pop-up dialogs
- ✿ How to add graphic effects to your web pages
- ✿ How to validate HTML forms and email yourself their contents
- ✿ How to detect the type and browser version that visitors to your web site are using
- ✿ How to advertise and display messages in banners on your web pages
- ✿ How to create VBScript cookies that store and retrieve information about the people that visit your web site
- ✿ How to integrate VBScripts with the WSH to automate a number of system tasks, such as creating new user accounts and managing your printer
- ✿ How to combine VBScript with another scripting language into Windows Script Files that allow you to leverage the strengths of both scripting languages
- ✿ How to use VBScript and the WSH to read and write to files and create logs and reports

- How to use VBScript and the WSH to work with the Windows Start Menu, shortcuts and the Quick Launch bar
- How to debug your VBScripts

Who Should Read This Book?

I wrote this book for anyone who wants to learn how to spice up his or her web pages or become more efficient by automating tasks on his or her Windows computers. This book was written for people new to VBScripting or programming in general, although it also provides an ideal quick start guide for more seasoned programmers who want to learn VBScript.

The only prerequisites are an understanding of basic computer concepts, a little experience with HTML, and some hands-on experience working with Internet Explorer and a Microsoft operating system. This means that you should already know how to manually perform such tasks as creating Windows shortcuts, moving and copying files and folders, and configuring the Windows Start menu. If you think that you could use a HTML refresher, you might want to first take a look at Premier Press's *Learn HTML In a Weekend*.

Of course, things will go quicker if you already have experience with another programming language, such as Visual Basic on which VBScript is based. However, this is not a prerequisite. Every programmer has to start learning someplace and VBScript makes a great first programming language. This book will provide you with a complete review of VBScripting basics and provide a variety of examples needed to get you going.

What You Need to Begin

Unlike some programming languages such as C++ or Visual Basic, VBScript does not require that you master a full-blown *integrated development environment* or *IDE*. In fact, all you really need to write VBScripts is a text editor that can save your files as plain text. This not only makes the learning curve a lot less steep, but also makes script development a straightforward process.

The following list outlines the tools that you will need to complete this book.

○ **A Windows computer**. You will need a computer running a Windows 95 or later operating system. All the examples that you will see in this book use Windows XP Home Edition or Windows XP Professional.

○ **Internet access**. If you plan to use VBScript in web page development then you'll need Internet access so that you can upload your web pages to your web site.

○ **The Internet Explorer browser**. VBScript works with the Microsoft Internet Explorer browser. You need the browser to test your web pages and see if your VBScripts are running as you expect.

○ **A web site host**. If you do not already have a web site set up, then you can probably arrange for your ISP to host your web pages. In addition, there are plenty of free web page hosting sites on the Internet that you can sign up with.

○ **WSH and VBScript 5.6.** If you are running Windows XP you already have this version of WSH. Otherwise you should download this version from **msdn.microsoft.com/scripting**.

○ **A text editor**. Any text editor that can save your scripts as plain text files will do. For example, the Windows Notepad application can be used. However, you will probably want to find yourself a more advanced script editor that features things such as the color coding of your script statements, syntax checking, and script templates.

○ **A graphics editor**. This tool will allow you to create graphics images that you can then incorporate into your web pages. However, it is optional and you may be able to get by without any graphics or by using free graphics that can be found on the Internet.

How This Book Is Organized

This book has been designed to allow you to read it in just seven sittings over the course of a weekend. Of course, you can read it any way that you wish. It begins on Friday evening where you'll learn the basic concepts of VBScript programming and continues into Saturday where you'll learn the programming statements that make up the VBScript language as well as how to add VBScripts to your web pages. The book ends on Sunday where you'll spend the day learning how to use VBScript and the WSH.

A more detailed outline of the organization of the book follows.

- **Friday Evening: "Introducing VBScript."** This chapter provides the conceptual framework that you'll need to complete the rest of the book. You'll be presented with a list of ideas of the kinds of things that you can do using VBScript. You'll also find a brief history of VBScript and a comparison of VBScript to the other languages in the Visual Basic programming family. Before the chapter ends you'll see your first VBScript examples and learn how to use VBScript to enhance your HTML pages and increase your efficiency when working with Windows operating systems.

- **Saturday Morning: "An Introduction to VBScript Programming."** This chapter provides you with your VBScript programming foundation. First, you start by learning about VBScript syntax. Then you learn the basic programming statements that make up the VBScript language. Among the VBScript programming constructs that you will learn about are constants, variables, expressions, conditional logic, looping, procedures, arrays, and the use of pop-up dialogs.

- **Saturday Afternoon: "Scripting Inside Internet Explorer."** This chapter introduces you to object-oriented programming and explains the VBScript object model. You learn about objects and their properties and methods. In addition, you review the most commonly used objects and learn how to incorporate them into your VBScripts. You also learn about browser events and how you can use VBScript to react to them and create interactive web pages.

○ **Saturday Evening: "Web Page Tricks."** This chapter continues the discussion on integrating VBScripts into your web pages. Here you will find specific examples of how to use VBScript to take control of the Internet Explorer Status bar and to perform an assortment of tricks, including the creation of navigation menus and graphics rollover effects. You also find examples that show you how to work with pop-up dialogs, as well as how to validate the contents of HTML forms and bake VBScript cookies.

○ **Sunday Morning: "Working with the Windows Script Host."** This chapter explains how the Windows Script Host works and how you can configure its operation. You also get exposed to a little XML to show you how to combine VBScript with other scripting languages into Windows Script Files. The chapter ends with an introduction to the WSH object model and explains how you can use it to create truly powerful scripts.

○ **Sunday Afternoon: "Working with Files and Folders."** This chapter shows you how to use VBScript and the WSH to take control over the Windows file system. You learn how to copy, move, and delete files and folders. You learn how to create new files and write to them. You also find out how to open them back up and read or modify their contents. By the time you finish this chapter you'll know everything that you'll need to begin creating log files and reports.

○ **Sunday Evening: "Desktop, Computer, and Network Automation."** This chapter presents a number of topics that will show you how you can automate various Windows tasks. An example of what you learn includes how to create shortcuts, work with Windows applications, and configure the Windows Start menu. You'll also see examples of how to perform advanced system administration tasks, including how to read Windows event logs, manage printers and stop and start Windows services.

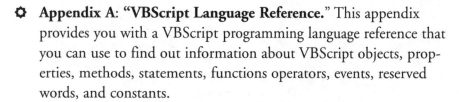

- **Appendix A**: **"VBScript Language Reference."** This appendix provides you with a VBScript programming language reference that you can use to find out information about VBScript objects, properties, methods, statements, functions operators, events, reserved words, and constants.

- **Appendix B: "What's on the Web Site."** This appendix gives you a primer about what is on the book's companion web site.

- **Glossary:** A consolidated list of the terms that you have seen throughout the book.

Conventions Used in This Book

This book uses a number of conventions to help make it easier for you to work with it, including:

Notes. Provide additional information that is good to know but which may not be essential to the topic being discussed.

Tips. Suggest alternative techniques and shortcuts that you can use to work faster and more efficiently.

Italics. Used to highlight new terms and emphasize key pieces of information.

Introducing VBScript

- ✪ Learn about the different uses of VBScript
- ✪ See how to integrate VBScript into HTML pages
- ✪ Examine Internet browser compatibility
- ✪ Examine the Windows Script Host architecture
- ✪ Learn how to use VBScript and the Windows Script Host

Good evening! Tonight you start down the road to VBScript programming by laying down some groundwork. This includes an explanation of VBScript's capabilities and limitations. This evening also includes a brief history of VBScript and explains its relationship to Visual Basic and Visual Basic for Applications.

After you have a little background about how VBScript came to be I'll introduce the first of this book's two major topics—using VBScript to enhance your personal web pages. I'll talk about how VBScript can be used to add interactivity to your web pages and to perform other useful functions. This chapter also shows you how to write your first web page containing VBScript so that you can see how VBScript and HTML can be combined and used together.

The last part of tonight's reading covers this book's second major topic, VBScript and the Windows Script Host. The Windows Script Host (WSH) is Microsoft's advanced scripting solution. It allows you to use scripting languages such as VBScript to automate an assortment of Windows tasks. This chapter concludes by showing you how to write and test your own VBScripts using the WSH.

What Is VBScript?

VBScript is a scripting language. It is designed to allow you to write scripts that can automate any number of activities, such as adding simple animation to a web page. Unlike some programming languages VBScript cannot run on its own. It requires an execution host. An *execution host* is another program, such as a web browser, that interprets and executes your script.

Like other scripting languages, VBScript is an interpreted language. This makes it different from other types of programming languages that compile their programs. Every script or software program must be compiled into *binary code* (those 0s and 1s that make up the language that only computers understand) before it can be executed. Programming languages such as C++ and Visual Basic require that you compile your programs prior to execution. The compile process interprets and converts the statements that make up your programs into binary code that the computer understands. After a program has been compiled it is ready to execute. Because it is already compiled, it executes quickly.

Scripting languages like VBScript do not compile their scripts until the moment they are actually executed or interpreted. This means that every time a VBScript is run, it must be interpreted and then executed. This makes scripts run slower than compiled programs.

Another difference between scripts and compiled programs is that compiled programs are syntax-checked during the compile process. If the program contains a syntax problem, an error occurs, and you are required to fix it. On the other hand, syntax errors in scripts do not appear until you run them.

You can create VBScripts using a simple text editor such as Notepad. VBScripts are stored as plain text files. Because VBScripts are stored as plain text files you can use any text editor to create them. This makes them easy to work with and modify.

TIP Most VBScript programmers have an editor that they like to work with. Script editors can usually support more than one scripting language allowing you to use it for multiple purposes. Modern script editors usually provide a number of handy features that make them far more useful than Notepad. These features include the automatic color-coding of your script statements, automatic indentation of statements, the ability to test a script, and code templates that help you with basic syntax. I used a very good editor called Home-Site when writing and testing all the scripts in this book. For your convenience, I have included a 30-day trial copy of HomeSite on the book's web site at **www.premier-pressbooks.com/downloads.asp**.

What Can VBScripts Do?

VBScript can be written to perform an infinite number of tasks. VBScripts are, however, limited by the constraints of their execution environments, which I'll cover in the next section. For example, when executed within Internet Explorer VBScripts cannot access a computer's file system to store or retrieve data. This protects web surfers by preventing web sites from being able to alter users' computers and their files. However, when a VBScript is run by the WSH it has full access to the Windows file system. In addition, it can access the Windows desktop and even manipulate the registry.

The following list provides you with ideas that you might want to implement when using VBScript in your web pages.

- Validating HTML forms before submitting their contents as email.
- Creating animation effects such as a rollover, which changes the appearance of a graphic, such as a button, when the mouse moves the pointer over it.
- Creating rotating banners.
- Interacting with visitors using pop-up dialogs to display messages and collect information.

○ Detecting browser type and redirecting visitors to HTML pages specifically suited for their browser version.

○ Posting messages on the Internet Explorer status bar and creating scrolling messages.

○ Using VBScript to better manage HTML frames.

○ Automatically opening multiple customized Internet Explorer Windows when people visit your web site.

○ Performing calculations based on user provided input.

○ Addressing visitors to your web site by name using VBScript to manage cookies.

Although VBScript embedded in an HTML page is limited in its ability to affect the operating system and other resources on a computer, VBScripts run with the WSH are not. In fact, the main purpose behind the WSH is to allow scripts to automate system tasks. This makes VBScripts run with the WSH especially good for automating repetitive and mundane tasks that may take you hours but which can be done by a script in a matter of moments. VBScripts are also well used for automating tasks that are not performed often but which may be complicated and lengthy and thus subject to human error. The following list presents just a glimpse at the kinds of tasks that you can automate using VBScript and the WSH.

○ Creating desktop shortcuts

○ Managing your file system by automatically copying, moving, archiving, and deleting files

○ Managing network resources on home and corporate networks

○ Generating reports that display system and status information

○ Working with other applications

○ Managing local and network printers

○ Setting up automated scripts that can run after-hours when your computer is not in use

⚙ Creating new user accounts

⚙ Managing operating system resources, such as services and event logs

VBScript Execution Environments

VBScripts cannot run on their own. They need an execution host environment to execute them. When Microsoft first introduced VBScript in 1996, it was designed to operate inside the Internet Explorer Internet browser. However, since then Microsoft has continued to expand VBScript's roles and capabilities. As a result, VBScript can now run in a number of different environments. Although this book focuses on two of these environments—HTML pages and the WSH—I thought I'd provide a brief overview of these and some other environments where VBScripts can be used. This will not only provide you with an understanding of the scope of VBScript's capabilities, but will also provide you with ideas for other avenues that you may later decide to pursue with your new VBScript programming skills.

⚙ **Internet Explorer.** When VBScript was first introduced it was only supported as a scripting language for the Internet Explorer 3 web browser. VBScript can be used to make web pages more interactive by responding to user input. It can also be used to validate forms and add graphical effects.

⚙ **Windows Script Host.** The Windows Script Host of WSH is Microsoft's solution for providing Windows operating systems with advanced scripting capabilities beyond those provided by each operating system's built-in batch scripting language. WSH provides VBScript with an execution environment that has access to Windows resources, such as the desktop, registry, file system, and network. Using WSH and VBScript, you can develop scripts that perform repetitive tasks and speed up complex and tedious chores.

⚙ **Internet Information Server and ASP.** *Internet Information Server* (*IIS*) is Microsoft's web server application. It allows you to create and administrator your own web site and is used by many companies on the Internet to run their Internet businesses. IIS uses *Active Server Pages* (*ASP*) to deliver information in the form of HTML pages to Internet users. VBScript plays a major role in ASP development by providing it with a powerful scripting language that can process incoming requests, access local databases, and return dynamically built HTML content.

○ **Outlook Express.** VBScript can be used to automate the behavior and functionality of the Outlook Express email client.

○ **Microsoft Windows Script Console.** This is a new capability that allows developers of third-party applications to incorporate scripting capabilities directly into their applications. This allows you to automate application functionality and expand its capabilities using VBScript or JScript.

A Brief History of VBScript

Microsoft first introduced VBScript in 1996 with Internet Explorer 3. However, it was not the first scripting to arrive on the scene. Netscape had already introduced LiveScript, later renamed JavaScript. VBScript did not fare well. At the time Netscape still had the dominant share of the Internet browser market and its scripting language had a head start. To make things more difficult on VBScript, the Netscape browsers did not support it, which meant that although both Internet Explorer and Netscape browsers support JavaScript, only Internet Explorer supported VBScripts. Nevertheless, Microsoft continued to develop and enhance VBScript.

NOTE If you want to learn more about JavaScript and how to use it for web page development I recommend that you read **Learn JavaScript In a Weekend**, written by Jerry Lee Ford, Jr. and published by Premier Press Books (ISBN 0-76156-3332-X).

Although the original version of VBScript supported scripting within the Internet browser, VBScript version 2, which was released with IIS 3, brought VBScripting to the web server. By embedding VBScripts into ASP pages, web developers could access local databases and build dynamic HTML pages that were then returned to the Internet browser.

VBScript version 3 was deployed to a number of environments, including:

✪ Internet Explorer 4

✪ IIS 4

✪ Outlook 98

✪ Windows Scripting Host

In addition to supporting both client and server based web development, VBScript version 3 provided scripting capabilities to Microsoft's email client and provided one of the two default scripting languages for Microsoft's new Windows Scripting Host. The other scripting language support by the WSH was JScript. *JScript* is the name that Microsoft gave to its own implementation of JavaScript.

VBScript version 4 was released as part of Microsoft Visual Studio development package. However, the language itself was unchanged from the previous version. The one major change that accompanied this version was the addition of file system support, allowing VBScripts to access and manipulate local file systems.

VBScript version 5 was released in 2000 with the introduction of Windows 2000 and Internet Explorer 5. The release of Windows XP Home Edition and Professional in 2001, along with Internet Explorer 6 and WSH 5.6, has brought with them the current version of VBScript, version 5.6. This is the version of VBScript that I will be using throughout this book to develop all of the web and WSH scripts that you'll see.

The Visual Basic Family of Programming Languages

VBScript is one of several languages that comprise Microsoft's family of Visual Basic programming languages. These programming languages include

⚙ Visual Basic

⚙ Visual Basic for Applications

⚙ VBScript

The original member of this family of programming languages is Visual Basic. Visual Basic was originally introduced in 1991. Over the last 10-plus years it has evolved into one of the most popular programming languages in the world. Visual Basic provides a powerful *Integrated Development Environment* (*IDE*) to support the building of desktop, networking, and web-based applications. Its current version is called Visual Basic .NET, reflecting its relationship to Microsoft's .NET web-based framework. Visual basic is generally used to create complete standalone programs.

 NOTE   Microsoft's .NET Framework is a development platform designed to support the creation of web applications using XML-based web services. .NET is designed to allow applications to exchange data over the Internet regardless of the programming languages or operating system being used. To learn more about .NET, check out **www.microsoft. com/net.**

Visual Basic for Applications (VBA) represents a subset of Visual Basic. VBA was first released in 1993. It is designed to provide Visual Basic-like programming capabilities to applications. The best example of this is Microsoft Office, which provides VBA to allow people to develop macros. *Macros* are programs that can be used to automate an application's functionality or to create a new application using VBA and the hosting application. For example, using VBA and Microsoft Excel, it's possible to develop an accounting or bookkeeping application. VBA can be compiled into p-code, which is like a partial compilation that allows VBA code to run fast (but not as fast as a regular compiled Visual Basic program).

VBScript, which was introduced in 1996, is a subset of VBA. VBScript cannot be compiled in advance and must be interpreted by an execution host at the time of execution. This makes VBScript the slowest member of the Visual Basic family. However, like VBA, VBScript provides the same easy to work with Visual Basic programming language, albeit scaled down as required to support scripting.

Table 1.1 provides a comparison of the major features of Visual Basic, VBA, and VBScript. As you can see, Visual Basic and VBA both provide an advanced IDE and the ability to compile their programs. However, only Visual Basic can be used to create standalone programs.

VBScript does not provide an IDE. However, this deficit can be partially overcome by purchasing a good third-party script editor. Because it is an interpreted language, VBScript cannot be compiled; however, there are some advantages to interpreted scripting languages. Because you do not have to compile them, you can go straight from development to execu-

TABLE 1.1 COMPARING VISUAL BASIC, VBA, AND VBSCRIPT

Language	IDE	Compiled	Standalone
Visual Basic	Yes	Yes	Yes
VBA	Yes	Yes	No*
VBScript	No**	No	No***

*VBA requires a hosting application such as Microsoft Office

**Although VBScript does not provide an IDE, you can use any of a number of excellent script editors that provide a reasonably good development environment

***VBScript requires an execution host such as Internet Explorer or the WSH

tion. If you find a problem, just reopen the text file containing your script, make the necessary correction, save it, and run it again. Sometimes it may take a number of tries to correct a problem before you fix it. Having to stop every time that you make a small change to compile your program before testing it can really slow you down.

VBScript does not support the development of standalone programs. You must run VBScripts inside an execution host; however, scripts are not meant for full-blown application development. They are meant to provide quick solutions or to glue other applications together. Therefore, this should not be seen as a missing feature but rather an unnecessary one.

Scripting Tools Needed for Web Page Development

You do not need much to create a web page, just a text editor and a web browser to test your web page. Because VBScript is just text embedded inside HTML pages, you won't need any additional tools. In fact, you can create and test web pages using Notepad and the copy of Windows Explorer that you currently have installed on your computer.

Because Notepad is such a simple text editor, I recommend that you find one that is better suited to scripting. That's why I've included a 30-day shareware copy of HomeSite on the book's web site at **www.premier-pressbooks.com/downloads.asp**. HomeSite, shown in Figure 1.1, is an HTML and script editor that provides a number of features found in many advanced script editors, including

❂ Color-coding of script statements that make scripts easier to read

❂ The capability to preview web pages while developing them

❂ HTML tag completion and code validation

❂ Support for other languages such as HTML, XHTML, and JavaScript allowing you to use it as an all purpose editor

❂ Templates that assist in writing HTML code

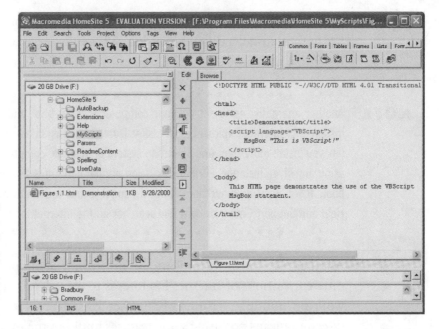

Figure 1.1

HomeSite 5.0 is a multi-purpose editor that provides a number of advanced script development features.

 NOTE

More information about HomeSite is available at **http://www.macromedia.com/software/homesite.**

Because VBScript has rapidly evolved over the years, each new version of Internet Explorer has had to adapt its support of VBScript to accommodate new VBScript features and functionality. This means that although Internet Explorer 6 supports all the features of VBScript 5.6, previous versions of the browser do not. The same can be said for earlier versions of the browser. For example, Internet Explorer 5 fully supports VBScript version 5 while versions 3 and 4 do not.

Because different versions of Internet Explorer will react differently to scripts written using different versions of VBScript, it's important to test your web pages using each version of the browser that you intend to support. Unlike Netscape, which lets you install different versions of the browser on the same computer, Internet Explorer only allows you to install one version of the browser at a time. My solution to this dilemma has been to install a different version of the browser on each computer on my home network.

NOTE Another alternative is to set up your computer to dual-boot and to install as many instances of Internet Explorer as necessary. Dual booting is an advanced procedure that lets you install more than one operating system on a single computer and then boot up using any given instance. Further discussion of dual booting is beyond the scope of this book. If you want to know more about it I suggest that you check out the Windows XP Help and Support Center or do a few searches on the Internet for more information.

Another way to try to mitigate the difficulties of supporting users with different versions of Internet Explorer is to write VBScript code that will work on multiple versions of Internet Explorer. Of course, going this direction means not using some features found in the most recent version of VBScript.

Yet another way to deal with the dilemma of trying to service multiple versions of Internet Explorer and other Internet browsers is to incorporate logic into your scripts that interrogate the browser to determine which type and version it is and then presents specifically tailored HTML pages. I'll show you how you can do this on Saturday.

Unfortunately, I cannot give you a perfect solution that will allow you to support all versions of all types of browsers. I am afraid that the Internet is still too new and growing too fast for Microsoft and the rest of the world to have agreed to a common set of standards.

Browser Compatibility

As I have already alluded to, Netscape browsers do not support VBScript. Instead they only support JavaScript. Therefore, when you opt to add VBScript to your web pages you are limiting your scripting support to users of Internet Explorer. Given Internet Explorer's increasing dominance as an Internet browser this provides you with the capability to reach most people.

NOTE Microsoft's dominance in the browser wars will probably continue for the foreseeable future. Microsoft has tightly integrated Internet Explorer into Windows XP making it impossible to ever get completely rid of it. In contrast, you have to download Netscape Communicator to use it. Most people will opt to use whichever browser they are initially presented with and this means Internet Explorer. In addition, the increasing size of modern software applications makes downloading them prohibitive to anyone without a high-speed Internet connection such as a DSL or cable. After all, Netscape Communicator 6.2.1, the most current version as of the writing of this book, is 26MB. Therefore, most people with a dial-up Internet connection, and this represents the majority of people on the Internet, are trapped with Internet Explorer.

Just because you add a little VBScript code to your web pages does not mean that you still cannot support your Netscape visitors. By appropriately using comments, which I'll show you how to do tomorrow morning, you can hide your VBScript code from Netscape browsers and allow them to still view your HTML pages.

NOTE There is another web browser called Opera that is gaining a small measure of popularity. This browser is based on the same code as Netscape Communicator. Therefore, your VBScripts won't work with it either.

Integrating VBScript and Your Web Pages

Up to this point I have gone over a lot of material, including browser compatibility and the tools that you'll need to get started writing VBScripts for your HTML pages. Now seems like a good time to introduce you to your first VBScript. This first script will be a basic one. Its purpose is to show you how easy it is to integrate VBScript into your HTML code and not to try to explain VBScript coding. We'll start discussing that topic in the next chapter.

VBScript is inserted or embedded into an HTML page using the <SCRIPT> and </SCRIPT> tags. The script tags can be placed in either the head or body section of an HTML page. There are two forms of the script tags that you'll see presented in this book. The most commonly used syntax is shown here:

```
<SCRIPT LANGUAGE="Script_Language" TYPE="TEXT/Language" SRC="url">
</SCRIPT>
```

This version of the script tags allows you to place any number of VBScript statements inside the opening and closing tags. The <SCRIPT> tag identifies the beginning of a script or script reference. LANGUAGE identifies the scripting language that is being used. Because this book is about VBScript, all the scripts that you will see will set the language attribute as follows.

```
LANGUAGE="VBScript"
```

Alternatively, if you prefer you can rewrite this attribute as follows:

```
LANGUAGE="VBS"
```

The TYPE attribute provides an alternative way to specify type of script. When used to identify a VBScript it is typed as follows:

```
TYPE="TEXT/VBScript"
```

Although the following format works just as well:

```
TYPE="TEXT/VBS"
```

In this book, I use the LANGUAGE attribute in all the scripts that you will see. If you prefer, you can store your VBScripts in separate text files and use the SRC attribute to reference their URL. The external VBScript file must have a file extension of .vbs. You might want to do this for several reasons, including

✿ To make your HTML code easier to read by keeping VBScripts in externally referenced files

✿ To separate lengthy VBScript files from your HTML code

✿ To create a library of sharable VBScripts, which multiple HTML pages can reference

The </SCRIPT> tag marks the end of the script or script reference.

The second version of the script tags that you'll see me use is shown here:

```
<SCRIPT FOR="Object" EVENT="Event_Type" LANGUAGE="Script_Language" >
</SCRIPT>
```

This version allows you to trigger the execution of VBScript code based on the occurrence of predefined events, such as a mouse click on a button created in an HTML form.

The FOR attribute specifies the HTML object to which the VBScript is being assigned. The EVENT attribute identifies the specific event that will trigger the script. An example of an event includes the onClick event, which automatically executes when a user clicks on an HTML object such as a form button.

I'll show you examples of how to use both versions of the scripts tags in the following two sections.

Writing Your First VBScript

In the next couple pages I'll show you how easy it is to add a simple VBScript to an HTML page. First, I'll start off by creating a simple HTML page as shown here:

```
<HTML>
  <HEAD>
    <TITLE>Script 1.1 - Adding VBScript to a HTML page</TITLE>
  </HEAD>
  <BODY>
    <H3>My first VBScript!</H3>
  </BODY>
</HTML>
```

As you can see this is a basic HTML page that contains a descriptive title in the head section and a simple heading in the body section. Now let's add our VBScript.

First, let's add the following lines to the HTML page in its head section:

```
<SCRIPT LANGUAGE="VBScript">
</SCRIPT>
```

These HTML statements will be used to contain the VBScript code. The first line tells the browser that VBScript code follows, which will need to be interpreted and processed. The last statement identifies the end of the VBScript.

Now insert the following lines of VBScript code between the script tags.

```
sub window_onload
  msgbox "Welcome to the world of VBScripting!"
end sub
```

These three lines of code make up your first VBScript. I'm not going to go over them in detail right now because I am just trying to show you how to integrate VBScript and HMTL. Let's get through my review of VBScript programming tomorrow morning before we worry too much about the specifics. In general what is happening here is that a VBScript subroutine has been defined containing a statement that will display a message in a pop-up Windows dialog when Internet Explorer loads the HTML page.

At this point your finished HTML page should look like the example shown here:

```
<HTML>
  <HEAD>
    <TITLE>Script 1.1 - Adding VBScript to a HTML page</TITLE>
    <SCRIPT LANGUAGE="VBScript">
      sub window_onload
        msgbox "Welcome to the world of VBScripting!"
      end sub
    </SCRIPT>
  </HEAD>
```

```
<BODY>
  <H3>My first VBScript!
</BODY>
</HTML>
```

Okay,, now that you have the HTML and script entered into your editor, save it. I have saved this script as `Script 1.1`. You'll find it and the rest of the scripts that you'll see in the book on the accompanying Web site at **www.premierpressbooks.com/downloads.asp**. You'll notice that this filename is the same as the file name shown in the HTML title tags. This is a convention that I will follow throughout this book to make it easy for you to identify any script and then locate it on the book's Web site.

NOTE

If you prefer, you can replace the file's .html file extension with .htm. Either file extension is supported by Internet Explorer and will not have any affect on your VBScript.

The following procedure shows how you can use Internet Explorer 6 running on Windows XP Professional to open and test your script. Although other Microsoft operating systems and versions of Internet Explorer may differ slightly, the procedure described here should still be accurate regardless of which version of these products you are using.

NOTE

Depending on what scripting editor you are using you may be able to load your HTML page and test your script without ever leaving your editor.

Testing Your VBScript

1. Click Start, All Programs and then Internet Explorer.
2. Click File and then select Open. The Open dialog appears.
3. Type the name of your HTML file, including its complete path and click OK or click the Browse and locate the HTML file that way and then click OK.

4. Internet Explorer opens the HTML page and immediately runs your VBScript as shown in Figure 1.2.

As you can see in Figure 1.2, Internet Explorer displayed the pop-up dialog specified in your VBScript code as soon as the web page was loaded.

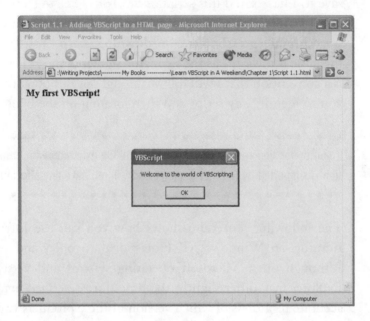

Figure 1.2

Testing your first VBScript.

Executing VBScripts in Response to Events

By setting up VBScripts to run when a user interacts with your HTML pages, you can add a great deal of interactivity to your web pages. For example, if a user clicks on a graphic, you can trigger a VBScript to execute and ask the user if they really want to perform a given action like open a link. If the user responds no, then your script can cancel the operation, otherwise it can allow it to continue normally. Similarly, if you have a web page that collects user information, you could create an event that triggers a VBScript. For example, you could add a Submit button to the form and use it to trigger the VBScript. The VBScript could then validate each entry in the form and ensure that it has been filled out correctly. If everything checks out okay, then the script can allow the form to be submitted.

The following example, demonstrates how to set up a VBScript to execute when the user clicks a form's button. In this case, the script displays a pop-up dialog demonstrating the script's ability to intercept events and react to them. Tomorrow I'll show you how to leverage this feature to create HTML pages that really communicate with the user.

```
<HTML>
  <HEAD>
    <TITLE>Script 1.2 - Processing events with VBScript</TITLE>
  </HEAD>
  <BODY>
    <FORM NAME="myForm">
      <INPUT TYPE=button NAME="myButton" VALUE="My Button">
      <SCRIPT FOR="myButton" EVENT="onClick" LANGUAGE="VBScript">
        msgbox "You clicked on My Button!"
      </SCRIPT>
    </FORM>
  </BODY>
</HTML>
```

In this example, the VBScript was embedded in the body section. In fact, I placed it right after the form object, in this case a button, for which it was defined. Although I could have moved the VBScript code anywhere, placing it right after the INPUT tag that defined the button makes it easy to see how the VBScript and the HTML form fit together. In this example, an HTML form button is created that displays the text message of My Button. The name assigned to the button is myButton. The FOR attribute on the first script tag specifies that the VBScript will execute when the onClick event for myButton is triggered. Thus when the user clicks the button, the VBScript code defined inside the script tags runs and displays a pop-up dialog as shown in Figure 1.3.

NOTE You'll learn a lot more about working with VBScript events tomorrow. You'll also find a list of events presented in Appendix A "VBScript Language Reference."

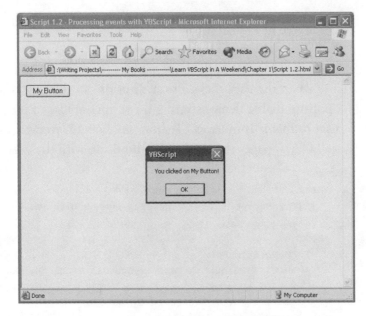

Figure 1.3

Using VBScript to create web pages that interact with your visitors.

Referencing External VBScripts

As I mentioned previously, you do not have to embed your VBScript code directly into your HTML pages. If you prefer you can store your VBScripts in external files. This way you can create a library of VBScripts. You can even use this approach to share a single VBScript with any number of HTML pages. In addition, separating your VBScript code from your HTML code can also make it both easier to view and to work with.

The following example demonstrates how to reference an external VBScript from within a HTML page. The HTML page is named Script 1.3.html and is shown here:

```
<HTML>
  <HEAD>
    <TITLE>Script 1.3 - Referencing an external VBScript</TITLE>
  </HEAD>
  <BODY>
    <SCRIPT SRC="Script 1.4.vbs" LANGUAGE="VBScript"> </SCRIPT>
  </BODY>
</HTML>
```

As you can see, there is no VBScript code embedded inside the script tags, which are located inside the HTML page's body section. Instead, the SRC attribute specifies the name of an external file called `Script 1.4.vbs`, which contains the VBScript code.

NOTE To place your VBScripts in external files, you must be sure that these files contain only VBScript statements and not HTML. Otherwise, your scripts will fail and you'll receive an error.

The contents of file `Script 1.4.vbs` is shown here:

```
'Script 1.4 - An example of an externally referenced VBScript
msgbox "Welcome to the world of VBScripting!"
```

As you can see, the external `.vbs` file only has two lines of code. The first is a <u>comment</u> that is used to identify the script and its function. I'll talk more about comments tomorrow morning. The second line is the VBScript. When referenced in this manner, the VBScript is inserted into the HTML and then interpreted just as if it were embedded directly into the HTML page.

Taking a Break

Why don't you take a quick break and relax before we jump into the second half of tonight's VBScript introduction. When you come back, I'll go over WSH in greater detail by examining its architecture and how it operates. I'll also provide you with a few useful links to some web sites where you can find some good information about VBScript not to mention some sample scripts that you can download and play with as you learn to write your own VBScripts.

Introducing the Windows Scripting Host

Although VBScript's role as a client-side Internet scripting language is somewhat murky, its role as a scripting language for WSH is clear. VBScript and JScript are the default scripting languages supplied by Microsoft with WSH. VBScript is the more popular of the two in this environment. VBScript is a great tool for tackling small tasks that require just a few lines of code where a full-blown Visual Basic solution would be overkill.

Windows XP, like earlier Windows operating systems, provides an intuitive *graphical user interface* (*GUI*) for working with the operating system. However, there are times that working with the GUI can be slow and tedious. For example, suppose you just purchased two new computers running Windows XP and needed to add 25 user accounts to each computer. Creating these accounts by hand could take an hour or two. However, in less than half that time you could write a script to do the job and once written you can use the script time and time again.

Besides the WSH, Microsoft also supplies its operating systems a built-in shell scripting capability. On Windows 95, 98, and ME the shell scripting capability is limited. To do any real scripting on these operating systems you must use the WSH. However, on Windows NT, 2000, and XP the built-in shell scripting language is a lot more robust and includes features such as variable support, conditional programming logic, looping, and procedures. In addition to shell programming statements, shell scripts can contain operating system commands and can execute Windows command line utilities. These scripts can also execute the utilities provided in the Windows resource kits. However, built-in Windows shell scripting falls far short of the power provided by the WSH.

NOTE •
If you want to learn more about Windows Shell Scripting I recommend that you check out **Microsoft Windows Shell Scripting and the WSH Administrator's Guide**, by Jerry Lee Ford, Jr. and published by Prima (ISBN 1-931841-26-8).
• •

The WSH is tightly coupled with the operating system and can access and manipulate a number of Windows resources. These resources include

- The Windows registry
- The Windows desktop
- The Windows file system
- The Windows Start Menu
- The Windows Quick Launch Bar
- Windows applications
- Network printers and drives
- Windows services
- User accounts

The WSH provides the most complete and powerful scripting solution for Windows operating systems and can be applied to all versions of the Windows operating systems starting with Windows 95. So unless you are supporting only Windows NT, 2000, and XP operating systems, the WSH should be your main scripting language.

NOTE There are other scripting languages available on Windows operating systems. These languages include REXX, Perl, and Python. Versions of each of these scripting languages can also be used in conjunction with the WSH.

The current version of WSH is 5.6. The previous versions were 2.0 and 1.0. If you have Windows XP, then you already have WSH version 5.6. If you have other Windows operating systems that you support, then you may already have previous versions of WSH installed. Table 1.2 provides a summary of Windows operating systems and the versions of WSH supplied with them.

You can install or upgrade to WSH version 5.6 on any Windows 95 or later operating system. You can download WSH 5.6 from **www.msdn. microsoft.com/scripting.**

TABLE 1.2 MICROSOFT OPERATING SYSTEM SUPPORT FOR WSH

Operating System	WSH Supported	Version
Windows 3.X	No	-
Windows 95	Yes*	-
Windows 98	Yes	1.0
Windows Me	Yes	2.0
Windows NT	Yes	**
Windows 2000	Yes	2.0
Windows XP	Yes	5.6

*Windows 95 never shipped with the WSH. However you can download and install it.
**WSH 1.0 is installed on Windows NT 4 when Service Pack 4 is installed.

WSH Architecture

WSH scripts are composed of language specific programming statements. By default WSH ships with VBScript and JScript. In addition, there are third-party supplied scripting language that also work with the WSH. These languages include REXX, Perl, and Python. Both Perl and Python are scripting languages evolved from UNIX and ported over to Windows. REXX is a scripting language that began on IBM mainframes and made its way to PCs, starting with the OS/2 operating system.

NOTE A WSH compatible version of Perl and Python can be found at **www.activestate.com**. IBM also provides a version of REXX called Object REXX that you can use with the WSH. Information on Object REXX is available at **www-4.ibm.com/software/ad/ obj-rexx**.

Because the WSH provides an extensible scripting host environment, it's possible that third-party developers will continue making additional scripting languages available to WSH. However, of all the languages supported by WSH, VBScript remains the most popular. This is because:

- ✿ It is one of the two default scripting languages supplied with the WSH.

- ✿ As a member of the Visual Basic programming family it has the advantage of being familiar to millions of Visual Basic and VBA programmers.

- ✿ It's a powerful yet easy to learn scripting language.

 NOTE

To use the WSH you must have a strong understanding of at least one scripting language. If you know more than one supported scripting language, the WSH will allow you to combine them into a special Windows Script File. Because all scripting languages have their own unique sets of strengths and weaknesses, WSH allows you to leverage the strengths of each scripting language. I'll talk more about Windows Script Files on Sunday and give you an example of how to create one using VBScript and JScript.

To work with WSH, it is helpful to have an understanding of its basic architecture and components as depicted in Figure 1.4.

The WSH runs as a 32-bit application on Windows operating systems. At the heart of the WSH architecture is the core object model. This component provides scripts with direct access to Windows resources such as the file system, network, and registry.

WSH provides two execution environments. Wscript.exe supports the execution of scripts from the Windows desktop and provides the ability to leverage the power of graphical pop-up dialogs. Cscript.exe, on the other hand, is designed to support the execution of scripts from the Windows command prompt.

You can use any WSH-supported scripting language to create your scripts and submit it to one of the execution environments. Except for the

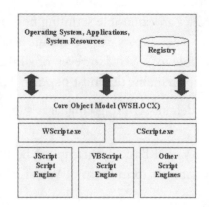

Figure 1.4

The WSH is composed of a modular architecture consisting of a number of components.

Wscript.exe execution environment's support for graphical pop-up dialogs, both execution hosts provide the same features and functionality.

As I have already stated, the WSH core object model exposes a number of Windows specific resources or objects. Examples of these objects include the Windows shortcuts, files, folders, and drives. Each object exposed by the WSH core object model has its own collection of properties and methods. A *property* is an attribute of an object that describes and controls a particular aspect of the object. For example, a shortcut object has a name property that can be programmatically changed. *Methods* are actions that can be taken by the object or used to affect it. For example, there are methods that allow you to create and delete files and folders when working with the Windows file system. By exposing Windows resources as objects and making their properties and methods accessible, the WSH core object model provides the capability to programmatically automate any number of Windows tasks. Don't worry if all this talk about objects, methods, and properties sounds a bit complex. I'll go over it more in greater detail in later chapters.

The VBScript implementation used with the WSH lacks Internet browser functionality. This means it does not work with things like forms, links, and frames because these objects are not used outside the Internet browser. Instead of embedding VBScripts inside HTML pages, VBScripts used with the WSH are stored as plain text files with a .vbs file extension.

Writing WSH VBScripts

When used with the WSH, a VBScript is saved as a plain text file using a `.vbs` file extension that uses only VBScript programming statements. The following example shows a simple two-line VBScript. The first line is a comment that describes the script and the second line displays a message when the script is run.

```
'Script 1.5 - An example of a WSH VBScript
Wscript.Echo "This script works differently depending on which WSH
execution environment runs it!"
```

Although the `Wscript.exe` and `Cscript.exe` execution environments provide equivalent functionality, they have different purposes. The `Wscript.exe` execution host supports the Windows GUI and the `Cscript.exe` supports the Windows command prompt. The previous script helps to demonstrate this difference. For example, if you run the script for the Windows GUI by double-clicking on its icon, you see the pop-up dialog shown in Figure 1.5 appear on your screen.

However, if you run the same script from the Windows command prompt you'll receive the output shown in Figure 1.6.

Figure 1.5

Running a WSH VBScript from the Windows graphical user interface.

Figure 1.6

Running a WSH VBScript from the Windows command prompt.

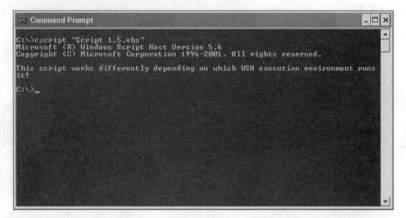

Working with the Windows Command Prompt

Even if you have used the Windows operating system for years, chances are that you have limited experience in working with its command prompt. If you are going to become a proficient VBScript programmer, then you will need to become comfortable working with Windows from the command prompt.

The Windows command prompt is a text-based interface between you and the operating system. To access the command prompt, open the Windows console. You can do this on Windows XP by clicking Start, All Programs, Accessories and then selecting Command Prompt. This opens the Windows Console shown in Figure 1.7.

Figure 1.7

Working with Windows via the command prompt.

NOTE   You can also access the Windows command prompt by clicking Start, Run, and then typing CMD and clicking OK.

The command prompt is displayed in the form of a drive letter followed by a colon, a backslash, and then the greater than character. To the right of the command prompt you'll see a blinking cursor. This indicates that the command prompt is ready to accept new input. For example, type

DIR and press Enter. The DIR command tells Windows to display a directory listing of all files in the current working directory as shown here:

```
C:\>dir
 Volume in drive C is IBMDOS_6
 Volume Serial Number is 2B6A-58F8

 Directory of C:\

11/10/2001  11:07 AM    <DIR>          DOS
06/29/1993  12:00 PM             9,349 WINA20.386
11/10/2001  12:40 PM               127 AUTOEXEC.BAT
11/10/2001  12:40 PM                90 CONFIG.SYS
11/10/2001  11:18 AM    <DIR>          WINDOWS
11/10/2001  11:43 AM                65 CONFIG.BAK
11/10/2001  01:24 PM    <DIR>          Program Files
11/10/2001  12:35 PM             1,330 SCANDISK.LOG
12/01/2001  10:45 AM            90,112 ffastunT.ffl
11/10/2001  01:01 PM    <DIR>          Documents and Settings
               6 File(s)        101,073 bytes
               4 Dir(s)     197,525,504 bytes free

C:\>
```

Windows processes the command then displays its output. The command prompt is then redisplayed indicating that it is ready to accept new commands.

The Windows command prompt provides an interface or shell between you and the operating system (see Figure 1.8). Any command that you type is translated into instructions that the operating system can understand. The command is then executed and any results returned by the operating system are then displayed in the Windows console.

You can use the following command to run a VBScript named Script 1.5.vbs, which is located in the current working directory:

```
Cscript "Script 1.5.vbs"
```

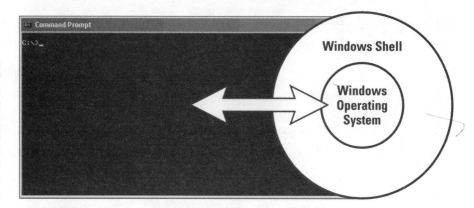

Figure 1.8

The Windows command prompt provides an interface or shell that isolates you from the complexities of the operating system.

This command tells Windows to run a VBScript named `Script 1.5.vbs` using the WSH `Cscript.exe` execution host. Because the filename contained a blank space I had to enclose it inside quotes. If you prefer, you could have also run the VBScript from the command prompt using the `Wscript.exe` execution host using the following command:

```
Wscript "Script 1.5.vbs"
```

Because the `Wscritp.exe` execution host is designed to work with the Windows GUI the output of the script will be displayed as a pop-up dialog.

NOTE Type EXIT and press Enter at the command prompt to close the Windows console.

NOTE There is not enough space or time for me to cover how to work with the Windows command prompt in great detail. If you think that you require more information than I have given you, I recommend that you check out the Windows Help system. You might also want to read **Microsoft Windows Shell Scripting and the WSH Administrator's Guide**, written by Jerry Lee Ford, Jr., and published by Prima (ISBN 1-931841-26-8).

Finding VBScript Source Code

There is no better way to learn VBScript than to sit down and start writing your own code. However, everybody needs a starting point. All the scripts that you'll see in this book are located on the book's Web site at **www.premierpressbooks.com/downloads.asp**.

What follows are a number of excellent web sites where I have found a lot to good VBScript information. These web sites are also great places to find examples of VBScript source code. I recommend spending some time visiting these and other sites that you may come across when surfing the World Wide Web. Try downloading some of the free scripts that you'll find and figure out how they work. An excellent way to learn is to try to make changes to the scripts and see if you can improve them. Many of these sites also will let you upload your own VBScript creations so that you can share them with the rest of the world.

The first place I'd check out is Microsoft's official VBScript documentation as shown in Figure 1.9. As of the writing of this book you can reach

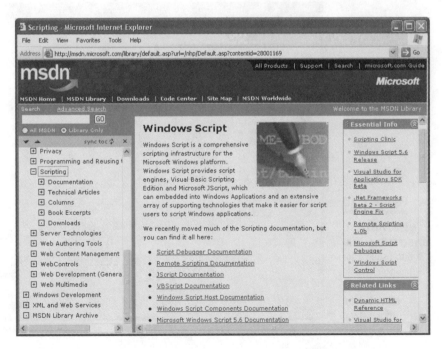

Figure 1.9

Examining Microsoft's VBScript and WSH documentation.

this site by typing **www.msdn.microsoft.com/scripting**. You are then redirected to this site. Here you will find complete VBScript user and reference guides. You'll also find plenty of VBScript examples. This is also the place to go for documentation on the WSH.

Another good web site is **www.vbscript.myscripting.com** shown in Figure 1.10. Here you will find information about VBScript books, links, and tutorials, as well as a host of example VBScripts.

You might also want to visit **www.win32scripting.com**, shown in Figure 1.11. Here you'll find a large collection of articles that include tons of coding examples. However, this is a subscription magazine, so to get at a lot of the good stuff you have to subscribe.

One more web site that I'd recommend you visit is **www.cwashington. netreach.net**, shown in Figure 1.12. Here you will find a large collection of VBScripts, links to pages with WSH information, and information on just about every aspect of scripting Windows operating systems.

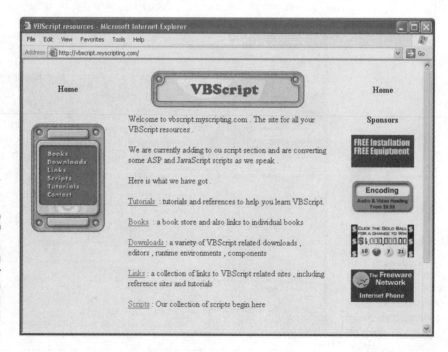

Figure 1.10

www.vbscript. myscripting.com is a good source for finding example VBScripts and other helpful information.

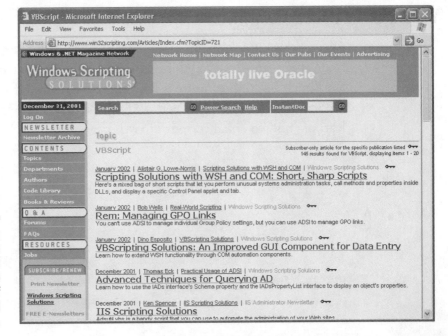

Figure 1.11

Windows Scripting Solutions is a subscription magazine that also provides a lot of free articles and content.

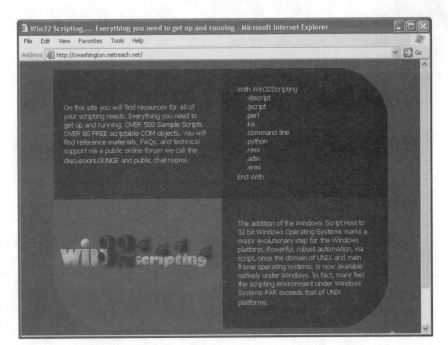

Figure 1.12

Win32scripting provides free access to a large collection of VBScripts.

What's Next?

Okay, I think that's about enough for tonight. Why don't you give your brain a rest and let everything that you have covered tonight soak in. We'll pick back up tomorrow morning by starting off with a review of VBScript programming. Then we'll spend the afternoon and evening learning how to enhance your HTML pages using VBScript.

An Introduction to VBScript Programming

- ✿ Learn the basics of VBScript syntax
- ✿ See how VBScript handles variables and constants
- ✿ Find out how to control script execution with conditional and looping logic
- ✿ See how to work with VBScript operators and expressions
- ✿ Find out how to organize your VBScripts into procedures
- ✿ Learn how to organize large groups of data using arrays

ood morning! I hope that you are rested and ready to get to work. Yesterday we looked at VBScript's history and capabilities. We also went over how to integrate VBScript into HTML pages and save it as WSH VBScript files. This morning we'll begin our examination of the programming statements that make up the VBScript programming language.

The major focus of this chapter is to provide you with everything you need to know to begin writing your own VBScripts. As I go over each different VBScript statement I'll point out its syntax and usefulness. I'll also supply examples of how the statements might be used in either a HTML page or a WSH VBScript file. I'll try to give equal coverage to both web and WSH scripting as we work our way through the chapter.

Getting Started

Now is a good time to be sure that you have all the tools that you'll need to begin writing your VBScripts. You'll need

- ✿ A script editor
- ✿ Internet Explorer 6
- ✿ Windows Script Host 5.6

Any editor will do as long as it can save your scripts in plain text. If you plan to use Notepad you can start it by clicking Start, All Programs, Accessories, and then Notepad.

NOTE

I will be using Windows XP Home Edition and Windows XP Professional for the testing and development of all the scripts that you will see in this book. However, any Windows 95 or later Microsoft operating system will work just fine.

If your computer runs Windows XP, then you already have Internet Explorer 6. However, if you are using an older operating system, you may want to visit **http://www.microsoft.com/windows/ie** and download it.

TIP

You might want to check out shareware sites such as **www.tucows.com**, **www.download.com**, or **www.jumbo.com** for some good script editors.

VBScript Syntax

VBScripts are written in plain text whether they are embedded inside HTML pages or stored as files with .vbs file extensions. As far as programming languages go, VBScript is pretty lenient. For example, VBScript variable names are not case sensitive. This means that as long as you spell a variable name correctly when you reference it within your scripts it will be correctly interpreted. For example, if you define a variable at the beginning of a script with a name of myVar and then refer to it later in the script as myvar or MYVAR, everything will still work. This is not the case in some other scripting languages where the slightest change in case will create an error.

VBScript is also very forgiving in other areas. For example, as long as you get the spelling correct, VBScript will allow you to reference objects, methods, and functions using a different case. For example, VBScript will treat all the following statements the same.

```
WScript.Echo "Good morning!"
WSCRIPT.ECHO "Good morning!"
Wscript.echo "Good morning!"
WsCrIpT.eChO "Good morning!"
```

However, it is best to stick with a consistent style of formatting when writing your VBScripts. Mixing case, even though VBScript allows its, makes scripts hard to read.

VBScript is a flexible language in that it provides you with a lot of leeway in formatting your scripts. For example, you can add blank lines between statements for readability and indent your statements multiple spaces to provide them with a visual organizational structure that is easy to read.

Avoiding Syntax Errors

Understanding VBScript syntax is a key part of learning to be a good VBScript programmer. Each VBScript statement has is own unique syntax that you have to follow. Otherwise, you'll get errors when you run your scripts. For example, the second line of the following VBScript contains an error.

```
'Script 2.1 - An example of a VBScript syntax error in a HTML page
MsgBox "Good morning
```

The syntax of the VBScript `MsgBox()` statement requires that the text message be enclosed inside matching quotes. But in the case of the previous example, the closing quote is missing. If you save this script as a file with a `.vbs` file extension and then run it using the WScript.exe execution host you'll see an error message like the one shown in Figure 2.l.

■ ■

Until you have been programming using VBScript for a number of years you are probably going to find yourself spending a lot of time looking up the syntax of VBScript statements. After you have put together your own collection of scripts you'll find that you can often get away with copying and pasting code statements from old scripts and modifying them to create new scripts. But even then you may need to double-check command syntax. You can always come back to this chapter and look at the examples presented here. In addition, don't forget about Appendix A "VBScript Language Reference." One other good resource is Microsoft's VBScript Language Reference, which you can find at **http://msdn.microsoft.com/scripting**.

■ ■

Figure 2.1

A VBScript syntax error occurring during the execution of a WSH VBScript.

You'll also get an error if you embed the script into an HTML page as shown here.

```
<HTML>
  <HEAD>
    <TITLE>Script 2.2 - An example of a VBScript syntax error in a
HTML page</TITLE>
    <SCRIPT LANGUAGE="VBScript">
      Sub Window_Onload
        MsgBox "Good morning!"
      End Sub
    </SCRIPT>
  </HEAD>
  <BODY>
  </BODY>
</HTML>
```

Depending on how you have Internet Explorer configured, you might not see the error when it occurs. By default, Internet Explorer suppresses all script errors. This way the visitors to your web site are not bothered by error messages if problems occur with your scripts.

NOTE
One reason that an error might occur would be if the visitor were running an old version of Internet Explorer that your script was not designed to accommodate.

If your copy of Internet Explorer is suppressing your VBScript error messages, then instead of an error all that you'll see is a yellow icon in the lower-left corner of the browser as shown in Figure 2.2.

If you double-click this icon you'll see the VBScript error message as demonstrated in Figure 2.3.

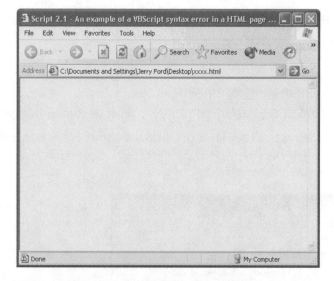

Figure 2.2

By default, Internet Explorer hides VBScript errors.

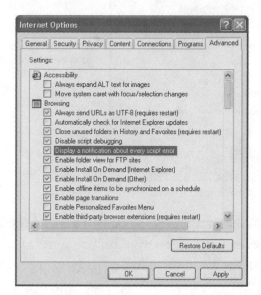

Figure 2.3

A VBScript error as reported by Internet Explorer.

When you are developing scripts for your HMTL pages it is generally a lot easier if you can see errors when they occur. You can configure Internet Explorer 6 to automatically display script errors by following the steps outlined in the following procedure.

...ring Internet Explorer 6 to display script errors

. Internet Explorer.

.....ct Internet Options from the Tools menu. The Internet
Options dialog appears.

3. Select the Advanced property sheet as shown in Figure 2.4.

4. Select the Display a notification about every script error option and
click OK.

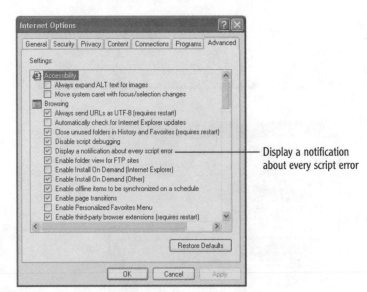

Figure 2.4

Configuring
Internet Explorer 6
to display script
error messages.

Hiding VBScript Statements from Non-Internet Explorer Browsers

Only Internet Explorer supports VBScript. If you are adding VBScripts
to your web site and someone with a non-Internet Explorer or a pre-
version 3 Internet Explorer browser visits not only will your VBScripts
not run, but the visitor will see your VBScript statements printed right in
the middle of your web page.

This is because browsers that do not understand VBScript treat your VBScript statements as text and display it. Obviously, this is not the effect you are looking for. The solution to preventing this from happening is the HTML comment tags and the VBScript comment statement.

The `<!--` is the opening HTML comment tag and the `-->` is the closing tag. All browsers are smart enough not to display anything located between HTML comments tags. Place these tags just after the opening `<SCRIPT>` tag and just before the ending `</SCRIPT>` tag as shown in the following example. Also place a VBScript comment at the beginning of the closing HTML comment tag.

```
<HTML>
  <HEAD>
    <TITLE>Script 2.3 - Hiding VBScript from non-supporting browsers
</TITLE>
    <SCRIPT LANGUAGE="VBScript">
    <!-- Start hiding VBScript statements
      Sub Window_Onload
        MsgBox "Good morning!"
      End Sub
  '   ' End hiding VBScript statements -->
    </SCRIPT>
  </HEAD>
  <BODY>
  </BODY>
</HTML>
```

Now, when a browser that does not support VBScript processes this page, it will view your script as a comment and simply ignore it. Browsers that support VBScript will recognize the opening HTML comment tag and ignore it. These browsers will also ignore the second HTML tag as a VBScript comment and ignore it as well. You'll find that I use this simple trick in the rest of the VBScript examples that you see in this book. I strongly recommend that you use it in all your embedded VBScripts.

VBScript Statements

VBScripts are made up of one or more VBScript statements. VBScript provides a complete collection of programming statements, which are outlined and explained throughout the rest of this chapter. The types of programming statements that we'll cover include

- ○ VBScript comments
- ○ Variable declaration and assignment
- ○ VBScript constants
- ○ Conditional statements
- ○ Looping statements
- ○ Functions and subroutines

Adding Comments to Your VBScripts

You can make your scripts a lot easier to work with by using comments. Comments allow you to make your scripts self-documenting. The VBScript interpreter ignores comments when it executes your scripts. Although adding comments to a script might slow it down during interpretation, the amount of time that might be lost by executing a script with a lot of comments is not discernable. Therefore, I strongly recommend that you liberally add comments to all your scripts. While you may understand exactly what your script is doing when you first write it, you may be less certain about what you were thinking a year later if you find yourself needing to make modifications to the script.

You can add comments to your scripts in either of two ways. Your first option is the Rem statement.

```
Rem Script 2.4 - Documenting your script with comments
MsgBox "This script was documented using the REM statement"
```

Alternatively, you can add comments to your scripts using the single quote character.

```
' Script 2.5 - Documenting your script with comments
MsgBox "This script was documented using the quotation character"
```

Regardless of which option you choose the results are the same.

VBScript is flexible in the application of comments, allowing you to place them on a line by themselves or on the same line as a program statement as demonstrated here. Just be sure that you have at least one blank space between the VBScript statement and the comment.

```
MsgBox "This is a VBScript!"      'This statement displays a message in
a pop-up dialog
```

● ●

You can also use Rem to add a comment at the end of a VBScript statement. However, you must also add a colon after the VBScript statement and before the Rem keyword.

```
MsgBox "This is a VBScript!" : Rem This statement displays a
message in a pop-up dialog
```

● ●

Another good use for comments is to build a script template. You can then use the template as a starting point each time you sit down to write a new VBScript. The following example shows the template that I'll be using in this book to document WSH VBScripts.

```
' *****************************************************
' * Script Name:     template.vbs
' * Description:     This script
' * Author:          Jerry L. Ford, Jr.
' * Address:         Hanover Virginia
' * Created:         01/05/02
' *****************************************************

' **** Script initialization statements go here ****

' *********** Main processing section ************

' ****** Subroutines & Functions go here ********
```

The template begins by providing a place to record basic information. The template outlines three sections: the first section is where I'll define and set variables and their initial values; the second section is where I'll write the script's main processing logic; the last section is where I will store any subroutines and functions defined by the script.

Working with Constants

A *constant* contains a value that never changes. For example, the value of PI is a constant. Use constants to define values that you know will never change during the execution of your script.

Like some other scripting languages, VBScript supplies a collection of predefined constants. You will find a list of VBScript constants in Appendix A. VBScript also allows you to define your own constants.

For example, you can define a constant that contains the name and path of a Windows folder as shown here.

```
Const cDefaultFolder = "C:\Temp"
```

In this example the name of the constant is `cDefaultFolder` and its statically assigned value is C:\Temp. Because this is a text value, it must be enclosed inside quotation marks. You need to leave off the quotation marks when defining constants with numeric values as shown here.

```
Const cMaxValue = 100
```

If you create a constant with a date value then you'll need to use the following format.

```
Const cFixedDate = #01-05-02#
```

As you can see, the value assigned to the date constant is enclosed inside # characters.

TIP

I recommend that you consider developing a naming convention for your constants. For example, all the examples of constants that you just looked at started with the lower-case letter c, which labels them as a constant, as opposed to a variable, which I'll talk about next. This makes your code more readable and helps to ensure that you do not get your constants and variables confused.

Storing Data in Variables

VBScript allows you to write scripts that can store data in memory while they execute. This way you can prompt the user of your WSH script or a visitor to your web site for information and then reference it over and over again as your script executes.

Unlike most other programming languages, VBScript only supports one type of variable called a *variant*. A *variant* can hold a number of different types of data. VBScript does a good job of recognizing the type of data stored in a variable and handling it accordingly. For example, if you assign a numeric value to a variable, then it will behave like a number, allowing you to use it in an expression that manipulates its value. On the other hand, if you assign a text message to it, the variable will behave like text.

Similar to the way you can define the type of data stored in a constant, you can control how VBScripts treat the values stored in variables by applying quotation marks. For example, if you create a variable and assign it a value of 100, it will be treated as a numeric value. But if you enclose the number in quotations, such as "100," it will be stored as a text value.

Although VBScript only supports the variant variable type, it does allow you to further classify a variable using variant subtypes. Table 2.1 lists the variant subtypes supported by VBScript.

VBScript lets you convert variant subtypes from one type to another using built-in conversion functions. A list of these functions is supplied in Appendix A. By using conversion functions, you can set a variant's subtype. For example, you can create a variant variable as shown here.

```
myBirthday = "November 20, 1964"
```

This stores the variable as a variant and tells VBScript to treat it like text. To convert the value of the variable to a date you would use the Cdate() function as shown here.

```
myBirthDate = Cdate(myBirthday)
```

TABLE 2.1 VBSCRIPT SUPPORTED VARIANT SUBTYPES	
Subtype	**Description**
Empty	Creates an uninitialized variable
Null	Establishes a variable with a null value
Boolean	Has a value of `true` or `false`
Byte	Sets an integer value between 0 and 255
Integer	Sets an integer value between 32,768 and 32,767
Currency	A currency value
Long	An integer value between 2,147,483,648 and 2,147,483,647
Single	A single-precision floating-point number
Double	A double-precision floating-point number
Date	A number representing a date
String	A text string
Object	An object
Error	An error number

Naming Variables

Before you add your first variable to a VBScript you need to know a few rules to follow.

- ✪ Variable names must be unique within their scope of use.
- ✪ Variable names cannot exceed 255 characters.
- ✪ Variable names must begin with an alphabetic character.
- ✪ Variable names cannot include an embedded period.

Although not a requirement, I recommend that you give your variables descriptive names that help document their contents. For example, a variable defined with a name of `totalValue` is easier to understand than one name `x`. Descriptive variable names will make your scripts easier to read and maintain.

Using Variables

Before you can use variables in your VBScripts you should declare them. You can declare a variable in a VBScript using either of two options. The first option is to simply reference the variable in your code.

```
userName = "JerryFord"
```

However, the preferred way to incorporate variables into your VBScripts is to formally declare them using the `Dim` keyword. Using the `Dim` keyword makes your scripts easier to read. Here is the syntax required to use `Dim`.

```
Dim variableName
```

`variableName` is the name of the variable being declared. So to use `Dim` to declare the variable shown earlier you would write.

```
Dim userName
```

After you have declared the variable, you can assign a value to it as shown here.

```
userName = "Jerry Ford"
```

If you have a script that will use a large number of variables, VBScript lets you declare more than one at a time by separating the variables with commas.

```
Dim userName, userBirthday, userAge, userId
```

It is considered good programming to formally declare a variable prior to using it. To force the formal declaration of variables in your VBScripts you can use the Option Explicit statement. When used, `Option Explicit` must be the first line in your script. `Option Explicit` tells

VBScript to generate an error if you attempt to use a variable that has not been previously defined using the Dim keyword.

For example, the following example demonstrates how you might use Option Explicit in a VBScript embedded in an HTML page.

```
<HTML>
  <HEAD>
    <TITLE>Script 2.6 - Using Option Explicit to enforce formal ➥
        variable declaration</TITLE>
    <SCRIPT LANGUAGE="VBScript">
    <!-- Start hiding VBScript statements
      Option Explicit
      Dim userName
      userName = "Jerry Ford"
    ' End hiding VBScript statements -->
    </SCRIPT>
  </HEAD>
  <BODY>
    <SCRIPT LANGUAGE="VBScript">
    <!-- Start hiding VBScript statements
      Sub Window_Onload
        MsgBox "Greetings " & userName
      End Sub
    ' End hiding VBScript statements -->
    </SCRIPT>
  </BODY>
</HTML>
```

In this example, a VBScript is embedded in the HEAD section of the HTML page where a variable is declared and then assigned a value. Another VBScript is embedded in the BODY section of the HTML page containing a subroutine, which executes when the HTML page is loaded by the browser. This VBScript displays the value assigned to the variable in a pop-up dialog box.

Examining Variable Scope

In the previous example a variable named userName that was declared in the HEAD section was referenced by another script in the BODY section of the HTML page. This is an example of a variable with a global scope. A *global scope* allows a variable's value to be accessed from any location in the script. A variable with a *local scope*, on the other hand, can only be accessed within the scope that it was created.

In VBScripts, local variables can be created only within procedures. VBScript supports two types of procedures—subroutines and functions—both of which are covered in greater detail later in the morning. For now I'll just say that a procedure is a collection of VBScript statements that can be called and executed from any point in the script. Procedures are used in VBScripts as a way to improve a script's organization.

The following example shows a WSH VBScript that defines both local and global variables.

```
' ****************************************************
' * Script Name:    Script 2.7.vbs
' * Description:    This script demonstrates the
' *                 use of local and global variables
' * Author:         Jerry L. Ford, Jr.
' * Address:        Hanover Virginia
' * Created:        01/06/02
' ****************************************************

' ***** Script initialization statements go here *****

Option Explicit

Dim userName
userName = "William Ford"

' ********** Main processing section ***************

WScript.Echo "Global Scope = " + userName
Display_Names()
WScript.Echo "Global Scope = " + userName

' ********* Subroutines & Functions go here *********

Function Display_Names()
  Dim userName
```

```
   userName = "Alexander Ford"
   WScript.Echo "Local Scope = " + userName
End Function
```

The script starts off with the `Option Explicit` option, which forces the formal declaration of all variables. Next a variable called `userName` is declared and then assigned a value. Because this variable is declared outside of a procedure, it is global in scope. Next, the value of this variable is displayed.

The script then calls a function named `Display_Names()`, which executes, displays a message, and then returns processing control back to the statement that follows the statement that called it.

Each variable within a VBScript must be unique within its scope. Because a procedure creates its own scope, you can create a new variable of the same name used by another variable elsewhere in the script. This variable will then have a scope that is local to the procedure. When the procedure ends, the variable is destroyed. Therefore when the `DisplayNames()` procedure executes and defines a variable called `userName`, it does not affect the variable of the same name created earlier in the script. The procedure then displays the value assigned to its variable.

When processing control is returned from the procedure another message is generated to show that the globally defined `userName` variable still exists and that its value has not changed. These results show what the output will look like if you run this script using the CScript.exe execution host.

```
C:\>CScript "Script 2.7.vbs"
Microsoft (R) Windows Script Host Version 5.6
Copyright (C) Microsoft Corporation 1996-2001. All rights reserved.

Global Scope = William Ford
Local Scope = Alexander Ford
Global Scope = William Ford

C:\>
```

Manipulating VBScript Variables with Operators

As you have already seen the VBScript = assignment operator is used to assign a value to a variable. When you are working with variables that contain numeric values, you can use any of the VBScript arithmetic operators, shown in Table 2.2, to change the value assigned to variables.

The following VBScript statements show how you can apply some of the operators listed in Table 2.2.

```
Option Explicit

Dim myAge
myAge = 37
WScript.Echo "myAge = " & myAge
```

TABLE 2.2 ARITHMETIC OPERATORS	
Operator	**Description**
^	Exponentiation
-	Negation
*	Multiplication
/	Division
\	Integer division
Mod	Modulus
+	Addition
-	Subtraction
&	Concatenation

```
myAge = myAge + 3
WScript.Echo "myAge = " & myAge

myAge = myAge - 10
WScript.Echo "myAge = " & myAge

myAge = myAge * 2
WScript.Echo "myAge = " & myAge
```

• •

You may have noticed the use of the & concatenation operator in the previous example. This operator is actually used to concatenate two pieces of text and was used to append the value of the variable (as text) to the end of a text message.

• •

If you were to save this script as part of a WSH VBScript and run it from the CScript.exe execution host then you'd see the output shown here.

```
myAge = 37
myAge = 40
myAge = 30
myAge = 60
```

VBScript performs arithmetic operations using a strict set of rules known as the order of operator precedence. This order is outlined in Table 2.2. As you can see exponentiation occurs before negation, which occurs before multiplication and so on. However, by enclosing portions of an expression inside parentheses you can change the order of operator precedence. Portions of expressions contained in parentheses are always computed first, although the order of precedence is still maintained within the parentheses.

Comparison Operators

VBScript provides a collection of operators that you can use to compare the values of expressions within your VBScripts. These operators are listed in Table 2.3.

TABLE 2.3 COMPARISON OPERATORS	
Operator	**Description**
=	Equal
<>	Not equal
<	Less than
>	Greater than
<=	Less than or equal to
>=	Greater than or equal to

Testing the values of variables in your scripts is something that you'll find yourself doing again and again. When combined with conditional execution logic, which I'll cover in just a bit, you'll be able to write scripts that can test for certain conditions and then switch between multiple execution paths based on the results of those tests.

Unlike arithmetic operators, there is no order of precedence to the execution of comparison operators. They are executed in the order in which they appear in a statement (e.g., they are evaluated starting from left to right).

For example, the following statement tests to see if values of two variables are equal.

```
Option Explicit
Dim myAge, yourAge
If myAge = yourAge Then
  WScript.Echo "Lets have a party"
End If
```

Similarly, you can test for greater than or less than values.

```
If myAge > yourAge Then
 WScript.Echo "May I see some ID?"
End If
If myAge < yourAge Then
 WScript.Echo "Would you like to see my ID?"
End If
```

Taking a Break

Okay, I think that this is a good place to take a quick break. We have gone over a lot of material since we started this morning. Why not give yourself a break and let things soak in. When you return I'll finish the review of VBScript programming by going over conditional logic, looping, procedures, arrays, and the use of pop-up dialogs. After you have completed this morning's work, you'll be ready to move on and begin writing VBScripts to spice up your HTML pages and automate your computer administration tasks.

Conditional Logic

VBScript provides two statements that allow you to add logic that can alter the logical execution of scripts. This way your scripts can make decisions based on user or environmental criteria. These statements are listed below.

- ✿ **If...Then...Else**. Guides the logical execution of a script based on one or more tested conditions.

- ✿ **Select...Case**. Guides the logical execution of a script based on multiple tests performed against the same condition.

If...Then...Else

The If...Then...Else performs a test of one or more conditions and alters script execution based on whether the test proves true or false. There are two versions of the If...Then...Else statement. This first version allows you to test a single condition. Its syntax is shown here.

```
If condition Then statement [Else statement]
```

Condition is an expression that evaluates to either true or false and statement represents a VBScript statement to be executed if the condition evaluates to true. Else provides an optional statement to execute if the tested condition proves false. For example, you can use this variation of the If...Then...Else statement to test whether two variables are equal as demonstrated here.

```
If unitsSent = unitsReceived Then MsgBox "This item is not in stock "
Else MsgBox " This item is in stock "
```

The previous example tests the values assigned to two variables, unitsSent and unitsReceived. If the value of these two variables is equal (or true) then a No inventory remaining message is displayed. If the values of these two variables are not equal (or false) a different message is displayed.

If you need to execute more than one VBScript statement as a result of your comparisons, then you'll need to use the following syntax for the If...Then...Else statement.

```
If condition Then
    statements
ElseIf condition-n Then
    statements
.
.
.
Else
    statements
End If
```

For example, you could modify the IF...Then...Else statement in the previous example as shown here.

```
If unitsSent = unitsReceived Then
  MsgBox "No inventory remaining"
```

```
  unitsOnhand = 0
Else
  MsgBox "This item is in stock"
  unitsOnhand = unitsSent - unitsReceived
End If
```

There is no limit to the number of statements that you can include in the multiline version of the `If…Then…Else` statement. If you include one or more `ElseIf` keywords you can expand the logic of the `If…Then…Else` statement to include tests for multiple conditions as demonstrated in the following example.

```
If unitsSent = unitsReceived Then
  MsgBox "No inventory remaining"
  unitsOnhand = 0
ElseIf unitsSent > unitsReceived Then
  MsgBox "Inventory error: Units sent cannot exceed _
    units received"
ElseIf unitsSent < unitsReceived Then
  MsgBox "This item is in stock"
  unitsOnhand = unitsSent - unitsReceived
End If
```

NOTE You may have noticed my use of the _ character in the previous example. The _ character is a continuation character that allows you to spread a lengthy VBScript statement across multiple lines.

As this example shows, you can use `ElseIf` to perform as many tests as required.

Sometimes you'll need to perform more complex analysis of a set of values than a single `If…Then…Else` statement can provide. VBScript addresses this need by allowing you to nest or embed `If…Then…Else` statements within other `If…Then…Else` statements in order to develop more complex tests as demonstrated in the following example.

```
If unitsSent < unitsReceived Then
  unitsOnhand = unitsReceived - unitsSent
```

```
    If unitsOnhand > 5 then
       MsgBox "Plenty of units left in stock"
    Else
       MsgBox "Time to re-order more units"
    End If
End If
```

As you can see the If statement tests whether or not there are any units left on hand. If units are still available the number of units is recorded in the unitsOnhand variable. This variable is then interrogated by a nested IF...Then...Else statement to determined whether or not it's time to reorder more units.

Select Case

The Select...Case statement provides functionality that is very similar to the If...Then...Else statement. However, although the If...Then...Else statement can test a large number of different conditions, the Select...Case statement is better equipped to test a large number of criteria against a single condition. The syntax of the Select...Case statement is

```
Select Case value
  Case expression
    statements
    .
    .
    .
  Case expression
    statements
  Case Else
    statements
End Select
```

Select...Case evaluates a single value as specified in the Select...Case statement and compares it against the values stored in each of the Case statements that follows as demonstrated in the following example.

```
Select Case myColor
  Case "blue"
    MsgBox "The matching color is blue"
```

```
Case "yellow"
  MsgBox "The matching color is yellow"
Case "red"
  MsgBox "The matching color is red"
Case Else
  MsgBox "No color match found"
End Select
```

Working with Loops

Like any advanced programming language VBScript provides a number of statements that allow VBScripts to loop or iterate repeatedly to quickly and efficiently process large amounts of data. These statements make it possible to write small scripts that are capable of processing enormous amounts of data.

VBScript provides five different types of loops, summarized here, each of which has its own unique purpose and advantages.

- ✪ **Do While**. Sets up a loop that iterates as long as a specified condition remains true.
- ✪ **Do Until**. Sets up a loop that iterates until a specified condition becomes true.
- ✪ **For...Next**. Sets up a loop to execute a specified number of times.
- ✪ **While...Wend**. Sets up a loop that executes as long as a condition remains true.
- ✪ **For...Each...Next.** Creates a loop that iterates through an object's properties.

Do While

The VBScript `Do While` statement is used to create loops that run while a condition remains true. There are two ways that you can set up `Do While` loops in your VBScripts. The syntax for the first method is

```
Do While condition
  statements
Loop
```

You can insert as many programming statements as you want to between the opening Do and closing Loop keywords. The While keyword is included at the beginning of the loop. Therefore if the condition being tested is already false, the loop will never execute. For example, the following VBScript statement shows a VBScript Do While loop that counts to 10. In this example, a variable called myCount is initialized with a value of 0 and then incremented by 1 each time the loop is executed. When the value of the variable finally exceeds 10 the loop terminates and processing continues with the next statement in the script. Therefore myCount is used to control the execution and termination of the loop.

```
' ******************************************************
' * Script Name:    Script 2.8.vbs
' * Description:    This script demonstrates the
' *                 use of the VBScript Do While
' *                 loop
' * Author:         Jerry L. Ford, Jr.
' * Address:        Hanover Virginia
' * Created:        01/13/02
' ******************************************************

' ***** Script initialization statements go here *****

Option Explicit

Dim myCount 'Counter used to control loop termination
myCount = 0

Dim crlf ' Contains carriage return and linefeed instructions
crlf = Chr(13) & Chr(10)

' ********** Main processing section ***************

WScript.Echo "Counting to 10 with a Do While loop" & crlf

Do While myCount < 10
  myCount = myCount + 1
  WScript.Echo(myCount) & crlf
Loop

' ********* Subroutines & Functions go here **********
```

NOTE   You may have noticed that I created a variable called `crlf` in the example and set it equal to a concatenated string made up of `Chr(13)` and `Chr(10)`. `CHR()` is a VBScript function that when called returns the value ANSI character code of the value passed to it. `Chr(13)` returns the value that equates to a linefeed and `Chr(10)` returns a carriage return value.

Figure 2.5 shows the results of running the previous example using the WSH Script.exe execution host.

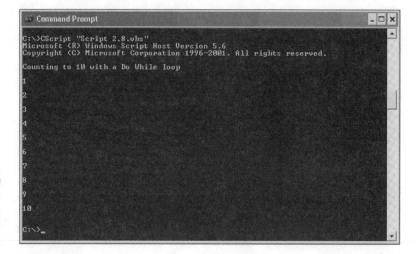

Figure 2.5

Do While loops process until a tested condition becomes false.

The second format of the Do While statement moves the While keyword to the end of the loop. The syntax for this format of the Do While loop is

```
Do
    statements
Loop While condition
```

The effect of moving the location of the While keyword from the beginning to the end of the loop is to force the loop to process at least one time even when the tested condition is initially false.

Do Until

The VBScript Do Until statement is used to create loops that run as long as the tested condition remains false. Like the Do While statement there are two versions of the Do Until statement. The syntax for the first form is

```
Do Until condition
  statements
Loop
```

For example, the following VBScript statements create a Do Until loop that sets up a loop that executes until the value assigned to a variable named myCount exceeds 9.

```
Option Explicit

Dim myCount
myCount = 0

WScript.Echo "Counting to 10 with a Do Until loop"
Do Until myCount > 9
  myCount = myCount + 1
  WScript.Echo(myCount)
Loop
```

If you save this example as a WSH VBScript and run it using the CScript execution host you will see the following output.

```
Counting to 10 with a Do Until loop
1
2
3
4
5
6
7
8
9
10
```

The syntax for the second form of the Do Until statement is shown next. This form of the Do Until statement ensures at least an execution of the loop.

```
Do
  statements
Loop Until condition
```

For example, the following VBScript statements set up a Do loop that will always execute at least one time.

```
Do
  statements
Loop Until condition
```

The following VBScript statements set up a loop that executes as long as the value of a controlling variable is not greater than 9.

```
Option Explicit

Dim myCount
myCount = 0

WScript.Echo "Counting to 10 with a Do Until loop"
Do
  myCount = myCount + 1
  WScript.Echo(myCount)
Loop Until myCount > 9
```

If you execute the statements exactly as shown previously, you'll see the same output that was generated in the previous example. However, try changing the initial value of the myCount variable to 10. You'll see that, unlike the previous example, the loop will execute and display the following output.

```
Counting to 10 with a Do Until loop
11
```

NOTE Be careful when creating loops within your scripts to be sure that they will end appropriately. Otherwise you could accidentally create an endless loop. One way to break out of a loop is with the Exit Do statement. As the following example shows, a variable called noOfExecutions is used to count the number of times that a loop iterates and to prevent it from executing endlessly. In the event that the loop runs more than 50 times, the Exit Do statement terminates the loop.

```
Option Explicit

Dim myCount
Dim noOfExecutions

myCount= 0
noOfExecutions = 0
Do Until myCount > 10
  myCount = myCount - 1
noOfExecutions = noOfExecutions + 1
  WScript.Echo(myCount)
  If noOfExecutions > 49 then
    WScript.Echo "Loop execution is out of control"
    Exit Do
  End If
Loop
```

For...Next

The VBScript For...Next statement is used to create loops that will execute for a specific number of operations. The syntax for the first method is

```
For counter = begin To end [Step step_value]
    statements
Next
```

Counter specifies the controlling variable. Begin specifies its initial value and end sets its ending value. Step_value is an optional parameter that specifies the value that will be used to increment the variable after each iteration.

For example, the following For...Next loop sets up a loop that will execute 10 times and display the value of the controlling variable i for each iteration. The variable i us used to control loop execution and is automatically incremented by 1 at then end of each execution of the loop.

```
Option Explicit
Dim i
For i = 1 To 10
  WScript.Echo i
Next
```

By adding the Step keyword you can control the value used to increment the counter.

```
Option Explicit
Dim i
For i = 1 To 10 Step 2
  WScript.Echo i
Next
```

In this example, the number of times that the loop will execute is cut in half. Instead of seeing the output display the number 1 through 10 you see the following.

```
C:\>CScript.exe test.vbs
Microsoft (R) Windows Script Host Version 5.6
Copyright (C) Microsoft Corporation 1996-2001. All rights reserved.

1
3
5
7
9
```

 NOTE You can force a For...Next loop to end prematurely using the Exit For statement.

While...Wend

The VBScript While...Wend statement is used to create loops that will execute as long as the tested condition remains true. The syntax for the first method is shown below.

```
While condition
  statements
Wend
```

The functionality provided by the `While...Wend` statement is duplicated by the Do loop. It is generally recommended that you use Do loops in place of it. However, just in case I'll give you an example of how to use it.

```
Option Explicit
Dim i

WScript.Echo "Counting to 10 with a While Wend loop"

i = 1
While i < 11
  WScript.Echo i
  i = i + 1
Wend
```

● ●

NOTE Even though I have tried to keep the previous examples as simple as possible to demonstrate how VBScripts statements operate without getting lost in complicated examples, I think it's best that I point something out. It is best to give your variables descriptive names that identify their contents. However, the one exception to this rule of thumb is that simple one-character variable names that are used to control loops are often easier to work with because their purpose is obvious and they make the code easier to read.

● ●

If you insert the preceding statements into a WSH VBScript and run it with the CScript execution host you see the following output.

```
Counting to 10 with a While Wend loop
1
2
3
4
5
6
7
8
9
10
```

For...Each...Next

VBScript allows you to work with objects such as disk drives and printers. Each object has a unique set of properties that describe and control its characteristics. For example, a file has a name as does a printer. Using the For...Each...Next statement you can create a loop that can process all the properties associated with an object.

The syntax of the For...Each...Next statement is

```
For Each element In collection
  statements
Next [element]
```

Element is a variable representing a property associated with the collection (or object). You can also use For...Each...Next statements to process the contents of arrays. An *array* is a related connection of index data that provides a more efficient way than using variables to store large amounts of related information. You will learn more about arrays a little later in the morning and will find examples of how to work with the For...Each...Next loop then.

Improving Script Organization with Procedures

So far the VBScript examples that you have examined in this book have been rather small. However, it's possible to create scripts that are many hundreds of lines long. As your scripts begin to grow in size and complexity you will find that they become more difficult to read and work with.

To help make your scripts easier to work with VBScript allows you to organize portions of your scripts into procedures. A *procedure* is simply a collection of related VBScript statements that are executed as a unit. For example, if you have a script that is designed to perform three tasks, you might break up each task into its own procedure and then call each procedure, when required from the main body of your script.

Procedures are also good for grouping a set of statements that may need to be executed repeatedly by different parts of a script. By grouping these

statements into a single procedure, you can then call
as many times as necessary throughout the script.

VBScript provides two different types of procedures.

- ✪ **Function**. A procedure that executes and then returns a result
  the statement that called it.

- ✪ **Subroutine.** A procedure that executes but does not return a result.

■■

TIP I recommend that you place all your procedures in a common location within your
scripts. This makes them easy to find and maintain. For example, most web page programmers embed their functions and subroutines in the HEAD section of their HTML
pages. This ensures that all procedures have initialized and are available for execution
before being called by VBScripts located in the BODY section. I recommend that you
locate all your procedures at the end of your WSH VBScripts using a template similar to
the one that I showed you earlier in this chapter.

■■

Functions

VBScript functions are collections of related VBScript statements that are
called and executed as a unit. Functions can also return a result to calling
statements. The syntax for creating a function is

```
[Public | Private] Function name [(arglist)]
  statements
End Function
```

Private and Public are optional keywords. The Private keyword is
used to set up a function that can only be called from within the script
where it has been defined. When used, the Public keyword allows the
function to be called by other scripts. Name identifies the function's name.
Arglist is used to specify one or more arguments that that can be passed
to the function.

To return a result to the statement that called the functions you must be
sure that the subroutine has a variable of the same name as the subroutine.

...outine assigned to this variable is what will be

...shows a WSH VBScript that has two functions.

```
' **********************************
' ...ript 2.9.vbs
' ...his script demonstrates how to
' ...rganize your scripts using
' ...unctions
' ...erry L. Ford, Jr.
' ...Hanover Virginia
' * Created:          01/13/02
' **************************************************

' ***** Script initialization statements go here *****

Option Explicit

Const cGreetingMsg = "Hello and welcome"

Dim userFirstName
Dim userLastName

' ********** Main processing section ****************

' Collect the user's first name
userFirstName = GetFirstName()

' Collect the user's last name
userLastName = GetLastName()

' Display welcome message
WScript.Echo cGreetingMsg & " " & userFirstName & " " & userLastName

' ********* Subroutines & Functions go here **********

function GetFirstName()
  GetFirstName = InputBox("What is your first name?")
End Function

function GetLastName()
  GetLastName = InputBox("What is your last name?")
End Function
```

example → next page

on them to execute

t to

The script is divided into three sections. In the first section a constant and a collection of variables used by the rest of the script are defined. The script's controlling logic is located in the main processing section and consists of two function calls and a statement that displays a message that uses information returned by the function calls.

The first function call is to the procedure called Get_First_Name(). This function displays an input dialog asking the user to type his first name. The name typed by the user is then passed back from this procedure and stored in the variable userFirstName. Similarly, the procedure named Get_Last_Name() is called and it collects the user's last name, which is then returned and stored in userLastName. The last statement in the main processing section then displays a message that addresses the user by his first and last names.

NOTE Don't worry about how the InputBox() statement works. I'll explain it in detail at the end of the morning.

NOTE You can also call functions by referencing them inside other VBScript statements. For example, you could have called the Get_First_Name() function and displayed its returned results as follows.

```
WScript.Echo "Hello and welcome " & Get_First_Name()
```

Subroutines

Subroutines work almost exactly like functions except that they are unable to return any results to the calling statement. The syntax for creating a subroutine is shown here.

```
[Public | Private] Sub name [(arglist)]
  statements
End Sub
```

`Private` and `Public` are optional keywords. The `Private` keyword is used to set up a subroutine that can only be called from within the script where it has been defined. When used, the `Public` keyword allows the subroutine to be called by other scripts. `Name` identifies the function's name. `Arglist` is used to specify one or more arguments that can be passed to the subroutine.

When a subroutine is called, it executes and then returns processing control to the statements that follow the calling statement. For example, the following example shows how you might use a subroutine in a VBScript embedded in an HTML page.

```
<HTML>
  <HEAD>
    <TITLE>Script 2.10 - Using a subroutine in your VBScript</TITLE>
    <SCRIPT LANGUAGE="VBScript">
    <!-- Start hiding VBScript statements
      Sub SayHello(name)
        MsgBox "Good morning " & name
      End Sub
    ' End hiding VBScript statements -->
    </SCRIPT>
  </HEAD>
  <BODY>
    <SCRIPT LANGUAGE="VBScript">
    <!-- Start hiding VBScript statements
      SayHello("Jerry")
    ' End hiding VBScript statements -->
    </SCRIPT>
  </BODY>
</HTML>
```

The subroutine is called `Say_Hello()` and is located in the HEAD section of the HTML page. When called it displays a text message in a pop-up dialog. The following statement, located in the BODY section of the HTML page, calls the subroutine.

```
Say_Hello("Jerry")
```

Working with Large Amounts of Related Data

VBScript allows you to store data in variables that you can then reference and manipulate. While there is no limit to the number of variables that you can create in a single VBScript, you'll find that trying to manage too many of them can become difficult.

VBScript provides another storage structure for managing large groups of related data known as an array. An *array* is an indexed collection of values that are managed as a unit. For example, rather than creating a whole series of individual variables to store a list of values such as people's names, you can create an array and assign each name as an array element.

VBScript supports the creation of single dimensional and multidimensional arrays. In fact, VBScript allows for the creation of arrays with as many as 60 dimensions, although you'll probably never need to work with anything bigger than one or two dimensions.

VBScript allows you to create an array using the Dim statement. The syntax of the Dim statement when used to establish an array is

```
Dim arrayname(dimensions)
```

Dimensions is a comma-separated list specifying the length of each of an array's dimensions. For example, the following statement defines a single dimension array called myArray that can hold up to four elements.

```
Dim myArray(3)
```

An array is an indexed list. The first value stored in the array is automatically assigned an index value 0. The second element stored in an array has an index value of 1, and so on. Because an array's index always begins with zero the actual length of an array dimension is equal to the number supplied in the declaration statement plus one. So the array defined above can hold up to 4 elements.

Once you have defined and array you can populate it as demonstrated here.

```
myArray(0) = "Ford, Jerry"
myArray(1) = "Mahoney, Mike"
myArray(2) = "Canzoneri, Nick"
myArray(3) = "Benson, Markland"
```

After you have populated an array you can reference its contents. For example, you could use the following statement to display the value stored as the third element in the array.

```
WScript.Echo myArray(2)
```

The following examples show how to create an array with more than one dimension. In this case, a two-dimensional array is created using the Dim statement that can store its data in a spreadsheet like format.

```
Dim myArray (4,4)
```

You can think of the array created by this example as having five rows by five columns. Remember, the length of any array dimension equals 1 plus the value that specified its length. Similarly, your could define a three-dimensional array by adding additional comma separated values in the Dim statement as shown here.

```
Dim myArray (4,4,4)
```

Processing Array Elements

Although you can access each element of an array a statement at a time, it is usually a lot more efficient to use the VBScript For...Each...Next loop. This loop provides a convenient and speedy way for your scripts to process every element stored in an array. The following example shows how a VBScript embedded in an HTML page can use a For...Each...Next loop to display the contents stored in an array using just a few lines of code.

```
<HTML>
  <HEAD>
    <TITLE>Script 2.11 - Processing the elements in a single ➥
        dimension array</TITLE>
  </HEAD>
```

```
<BODY>
  <SCRIPT LANGUAGE="VBScript">
  <!-- Start hiding VBScript statements

    Option Explicit

    Dim i ' Variable used to control a For...Each loop

    Dim myArray(3)
    myArray(0) = "Ford, Jerry"
    myArray(1) = "Mahoney, Mike"
    myArray(2) = "Canzoneri, Nick"
    myArray(3) = "Benson, Markland"

    Document.Write "<B>My little test array:</B> <BR>"

    For Each i IN myArray
      Document.Write i & "<BR>"
    Next


  ' End hiding VBScript statements -->
  </SCRIPT>
  </BODY>
</HTML>
```

As you can see the VBScript begins with the Option Explicit statement and then defines a variable. This variable, i, will be used by the For...Each...Next loop later in the script to control loop execution. Next an array called myArray is defined and populated with four elements. Then the Document.Write statement displays an HTML message.

NOTE Document is an Internet browser object that VBScript can access to manipulate the currently displayed web page. Write is a method belonging to the Document object that provides a means of displaying text on an HTML page. You'll learn more about working with the Internet Explorer object model this afternoon. For now just know that Document.Write lets you print text information on web pages and that it can do so while supporting HTML formatting tags like the bold <B></B> tags.

Next comes the `For...Each...Next` loop that iterates its way through the array beginning at index position 0 and continuing to the end of the array. A `Document.Write` statement executes with each iteration, displaying the value of the array element currently being processed.

Figure 2.6 shows the results that you will see if you run this script.

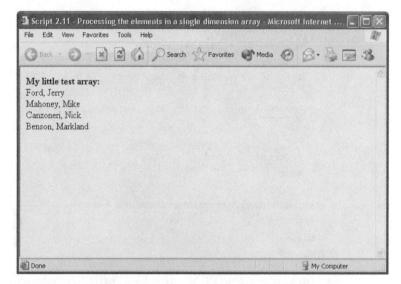

My little test array:
Ford, Jerry
Mahoney, Mike
Canzoneri, Nick
Benson, Markland

Figure 2.6

Processing the contents of an array using a `For...Each...Next` loop.

Dynamically Changing the Size of Arrays

The previous example shows an array where its size was statically set before it was populated. Sometimes, however, it may be useful to change the size of an array. For example, if you are collecting user input and the user wants to provide more data than was anticipated.

One way to set up an array so that you can change its size later in the script is by specifying the `Dim` statement with an empty set of parentheses as shown here:

```
Dim myArray()
```

Defining an array in this manner allows you to set the array's size later in the program, perhaps after asking the user how much data he plans to provide. You use the ReDim statement to change the size of an array. For example, the following statement sets the size of the array to five elements.

```
ReDim myArray(4)
```

Another way to create an array in your scripts that you may need to later resize is to use the ReDim statement to define the array instead of the Dim statement.

Be careful when changing the size of an array that has already been populated with data. For example, the following statement not only expands the size of the array to contain eight elements but also clears out all the array's initial elements, leaving it empty.

```
ReDim myArray(7)
```

If you want to delete the contents of an array, the previous statement works fine, but if you want to preserve the contents in the redefined array, you'll need to add the Preserve keyword to the ReDim statement as shown here.

```
ReDim Preserve myArray(7)
```

Once the array has been resized, you can continue to populate it without loosing any existing data. For example, the following HTML page contains a VBScript that defines an array using the ReDim statement that can hold four elements. It then populates the array and uses a For...Each...Next loop to display the array's contents. A second ReDim statement uses the Preserve keyword to increase the size of the array. New elements are then added to the array and then another For...Each...Next loop is used to display the expanded array's contents.

```
<HTML>
  <HEAD>
    <TITLE>Script 2.12 - Resizing a array</TITLE>
  </HEAD>
  <BODY>
    <SCRIPT LANGUAGE="VBScript">
    <!-- Start hiding VBScript statements
```

```
Option Explicit

Dim i ' Variable use to control a For...Each loop

ReDim myArray(3)
myArray(0) = "Ford, Jerry"
myArray(1) = "Mahoney, Mike"
myArray(2) = "Canzoneri, Nick"
myArray(3) = "Benson, Markland"

Document.Write "<B>My little test array:</B> <BR>"

For Each i IN myArray
  Document.Write i & "<BR>"
Next

ReDim Preserve myArray(6)

myArray(4) = "Ford, Alexander"
myArray(5) = "Ford, William"
myArray(6) = "Ford. Molly"

Document.Write "<P><B>My expanded test array:</B> <BR>"

For Each i IN myArray
  Document.Write i & "<BR>"
Next

  ' End hiding VBScript statements -->
    </SCRIPT>
  </BODY>
</HTML>
```

Figure 2.7 shows the results that you will see if you run this script.

NOTE   Be careful when using the ReDim statement not to reduce the size of an array because you'll lose some of your data. For example, if you defined an array capable of holding ten entries and then populated an array with a list of ten names and then resized it to be half its original size, the final five names that were added to the array are lost.

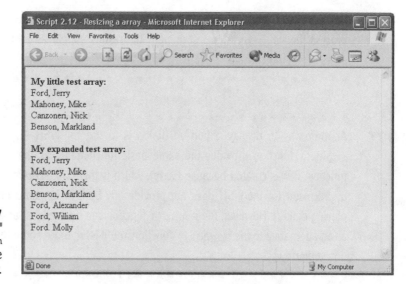

Figure 2.7

Using the ReDim statement to resize a dynamic array.

VBScript Pop-Up Dialogs

VBScript provides two built-in functions that allow you to add pop-up dialogs that you can use in your VBScripts to communicate with users. You can call on these functions to execute within your scripts just like you would any function that you wrote yourself.

These two functions are available regardless of whether you are embedding your VBScripts into HTML pages or writing WSH scripts. Both of these functions are described here.

○ **MsgBox()**. A procedure that executes and then returns a result to the statement that called it.

○ **InputBox()**. A procedure that executes but that does not return a result.

NOTE You have already seen examples in this book of pop-up dialogs created using the WScript.Echo statement. Echo is a method belonging to the WSH WScript object that allows you to display messages to the user that vary depending on which execution host processes them. If the WScript execution processes a WScript.Echo command, it displays the results in a pop-up dialog. However, if the CScript execution host is used to process the `WScript.Echo` statement the results appear as printed text in the Windows command console. You'll learn more about `WScript.Echo` tomorrow.

NOTE   Another way to display a pop-up dialog is to use the WSH `Popup()` function. The `Popup()` function provides the same basic functionality as the VBScript `MsgBox()` function. It was created because JScript, which is the other scripting language supplied by Microsoft for the WSH does not provide any built-in functions or methods for displaying dialogs. However, the `Popup()` function can be used just as easily in a VBScript as an alternative to the `MsgBox()` function. You'll learn more about the `Popup()` function tomorrow.

The VBScript MsgBox Function

The `MsgBox` function provides a way for you to display a pop-up dialog and ask the user to respond by clicking the appropriate button. The syntax of the `MsgBox` function is shown here.

```
MsgBox(prompt [, buttons] [, title] [, helpfile, context])
```

`Prompt` is the text message displayed by the dialog and can be as many as 1,024 characters long. `Button` is a numeric expression or value that is the sum of a number of other values that specify.

○ The types of buttons to display

○ The type of icon to be displayed in the dialog

○ The button to be selected by default

○ The modality of the dialog

Each of the possible numeric values of these four button attributes is outlined in the following four tables. Table 2.4 lists the numeric values that specify the number and types of buttons that will be displayed on the dialog.

Table 2.5 lists the numeric values that specify the type of icon that will be displayed on the dialog.

Table 2.6 lists the numeric values that specify which button on the dialog will be set as the default button.

Table 2.7 lists the numeric values that specify the type modality that will be applied to the dialog.

TABLE 2.4 VBSCRIPT MSGBOX BUTTONS

Constant	Value	Description
vbOKOnly	0	Display OK button
vbOKCancel	1	Display OK and Cancel buttons
vbAbortRetryIgnore	2	Display Abort, Retry, and Ignore buttons
vbYesNoCancel	3	Display Yes, No, and Cancel buttons
vbYesNo	4	Display Yes and No buttons
vbRetryCancel	5	Display Retry and Cancel buttons

TABLE 2.5 VBSCRIPT MSGBOX ICONS

Constant	Value	Description
vbCritical	16	Display critical icon
vbQuestion	32	Display question icon
vbExclamation	48	Display exclamation mark icon
vbInformation	64	Display information icon

TABLE 2.6 VBSCRIPT MSGBOX BUTTON DEFAULTS

Constant	Value	Description
vbDefaultButton1	0	Makes the first button the default
vbDefaultButton2	256	Makes the second button the default
vbDefaultButton3	512	Makes the third button the default
vbDefaultButton4	768	Makes the fourth button the default

TABLE 2.7 VBSCRIPT MSGBOX MODAL SETTING

Constant	Value	Description
vbApplicationModal	0	User must respond before the script can continue
vbSystemModal	4096	User must respond before the script can continue. Also the pop-up dialog remains displayed on top of other active applications

NOTE A dialog's modality governs its behavior. For example, when a dialog is set to be application modal the user is forced to respond to the dialog before the VBScript can continue executing.

The remaining parameters of the MsgBox function are the title, helpfile, and context. Title is an optional text message that will be displayed in the pop-up dialog's title bar. Helpfile and context allow you to associate a help file with the dialog.

The best way to see how to work with the MsgBox() function is to look at a few examples. This first example uses the MsgBox() function in its simplest form as demonstrated below. Only the required `prompt` parameter is supplied.

```
Option Explicit
Dim myCount
MsgBox("Thank you for visiting and come back again soon!")
```

When executed, these statements tell VBScript to display the dialog that you see in Figure 2.8. By default only the OK button is displayed on the dialog. Therefore, the `MsgBox()` function uses the `vbOKOnly` constant by default. Refer to Table 2.4 to see the `vbOKOnly` constant and its value.

Figure 2.8

Using the `MsgBox()` function to display a notification message.

When you execute the `MsgBox()` function as shown previously no value is returned. However if you restructure the way that the `MsgBox()` function was used, VBScript can return a value indicating the button that the user clicks. Table 2.8 provides a list of the possible return values that the `MsgBox()` function can return.

For example, the following statements create a dialog that has two buttons, OK and Cancel, by specifying a value of 1 for the `MsgBox()` button argument. A value of 1 specifies the `vbOKCancel` constant as shown in Table 2.4. In addition, both a prompt message and a title bar message are displayed. Once executed, the value of the button selected by the user is assigned to a variable named `myResponse`. You can then programmatically interrogate the value of this variable. The variable has a value of 1 if the user clicks the OK button and a value of 2 if the user clicks the `Cancel` button.

```
Option Explicit
Dim myResponse
myResponse = MsgBox("Do you wish to quit?", 1, "What do you wish to do?")
```

TABLE 2.8 VBSCRIPT MSGBOX RETURN VALUES

Constant	Value	Description
vbOK	1	User clicked the OK button
vbCancel	2	User clicked the Cancel button
vbAbort	3	User clicked the Abort button
vbRetry	4	User clicked the Retry button
vbIgnore	5	User clicked the Ignore button
vbYes	6	User clicked the Yes button
vbNo	7	User clicked the No button

NOTE If the user presses the ESC key then the value returned will be a 2, supplying the same value as if the Cancel button had been clicked.

This next example shows how to mix up things a bit more. This time we are going to display a message box that has both the OK and Cancel buttons, as well as the Critical icon. In your reference to Table 2.4 you will see that in order to display the OK and Cancel buttons you'll need to use the vbOKCancel constant that has a value of 1. In addition, Table 2.5 shows that to display the Critical icon you'll have to specify the vbCritical constant that has a value of 16. By summing the values of these two constants you come up with a value of 17, which is what you will use in the example shown here.

```
Option Explicit
Dim myResponse
myResponse = MsgBox("Do you wish to quit?", 17, "What do you wish to
do?")
```

As Figure 2.9 shows, the dialog contains all three elements.

Figure 2.9

Displaying a dialog with an OK and Cancel button, as well as a critical icon.

Just to be sure that I have made clear the way to sum up the values of the VBScript constants that represent the features you want to appear on the MsgBox() pop-up dialog, let's do one more example. This time let's create a pop-up dialog that has OK and Cancel buttons, as well as a critical icon and let's set the default button to be the second button, which will be the Cancel button.

To create a dialog that satisfies all these criteria you'll need to use the following VBScript constants.

- **vbOKCancel** that has a value of 1
- **vbCritical** that has a value of 16
- **vbDefaultbutton2** that has a value of 256

By adding up the values associated with these three VBScript constants you come up with 273 which is the number used in this example.

```
Option Explicit
Dim myResponse
myResponse = MsgBox("Do you wish to quit?", 273, "What do you wish to
do?")
```

The VBScript InputBox Function

The InputBox() function provides a way for you to display a pop-up dialog that prompts the user to supply text input. The InputBox allows you to ask the user questions and collect text input. The syntax of the InputBox() function is shown here.

```
InputBox(prompt [, title] [, default] [, xpos] [, ypos] [, helpfile,
context])
```

`Prompt` is the text message displayed by the dialog and can be as many as 1,024 characters. `Title` is an optional text message that will be displayed in the pop-up dialog's title bar. You can include the `default` parameter to specify a default answer in the dialog's text field. `Xpos` and `ypos` can be used to optionally specify the initial location of the dialog. Finally `helpfile` and `context` allow you to associate a help file with the dialog.

For example, the following statements prompt the user to type the name of the country in which he or she resides.

```
Option Explicit
Dim myInput
myInput = InputBox("What country do you reside in?")
```

The only parameter passed to the `InputBox()` function is the `prompt` text. As Figure 2.10 shows, two buttons are displayed on the dialog—the `OK` and `Cancel` buttons. If the user clicks `OK` or presses the Enter key, then the text, if any, that was typed by the user is assigned to the `myInput` variable. If the user clicks on `Cancel` or clicks on the Close button, then a zero-length string is assigned to the `myInput` variable.

Figure 2.10

A typical pop-up dialog created by the `InputBox()` function.

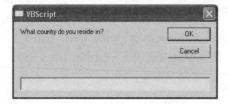

The following example demonstrates how to display a message in the pop-up dialog title bar as well as how to provide the user with a default answer.

```
Option Explicit
Dim Input
Input = InputBox("What country do you reside in?", "Welcome to my
script!", "USA")
```

Figure 2.11 shows the dialog displayed when these statements execute.

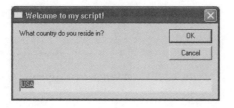

Figure 2.11

Adding a title bar
message and
default answer to a
pop-up dialog.

If you want to display a large amount of text in the dialog and you want
to get fancy you can format the `prompt` text displayed using `Chr(13)`
and `Chr(10)`. `Chr(13)` equates to a carriage return while `Chr(10)` provides for a linefeed character. The following example demonstrates a typical formatting example.

```
Option Explicit
Dim Input
Input = InputBox("What country do you reside in? If you prefer not"
        + Chr(13) + Chr(10) + "to provide this information please type
NA.", "", "USA")
```

Figure 2.12 shows the dialog box created from the previous example.

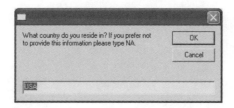

Figure 2.12

Creating pop-up
dialog with
formatted text.

What's Next?

Well now, I'd say that we've gone over a pretty good amount of material
for a single morning. Now is probably a good time for you to put this
book down, stretch your legs, and get a little something to eat. We'll pick
back up this afternoon and begin the first of two chapters that cover the
integration of VBScript into your HTML pages. By the time the day is
over you'll be ready to begin spicing up your web pages.

Scripting Inside Internet Explorer

- ✪ Examine the object models supported by Internet Explorer
- ✪ Learn how to manipulate browser objects using their methods and properties
- ✪ See how to post messages on the Internet Explorer status bar
- ✪ Learn how to react to keyboard keystrokes and mouse clicks
- ✪ Find out how to track and respond to mouse movements

Welcome back. I hope you are ready for an afternoon full of work. This morning you learned all the basic programming statements that make up the VBScript language. This included learning how to work with variables, constants, conditional logic, procedures, looping and arrays.

This afternoon you'll complete the first of two chapters devoted to showing you how to apply your new VBScript programming skills to your HTML pages. You will see how VBScript interacts with Internet Explorer and uses object models to control a number of browser features, such as opening and closing browser windows. You'll also learn to work with a number of Internet Explorer objects that allow you to write scripts that can display pop-up dialogs, control browser navigation, and react to browser and user events such as mouse clicks and double clicks.

NOTE Internet Explorer supports VBScript but Netscape Communicator does not. This also means that the Opera browser, which is based on Netscape Communicator's open source code, does not support VBScript. However, there are many other Internet browsers on the market, a large number of which are based on the Internet Explorer engine giving VBScript a much wider support base than most people realize. For example, America Online supports a number of custom browsers. Some are based on Netscape and others on Internet Explorer. However, the browser that AOL distributes to its subscribers is based on Internet Explorer and therefore supports VBScript. It probably won't surprise you then that the MSN Explorer browser that Microsoft distributes to its MSN customers

also supports VBScript. In total I know of at least a dozen Internet browsers that are based on Internet Explorer and support VBScript. These include

Internet Explorer	MSN Explorer	AOL
EarthLink LiteAOL	CompuServe	Oligo
UltraBrowser	CrystalPort	NeoPlanet
Kidnet	ExplorerRapidBrowser	SmartExplorer
Fast Browser Pro		

I am sure that there are more browsers based on Internet Explorer (which also support VBScript) than I have listed here. These are just the ones that I have heard of and tried.

Programming Using Objects

A browser-based object is a programming construct that contains methods and properties and represents a specific feature or piece of browser functionality. Internet Explorer exposes objects based on the content of HTML pages. You can then use VBScript to manipulate the properties and methods associated with objects to affect the operation of Internet Explorer and the currently loaded HTML page.

Each version of Internet Explorer provides its own object model. This model has been modified and expanded with each new release. Therefore, some objects, methods, and properties found in Internet Explorer 6 are not supported by earlier versions of the browser. What this means is that if you create a VBScript that works with objects, methods, or properties introduced by a later version of Internet Explorer they won't be available in earlier versions and your scripts will experience run-time errors. This makes script development difficult.

Some people choose to write scripts that ignore newer objects, methods, and properties and stick to a collection of objects supported by all versions of the Internet explorer. This way they know that their scripts will always run as expected. However, this can limit the things that you can

do with your scripts. Other pe[...]
tage of the features found in [...]
expect their visitors to keep th[...]
body that visits your web pag[...]
develop multiple versions of y[...]
different versions of the brov[...]
to test each visitor's browser[...]
redirect them to pages appr[...]
to proceed, of course, is up to you.

Given that there have already been four major versions of Internet Explorer since the introduction of VBScript (versions 3.X, 4.X, 5.X, and now 6.X) there is no way I can discuss in this book every object, method, and property specific to each version. Instead, to provide you with a quick foundation for VBScript web page development I am going to cover those objects that you are most likely to need to work with, and demonstrate various ways of using them.

NOTE

As I stated at the beginning of the book, I am using Internet Explorer 6 to test each VBScript that I embed in the HTML pages shown in this book. You may want to test your scripts on multiple versions of Internet Explorer before adding them to your web site to be sure that they operate correctly for each version of Internet Explorer that you intend to support.

Understanding Object Organization

Objects are logically organized into a tree-like structure with parent, child, and sibling relationships. For example, take a look at the following HTML page. As you can see it only contains a few elements.

```
<HTML>

  <HEAD>
    <TITLE>Script 3.1 - A simple HTML page</TITLE>
  </HEAD>
```

```
<BODY>
  <P>Good morning.</P>
  <P>Welcome to my web page!</P>
 </BODY>

</HTML>
```

When you create web pages using only HTML you do not need to be concerned with the logical tree structure of your pages. However, you need to know at least a little to successfully add VBScripts. Let's take the preceding example and depict its organizational tree structure, which is shown in Figure 3.1.

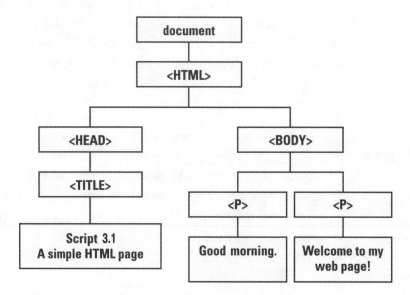

Figure 3.1

Examining the organizational tree structure of a HTML page.

As you can see the document object, which I'll go over in greater depth in a bit, is always at the top of the tree. The rest of the tree is composed of the HTML tags and their contents. For example, the document object's child is the <HTML> element. The <HTML> element has two children of its own, the <HEAD> and <BODY> elements. Likewise these two elements have their own children.

Object Properties

An object's *properties* are attributes that store values representing certain aspects of the object. For example, the `document` object, which I mentioned previously has a pair of properties called `bgColor` and `fgColor`. You can manipulate these properties to change the background and foreground colors on a HTML page.

In order to reference an object from within a VBScript you type the object's name followed by a period and then the name of the property as demonstrated here.

```
document.bgColor
document.fgColor
```

For example, the following HTML page contains a VBScript that reverses the default black on white foreground and background colors on the HTML page.

```
<HTML>

  <HEAD>
    <TITLE>Script 3.2 - Working with document object
        properties</TITLE>
  </HEAD>

  <BODY>
    <SCRIPT LANGUAGE="VBScript">
    <!-- Start hiding VBScript statements
      document.bgColor="black"
      document.fgColor="white"
     ' End hiding VBScript statements -->
    </SCRIPT>
    <P>Good morning.</P>
    <P>Welcome to my web page!</P>
  </BODY>

</HTML>
```

Figure 3.2 shows how the preceding example appears when loaded by Internet Explorer. As you can see the two VBScript statements shown earlier have been added to the HTML page. They manipulate properties of the `document` object, which resides at the top of the page's object tree.

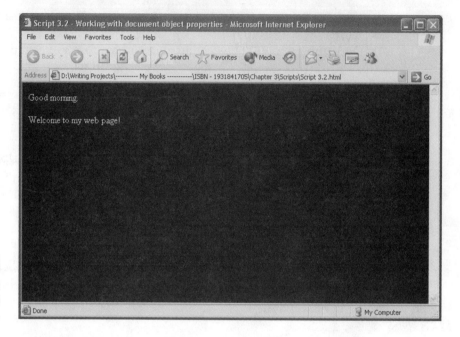

Figure 3.2

Manipulating the
properties of the
document object.

Object Methods

An object's *methods* are functions that manipulate the object or its data. For example, the window object is the parent of the document object. The window object provides a method called alert() that you can use in your VBScripts to display messages in pop-up dialogs as demonstrated here.

```
window.alert("Welcome to my web site!")
```

When referencing an object's methods you first type the name of the object, a period, the name of the method, and a pair of parentheses containing a comma-separated list of arguments that the method is to process. You must also supply the () characters even if you are not going to pass any parameters to the method for processing. For example, the following VBScript uses the window.alert method to welcome visitors.

```
<HTML>

  <HEAD>
    <TITLE>Script 3.3 - Working with window object's alert ➥
        method</TITLE>
  </HEAD>

  <BODY>
    <SCRIPT LANGUAGE="VBScript">
    <!-- Start hiding VBScript statements
      window.alert("Welcome to my web site!")
      ' End hiding VBScript statements -->
    </SCRIPT>
    <P>Good morning.</P>
    <P>Welcome to my web page!</P>
  </BODY>

</HTML>
```

Object Events

An *event* represents the occurrence of an action within Internet Explorer. Examples of events include such things as mouse movement or a mouse click. For example, if you create a form on a HTML page, events fire whenever a visitor moves the pointer over any form element, when data is typed into a text field, and when mouse clicks occur on form buttons, checkboxes, and radio buttons.

You can define event handlers within VBScripts that can react to events. This way your scripts can interact with visitors as they point and click their way round your web pages. I'll provide more information and examples on how to work with events later this afternoon.

An Overview of Internet Explorer Object Models

In addition to the difficulty of developing scripts in a world where visitors to your web pages may use any of four versions of Internet Explorer, you also need to know something about working with two different

Internet Explorer object models. That's right, there are two different object models.

Internet Explorer versions 3 and 4 support a single object model known as the DHTML object model. This model provides access to most of the elements found on an HTML page.

In recent years a group known as the World Wide Web Consortium has developed an object model standard known as the *Document Object Model* or *DOM*. This model provides access to every element on a HTML page and is gradually being adopted by all major Internet browser developers, including Microsoft Internet Explorer.

 NOTE
If you are interested in learning more about this object model check out **www.w3c. org/DOM**.

The DHTML Model

Internet Explorer versions 3 and 4 support variations of the DHTML model. This model is also supported by Internet Explorer versions 5 and 6 thus providing for backward compatibility. The DHTML model views a HTML page as a hierarchy of objects. To manipulate any object in the tree you must be able to refer to it by name. For example, you might define a form on your HTML as shown here.

```
<FORM NAME="myForm">
  <INPUT NAME="myButton" TYPE="button" VALUE="Click on me!">
</FORM>
```

To reference the button on the HTML form from within your VBScript you must add the NAME attribute to both the HTML FORM and INPUT tags and specify a name. For example, the name assigned to the form is myForm while the button on the form is named myButton.

NOTE Absent from the DHTML model is the capability to specify a particular object in the tree and then programmatically navigate up, down, or sideways in the tree. The DOM model discussed later in this chapter provides this capability.

At the top of the DHTML model is the window object. Every HTML page has a single window object—except when frames are used—in which case there is a separate window object for each frame and a parent window object, which represents the page that defined each frame.

The window object provides access to a number of child objects as depicted in Figure 3.3. The window object provides properties and methods that allow it to do many things, including:

⚙ Place text messages in the Internet Explorer status bar

⚙ Open a new window and load a URL into it

⚙ Close a window

⚙ Create pop-up dialogs that display messages, prompt the user to click on preset options, or type in a text response

Objects under the window object include:

⚙ **Navigator object.** Provides information about the browser that has loaded the HTML page, including the browser type and version.

⚙ **History object.** Provides methods that can be used to navigate through the document object's history list (for example, the places visited since the browser window was opened).

⚙ **Document object.** Represents the HTML page currently displayed by Internet Explorer and provides properties and methods for manipulating it.

⚙ **Location object.** Provides information about the currently loaded URL and provides the capability to reload HTML pages or load a new URL.

⚙ **Frames collection.** Provides an indexed list (an array) of the frames currently located in the browser window.

Figure 3.3

Examining some of the `child` objects under the `window` object.

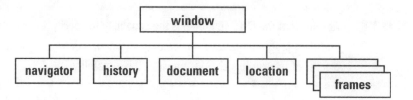

• •

A **collection** is simply an array containing references to objects of the same type on an HTML page. For example, the `frames` collection is an array that lists all the frames in the currently loaded HTML page, while the `forms` array contains a list of all the forms on the current HTML page.

• •

The object that you'll find yourself working with the most in your VBScripts is the document object. It provides access to a number of other objects and collections. Figure 3.4 depicts some of the objects and collections that are located under the document object. We will take a closer look at these objects as the afternoon progresses.

The Document Object Model

There are a number of DOM standards. Internet Explorer 5 supports most of the DOM Level 1 standard. Internet Explorer 6 comes even closer to supporting this standard. However, neither version is 100 percent compliant.

Besides helping to standardize the object model for modern browsers, this model, which is sometimes referred to as the W3C DOM, also provides more comprehensive control over a script's ability to navigate a HTML page and change its contents. In fact, all the objects that are available in the DHTML object model are still available but now they are more accessible. Each of these objects still has its own unique set of methods and properties. However, under the DOM the objects have a second set of methods and properties, which are used to navigate the HTML pages tree hierarchy.

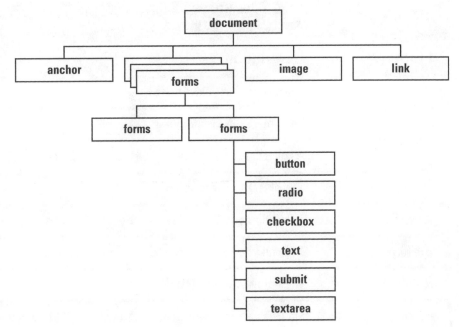

Figure 3.4

Examining the child objects of the document object.

Unlike the DHTML model where you must address the various elements in a HTML page directly by name the DOM lets you access the elements on a HTML page using any of the following properties as shown in Table 3.1.

The best way that I can think of to explain how these properties are used is to show you an example. First, let's create a simple HTML page as shown here.

```
<HTML>
  <HEAD>
    <TITLE>Script 3.4 - Advanced DOM Example</TITLE>
  </HEAD>

  <BODY ID="myBodyNode"
    <P ID="paraTag1" Name="Tag1">This is paragraph one.</P>
    <p ID="paraTag2">This is paragraph two.</P>
  </BODY>
</HTML>
```

TABLE 3.1 **DOCUMENT OBJECT MODEL PROPERTIES**	
Property	**Description**
firstChild	The object's first child node
lastChild	The object's last child node
childNodes	A collection/array of all an object's child objects
parentNode	The object's parent object
nextSibling	The child node that follows next in the DOM tree
prevSibling	The child node that precedes the current child
nodeName	The name of the HTML tag
nodeType	Specifies a value representing the type of HTML element (tag, attribute, or text)
nodeValue	The value assigned to a text node
data	The value of the specified text node
specified	Specifies whether an attribute has been set
attributes	A collection/array of all an object's attributes

Next, let's make a model representing the tree structure of this HTML page as shown in Figure 3.5. As Figure 3.5 shows, the document object is the root of the tree. It has only one child object—the documentElement—which equates to the first <HTML> tag on the page.

Now let's add a VBScript to the HTML page that demonstrates how to use DOM properties and methods to navigate the HTML page and manipulate its contents.

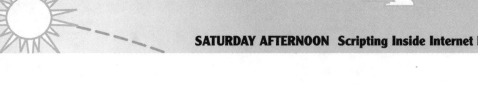
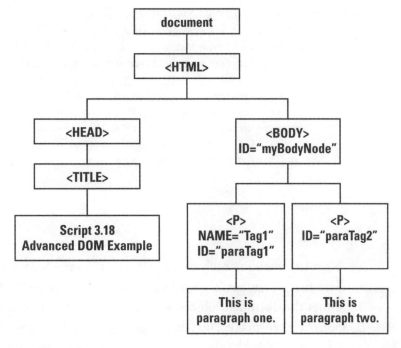

Figure 3.5

A graphical
representation of
the HTML page.

```
<HTML>
  <HEAD>
    <TITLE>Script 3.5 - Advanced DOM Example</TITLE>
  </HEAD>

  <BODY ID="myBodyNode"
    <P ID="paraTag1" Name="Tag1">This is paragraph one.</P>
    <p ID="paraTag2">This is paragraph two.</P>

    <SCRIPT LANGUAGE="VBScript">
    <!-- Start hiding VBScript statements
      window.alert("The ID for the first element is: " & ➥
          document.documentElement.firstChild.tagName)
      window.alert("The ID for the second element is: " & ➥
          document.documentElement.firstChild.nextSibling.tagName)
      window.alert("The ID for the child of the first element is: " ➥
          & document.documentElement.firstChild.firstChild.tagName)
      window.alert("The type of tag associated with the myBodyNode ➥
          ID is: " & myBodyNode.tagName)
```

```
    window.alert("The type of tag associated with the paraTag2 ➡
        ID is: " & paraTag2.tagName)
    window.alert("The Value associated with the paraTag2 element ➡
        is: " & document.getElementById("paraTag2").firstChild.➡
        nodeValue)
    window.alert("When you click on OK the value associated with ➡
        the paraTag2 " & "ID will be changed.")
    document.getElementById("paraTag2").firstChild.nodeValue=➡
        "This is the " & "new and improved paragraph two!"
    ' End hiding VBScript statements -->
    </SCRIPT>

    </BODY>

</HTML>
```

Now let's examine each of the statements in the VBScript one at a time. The first statement, shown here, displays the tag name of the first child under the document object, which is the `<HEAD>` tag. Look at each component that makes up the `tagname` reference (for example, `document.documentElement.firstChild.nextSibling.tagName`) and compare it to the tree hierarchy shown in Figure 3.5.

```
window.alert("The ID for the first element is: " & _
    document.documentElement.firstChild.tagName)
```

Figure 3.6 shows the pop-up dialog that appears when this statement is executed.

Figure 3.6

The Internet Explorer DOM lets you access every element on an HTML page.

The next VBScript statement displays the tag name of the BODY tag using the `nextSibling` property.

```
window.alert("The ID for the second element is: " & ➡
    document.documentElement.firstChild.nextSibling.tagName)
```

The next VBScript statement displays the tag name of the first child of the first child of the document object, which is the TITLE tag.

```
window.alert("The ID for the child of the first element is: " & ➡
  document.documentElement.firstChild.firstChild.tagName)
```

Each of the preceding statements has referenced a specific element in the HTML page by referencing it starting from the document element down to its location in the page. The next VBScript statement displays the tag name of the BODY tag by specifying its ID.

```
window.alert("The type of tag associated with the myBodyNode ID ➡
  is: " & myBodyNode.tagName)
```

The next VBScript statement displays the tag name of the <P> tag whose ID is paraTag2.

```
window.alert("The type of tag associated with the paraTag2 ID is: " ➡
  & paraTag2.tagName)
```

The next VBScript statement shows how to display the value of the first child of the <P> tag whose ID is paraTag2 using the DOM getElementById() method.

```
window.alert("The Value associated with the paraTag2 element is: " ➡
  & document.getElementById("paraTag2").firstChild.nodeValue)
```

Figure 3.7 shows the pop-up dialog produced by the previous statement.

Figure 3.7

Displaying the value of the <HTML> tag.

Next, the following statement informs the user that when the OK button is clicked the script will change the value stored in the second <P> tag.

```
window.alert("When you click on OK the value associated with the ➡
  paraTag2 " & "ID will be changed.")
```

Finally, the last VBScript statement changes the text displayed in the second <P> tag.

```
document.getElementById("paraTag2").firstChild.nodeValue="This is ➥
  the " & "new and improved paragraph two!"
```

This statement can be broken down as follows.

- ✪ Start with the `document` object
- ✪ Add the `getElementById()` method and specify `paraTag2`. This gets you to the second <P> tag.
- ✪ Add references to the `firstChild` and `nodeValue` properties. This creates a reference to the text stored in the <P> tag.

Figure 3.8 shows how the HTML page appears after the text stored in the second paragraph has been modified.

As you can see, the DOM provides powerful capabilities for navigating a HTML page and manipulating its content. This can be a powerful pro-

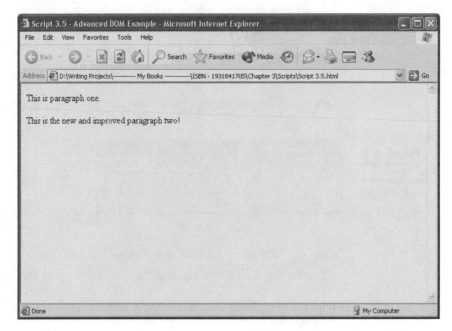

Figure 3.8

Using properties and methods of the document object to navigate a HTML page and alter its content.

gramming technique; however, it also adds a level of complexity to your VBScripts. Complete coverage of how to implement all of the objects, methods, and properties of the DOM would take more space than is available in this book. You can go to **www.w3c.org/DOM** to learn more about this object model. Also a lot of good information can also be found by searching **www.microsoft.com**.

One big problem with using the DOM is that Internet Explorer browsers prior to version 5 do not support it, which means that many of the visitors to your web pages may not be able to work with your HTML pages.

The bottom line here is that we are still in a state of infancy as far as web page development is concerned. Standards and their adoption and implementation are in a constant state of change. Any time you choose to implement the latest Internet Explorer features like the objects, properties, and methods of the DOM, you risk creating HTML pages that will not support everyone. Using DOM properties and methods of the `document` also adds to the complexity of your VBScripts. However, while not using new features may let you develop HTML pages suited to a broader audience, you are limiting yourself to yesterday's technology. Neither choice is ideal and there is no right answer. Therefore it is really just a matter of personal choice as to how you work with the available object models.

As far as this book goes, I'll rely on demonstrating examples that leverage the DHTML model. This will make my VBScript examples easier to follow and help to simplify their presentation.

Commonly Used Browser Objects

So far I have spent a lot of time discussing the concept of objects and their methods and properties. I also spent a great deal of time trying to explain the basics of working with the object models supported by Internet Explorer. Don't worry if your head is spinning and if you did not

understand every thing that you read. Object models are an advanced programming concept and it can take a while for them to sink in. In fact, you may want to come back in a few weeks and read the first part of this chapter again. However, I'd also recommend searching the Internet and finding as much additional information as you can on both the DHTML and DOM object models.

Next, let's spend a little time getting to know some of the objects that you'll find yourself using in your VBScripts. These objects include the following:

- ✪ window
- ✪ document
- ✪ location
- ✪ history
- ✪ navigator

The window Object

The window object is at the top of the object model hierarchy and is the parent of the document object. If frames are being used, then a window object will be created for each frame with an additional parent window representing the HTML page that defined the frameset. The window object provides access to the following.

- ✪ window object methods
- ✪ window object properties
- ✪ Other objects
- ✪ Collections

You can manipulate the window object's properties and execute its methods to affect the browser in a number of ways. The following example shows how you can use the window object's prompt() and alert() methods to greet visitors by name.

```
<HTML>

  <HEAD>
    <TITLE>Script 3.6 - Working with the Window object's prompt and ➥
       alert methods</TITLE>
  </HEAD>

  <BODY>
    <H3>ABC Company web page<H3>

    <SCRIPT LANGUAGE="VBScript">
    <!-- Start hiding VBScript statements
      visitorName = window.prompt("What is your name?", "")
      window.alert("Welcome to my Web Page " & visitorName & "!")
    ' End hiding VBScript statements -->
    </SCRIPT>

  </BODY>

</HTML>
```

The following statement assigns the text value returned from the
`prompt()` method to a variable name `visitorName`.

```
visitorName = window.prompt("What is your name?", "")
```

The `alert()` method is then used to display a greeting message to which
the value of `visitorName` is appended using the & concatenation operator as shown here.

```
window.alert("Welcome to my Web Page " & visitorName & "!")
```

Figures 3.9 and 3.10 show how the interaction appears to the visitor.

Figure 3.9

Using the `window`
object's prompt
method to collect a
user's name.

Explorer User Prompt

Script Prompt:
What is your name?

OK
Cancel

Jerry

Figure 3.10

Using the `window` object's alert method to greet a user by his or her name.

This next example uses the window object's confirm(), alert(), and close() methods.

```
<HTML>

  <HEAD>
    <TITLE>Script 3.7 - Working with the Window object's confirm, ➡
        alert and close methods</TITLE>
  </HEAD>

  <BODY>
    <H3>ABC Company web page<H3>

    <SCRIPT LANGUAGE="VBScript">
    <!-- Start hiding VBScript statements
      decision = window.confirm("Click on OK to exit or Cancel to ➡
        stick around?")
      If decision = "True" Then
        window.alert("Bye. Please visit again soon!")
        window.close()
      Else
        window.alert("Great. Thanks for sticking around!")
      End If
    ' End hiding VBScript statements -->
    </SCRIPT>

  </BODY>

</HTML>
```

The confirm() method is used to display the pop-up dialog shown in Figure 3.11. Here the visitor is presented with two options: either click OK to leave or Cancel to remain at your web site. Clicking OK returns a

value to `true` in which case the `window` object's `alert()` method displays a message asking the visitor to come back again. When the visitor clicks OK the `close()` method is executed, which then closes the Internet Explorer window. However, if the visitor clicks Cancel when first prompted a value of `false` is returned and the `Else` part of the `If...Then...Else` statement displays a message thanking the visitor for sticking around.

Figure 3.11

Using the `window` object's `confirm()` method to ask the user if they really want to leave your web site.

As the following VBScript shows, you can do more with the `window` object than just display pop-up dialogs. This script contains a HTML form with three buttons. When the HTML page is initially loaded the `onLoad` statement embedded in the `<BODY>` tag displays a message in the Internet Explorer status bar by assigning a value to the `window` object's `status()` property.

A VBScript is embedded in the `HEAD` section of the HTML page that defines three functions. Each function executes when one of the form's buttons is clicked and each displays a different message in the browser's status bar.

NOTE

These three functions are executed when the `onClick` event fires for each one's associated button. You can tell which button each function is associated with by looking at the first half of the function's name. I'll discuss in greater detail how VBScript events work a little later in the afternoon.

```
<HTML>

  <HEAD>
    <TITLE>Script 3.8 - Posting Messages to the IE Status Bar</TITLE>

    <SCRIPT LANGUAGE="VBScript">
    <!-- Start hiding VBScript statements
      Sub myButton1_onclick
        window.status = "You should see message 1 displayed in the ➥
          statusbar"
      End Sub

      Sub myButton2_onclick
        window.status = "You should see message 2 displayed in the ➥
          statusbar"
      End Sub

      Sub myButton3_onclick
        window.status = "You should see message 3 displayed in the ➥
          statusbar"
      End Sub
    ' End hiding VBScript statements -->
    </SCRIPT>

  </HEAD>

  <BODY onLoad="window.status = 'This message is displayed on the ➥
        IE status bar when the HTML page loads'">

    <H3>Taking Control of the IE Status Bar!</H3>

    <FORM>
      <INPUT NAME="myButton1" TYPE="button" VALUE="Display Message ➥
        # 1"> <P>
      <INPUT NAME="myButton2" TYPE="button" VALUE="Display Message ➥
        # 2"> <P>
      <INPUT NAME="myButton3" TYPE="button" VALUE="Display Message ➥
        # 3">
    </FORM>

  </BODY>

</HTML>
```

Figure 3.12 shows how the HTML page created in the prev... appears when executed.

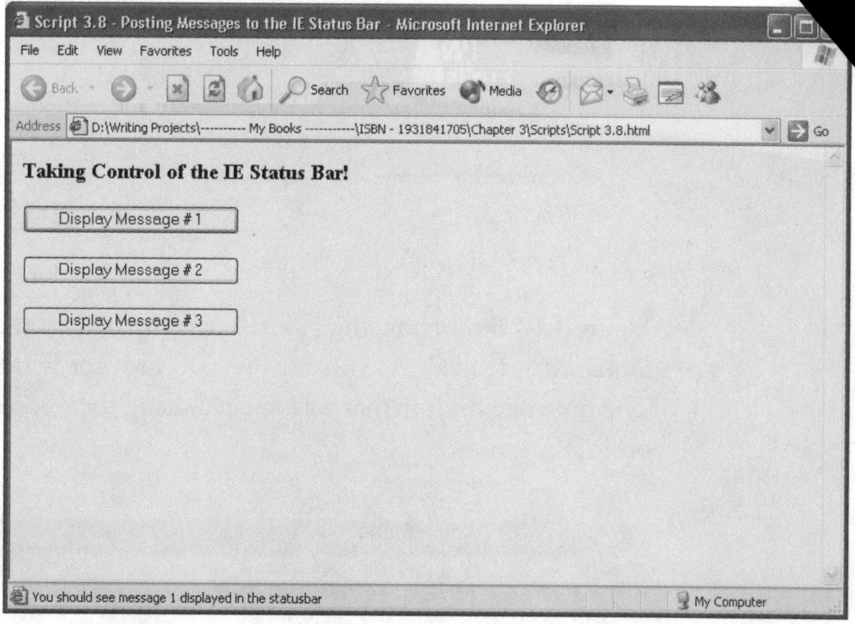

Figure 3.12

By manipulating the `window` object's status property you can post messages on the Internet Explorer status bar.

A final example demonstrates how to use the `window` object's `open()` method to open a second browser window and customize its appearance. By applying this example to your own web pages, you can easily create web sites that open any number of browser windows when a visitor loads your home page. This way you can load pages that display advertising pages, provide controlling menus, and a host of other information.

```
<HTML>

  <HEAD>
    <TITLE>Script 3.9 - Working with the Window object's open ➥
        method</TITLE>

    <SCRIPT LANGUAGE="VBScript">
    <!-- Start hiding VBScript statements
```

```
                        "http://www.premierpressbooks.com", "Window1", ➥
           no", _
           , "scroolbar=no"
           3Script statements -->
```

```
<BODY>
  <H3> Welcome to my web page!</H3>
</BODY>

</HTML>
```

Figure 3.13 shows how the HTML page created by the previous example looks when loaded. As you can see two browser windows are displayed. The browser window that was opened using the open() method appears on top.

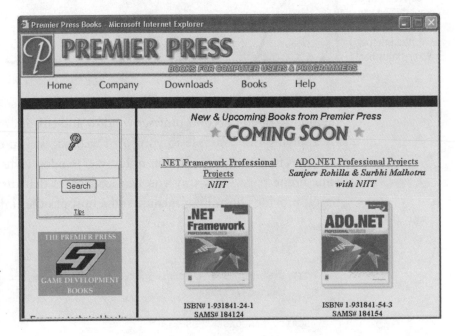

Figure 3.13

The window object's open() method lets you open new browser windows and load new web pages in them.

Take a Break

I don't know about you but all this talk about object models, properties, methods, and events has worn me out. Let's take a 15-minute break and give things some time to sink in. When you come back we'll finish the afternoon by examining a few more browser objects and then dive into event handling a lot deeper. You'll learn how to create event handlers that can respond to both keyboard and mouse events as well as events generated by the browser, such as when it loads or unloads a HTML page.

The `document` Object

The `document` object is a child of the `window` object and is the object that you'll find yourself using most often. It represents the currently loaded HTML page. You can use its properties and methods to manipulate HTML pages in a number of ways. For example, the following VBScript changes the value assigned to the `document` object's `bgColor` and `fgColor` properties and then uses the `write()` method to display text on the HTML page.

```
<HTML>

  <HEAD>
    <TITLE>Script 3.10- Working with the document object's ➡
       properties and methods</TITLE>
  </HEAD>

  <BODY>
    <H3>Gathering Browser and Operating System Information</H3>

    <SCRIPT LANGUAGE="VBScript">
    <!-- Start hiding VBScript statements
      document.bgColor="black"
      document.fgColor="white"
      document.write("<B>Document Title:</B> "  & document.title ➡
         & "<P>")
      document.write("<B>Last Modified on:</B> " & ➡
         document.lastModified & "<P>")
      document.write("<B>Document URL:</B> "  & document.URL)
```

```
' End hiding VBScript statements -->
</SCRIPT>

</BODY>

</HTML>
```

This example also demonstrates how you can intermix HTML tags with your VBScript statements using the & concatenation operator. Figure 3.14 shows how the HTML page generated from this example appears.

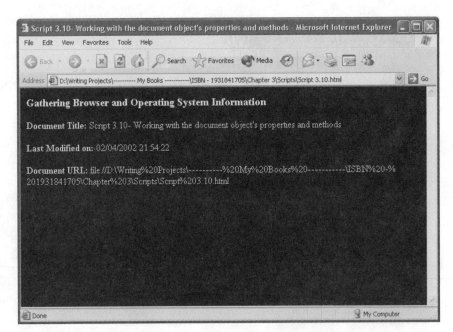

Figure 3.14

You can affect the appearance of web pages by manipulating the document object's properties.

Other document object properties that you may want to experiment with include

○ **linkColor**. Specifies the color of document links

○ **alinkColor**. Specifies the color of active document links

○ **vlinkColor**. Specifies the color of visited links

- ✿ **anchor**. An object whose length property specifies the number of anchors on the HTML page
- ✿ **link**. An object whose length property specifies the number of links on the HTML page
- ✿ **cookie**. Provides the ability to create, store, and retrieve cookies on visitor's computer
- ✿ **elements**. An object whose length property specifies the number of controls on a form
- ✿ **form**. Represents a form on a HTML page
- ✿ **lastModified**. Retrieves the date and time that the current HTML page was last modified
- ✿ **title**. Retrieves values stored in the HTML page's TITLE tags

The `location` Object

The `location` object lets you programmatically control the URL loaded into the browser. Using this object's href property you can retrieve the currently loaded HTML page's URL. Using the `location` object's `replace()` and `reload()` methods you can replace or refresh the HTML page displayed by Internet Explorer.

The following example demonstrates how to create a custom control that can change the HTML page loaded by Internet Explorer.

```
<HTML>

  <HEAD>
    <TITLE>Script 3.11 - Creating a manual custom navigation ➡
        control</TITLE>
  </HEAD>

  <BODY>
    <H3>Select an on-line bookstore</H3>

    <SCRIPT LANGUAGE="VBScript">
    <!-- Start hiding VBScript statements
```

```
        Function myButton_onClick()
           window.location=document.myForm.myList.value
        End Function
   ' End hiding VBScript statements -->
   </SCRIPT>

     <FORM NAME="myForm">
       <SELECT NAME="myList" size=3>
       <OPTION VALUE="http://www.amazon.com"> Amazon.com
       <OPTION VALUE="http://www.bn.com"> Barnes & Noble
       <OPTION VALUE="http://www.bamm.com"> Books-A-Million
       </SELECT>
       <INPUT NAME="myButton" TYPE="button" VALUE="Visit bookstore">
     </FORM>
   </BODY>

</HTML>
```

The HTML form is made up of a statically sized drop-down list and a button. When the visitor selects one of the selections in the drop-down list and then clicks on the button (named `myButton`) the `myButton_onClick` function is executed. This function changes the currently loaded URL by assigning the URL associated with the selected option to the location object as shown here.

```
window.location=document.myForm.myList.value
```

NOTE The `window` object is not required when referencing its `child` objects. In other words, both of the following statements will work just fine.

```
window.location=document.myForm.myList.value
location=document.myForm.myList.value
```

I am simply using the longer version to make my examples easier to follow.

Figure 3.15 displays the HTML page produced by the previous example.

This next example contains two VBScripts. The first VBScript is embedded in the HEAD section. It defines two subroutines. `ppBooks_onClick`

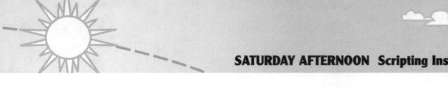

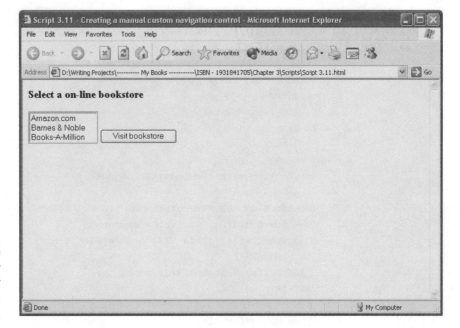

Figure 3.15

Giving the user more control over the custom navigation control.

uses the `location object's` `replace()` method to load a new URL into the Internet Explorer window. The `reload_onClick` subroutine executes the `location` object's `reload()` method, which refreshes the currently loaded HTML page.

The second VBScript is embedded in the BODY section of the HTML page. It consists of a single VBScript statement. This statement uses the `document` object's `write()` method to display a text message on the HTML page that includes the value stored in the `location` object's `href` property.

```
<HTML>

  <HEAD>
    <TITLE>Script 3.12 - Working with the location object</TITLE>

    <SCRIPT LANGUAGE="VBScript">
    <!-- Start hiding VBScript statements
      Sub ppBooks_onClick
        location.replace("http://www.premierpressbooks.com")
```

```
      End Sub
      Sub reload_onClick
        location.reload()
      End Sub
    ' End hiding VBScript statements -->
    </SCRIPT>

</HEAD>

<BODY>
  <H3>Working with the Location Object</H3>

  <SCRIPT LANGUAGE="VBScript">
  <!-- Start hiding VBScript statements
    document.write("This HTML page's URL is: " & location.href
        & "<BR>")
  ' End hiding VBScript statements -->
  </SCRIPT>

  <FORM NAME="form1">
    <INPUT NAME="ppBooks" TYPE="button"
        VALUE="www.premierpressbooks.com">
    <INPUT NAME="reload" TYPE="button" VALUE="Reload this page">
  </FORM>
</BODY>

</HTML>
```

Figure 3.16 displays the web page generated when Internet Explorer loads the HTML page.

The `history` Object

The `history` object provides another means of controlling Internet Explorer navigation. This object provides a means of moving backward and forward through the `document` object's history list.

The following example shows a VBScript that uses the `history` object's `back()`, `go()` and `forward()` methods. It places each of these methods in a separate subroutine located in the VBScript in the HTML page's HEAD section.

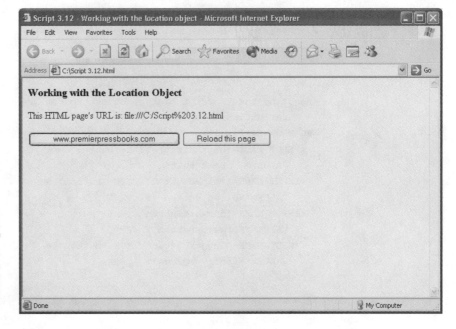

Figure 3.16

The location object's methods allow you to load any URL or reload the current URL.

```
<HTML>

  <HEAD>
    <TITLE>Script 3.13 - Working with the history Object</TITLE>

    <SCRIPT LANGUAGE="VBScript">
    <!-- Start hiding VBScript statements
      Sub backButton_onclick
        history.back()
      End Sub
      Sub reloadButton_onclick
        history.go(0)
      End Sub
      Sub forwardButton_onclick
        history.forward()
      End Sub
      Sub lengthButton_onclick
        alert("Number of entries in the history queue = " & ➥
               history.length)
      End Sub
```

```
    ' End hiding VBScript statements -->
    </SCRIPT>

  </HEAD>

  <BODY>
    <H3>Using the VBScript history object to control browser ➥
        navigation!</H3>
    <FORM NAME="form1">
      <INPUT NAME="backButton" TYPE="button" ➥
         VALUE="    Back Button    "> <P>
      <INPUT NAME="reloadButton" TYPE="button" ➥
         VALUE="Reload Button "> <P>
      <INPUT NAME="forwardButton" TYPE="button" ➥
         VALUE="Forward Button"> <P>
      <INPUT NAME="lengthButton" TYPE="button" ➥
         VALUE="History  Queue">
    </FORM>
  </BODY>

</HTML>
```

The `backButton_onclick` subroutine executes the `back()` method as
shown here. This method is used to load the previously visited URL into
the browser window.

```
history.back()
```

The `reloadButton_onclick` subroutine executes the `history` object's
`go()` method as shown next. In this case, the currently loaded URL is
simply refreshed.

```
history.go(0)
```

By entering a numeric value inside the `go()` method's parentheses, you
can load the different URLs. For example, a `go(-1)` loads the URL
stored back one level in the `document` object's history list and `go(1)`
loads the URL located one level ahead in the list.

The `forwardButton_onclick` subroutine executes the following statement.

```
history.forward()
```

The forward() method, like the go() method lets you load a URL by specifying how far ahead it is stored in the document object's history list. Figure 3.17 shows the results of loading the previous example into Internet Explorer.

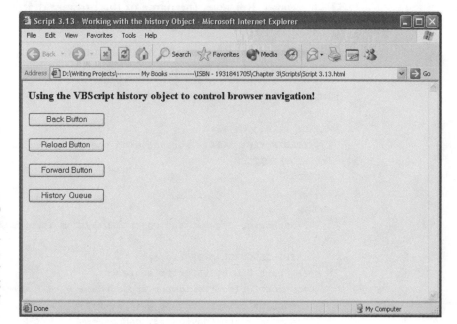

Figure 3.17

You can use the history object's methods to programmatically navigate Internet Explorer's history list.

The navigator Object

The navigator object contains properties that provide information about the browser that has loaded the HTML page. You can use properties of the navigator object to determine both the browser and operating system used by the people that visit your web pages and add programming logic to handle things accordingly. For example, you might automatically redirect visitors running Internet Explorer to different HTML pages that are specifically designed to support their browser version.

The following example displays a number of navigator properties. These properties include

○ **appCodeName**. Retrieves the code name of the browser that has loaded the HTML page.

○ **AppName**. Retrieves the name of the browser that has loaded the HTML page.

○ **appVersion**. Retrieves version information about the browser that has loaded the HTML page.

```
<HTML>

  <HEAD>
    <TITLE>Script 3.14 - Working with the navigator object's
properties</TITLE>
  </HEAD>

  <BODY>
    <H3>Gathering Browser and Operating System Information</H3>

    <SCRIPT LANGUAGE="VBScript">
    <!-- Start hiding VBScript statements
      document.write("navigator.appCodeName = <B>" & ➡
        navigator.appCodeName & "</B><P>")
      document.write("navigator.appName =      <B>" & ➡
        navigator.appName & "</B><P>")
      document.write("navigator.appVersion =  <B>" & ➡
        navigator.appVersion & "</B>")
    ' End hiding VBScript statements -->
    </SCRIPT>

  </BODY>

</HTML>
```

Figure 3.18 shows the results that are displayed when the HTML page is loaded by an Internet Explorer browser on a computer running the Windows XP operating system.

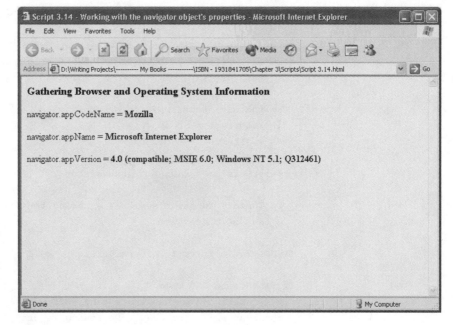

Figure 3.18

Collecting information about the browser using the `navigator` object's properties.

The application code name is `Mozilla`. You probably won't use this property too much. The application name that is returned is `Microsoft Internet Explorer`. Finally the application version is `4.0 (compatible; MSIE 6.0; Windows NT 5.1; Q312461)`.

The following example shows a VBScript that interrogates the values of both the `appName` and `appVersion` properties to determine where to redirect the visitor's browser.

```
<HTML>

  <HEAD>
    <TITLE>Script 3.15 - Detecting browser type and version</TITLE>
  </HEAD>

  <BODY>
    <H3>Gathering Browser and Operating System Information</H3>

    <SCRIPT LANGUAGE="VBScript">
    <!-- Start hiding VBScript statements
```

```
browserName=navigator.appName

If browserName = "Microsoft Internet Explorer" Then
  document.write("Your browser is <B>" & browserName & ➥
      "</B><P>")

  'Use the navigator appVersion property to collect ➥
      information about
  'the visitor's Internet browser and operating system

  browserVersion = navigator.appVersion

  'The Instr() function searches a string for a specified ➥
      set of characters

  findString = Instr(1, browserVersion, "MSIE")

  If findString = 0 Then
  'If findString = 0 then the string MSIE was not found
    document.write("Hum...... Something is wrong!")
    'window.location="http://www.myHtmlPages.com"
  Else
    findString = findString + 5
    'Below gives me the version number
    versionNumber = Mid(browserVersion, findString, 3)
    document.write("Your IE browser is at version number ➥
        <B> " & versionNumber & "</B>")
    'window.location="http://www.myVbscriptPages.com"
  End If

Else
  document.write("You are not using an Internet Explorer ➥
      browser <P>")
  'window.location="http://www.myHtmlPages.com"
End If

' End hiding VBScript statements -->
</SCRIPT>

</BODY>

</HTML>
```

Let's break down this example and look at it a piece at a time. First, the VBScript assigns the value of the navigator object's appName property to a variable named browserName as shown here.

```
browserName=navigator.appName
```

Then, the value of browserName is interrogated to see if the browser being used is Microsoft Internet Explorer. If it is, then the value of browserName is displayed in a pop-up dialog.

```
If browserName = "Microsoft Internet Explorer" Then
  document.write("Your browser is <B>" & browserName & "</B><P>")
```

Next, the value of the navigator object's appVersion property is assigned to a variable named browserVersion.

```
browserVersion = navigator.appVersion
```

Then, the Instr() function, which returns the position of the first occurrence of one string within another string, is used to locate the MSIE characters in a string assigned to browserVersion.

```
findString = Instr(1, browserVersion, "MSIE")
```

Next, the value of findString is interrogated. If it equals 0 then something strange has happened because every version of Internet Explorer should have this string. The Else portion of the If…Then…Else statement should therefore execute. It will add 5 to the character position of the MSIE string (which should be 18), to identify the starting position of the browser version number (e.g., the twenty-third character position). Next the Mid() function is used to obtain the next three characters from browserVersion (characters 24–26). Finally, this value is assigned to a variable name versionNumber, which is then displayed.

```
If findString = 0 Then
'If findString = 0 then the string MSIE was not found
  document.write("Hum...... Something is wrong!")
  'window.location="http://www.myHtmlPages.com"
Else
  findString = findString + 5
  'Below gives me the version number
```

```
    versionNumber = Mid(browserVersion, findString, 3)
    document.write("Your IE browser is at version number <B> " &
versionNumber & "</B>")
    'window.location="http://www.myVbscriptPages.com"
End If
```

You'll probably want to make some changes to this example before using it on your own HTML pages. There really is not much point to displaying the browser name and version number. Instead you'll probably want to uncomment the following statements found in the VBScript.

```
'window.location="http://www.myHtmlPages.com"
'window.location="http://www.myVbscriptPages.com"
```

These statements redirect the browser to HTML pages that are appropriate for the browser. Figure 3.19 shows how the HTML page looks when the script is executed on a Windows XP computer using the Internet Explorer browser.

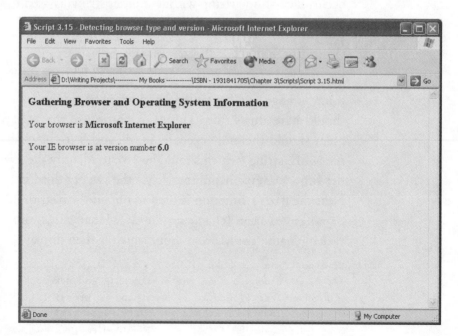

Figure 3.19

Redirecting visitors based on their browser type and version.

NOTE The preceding VBScript will not do you much good if a Netscape browser opens it because Netscape browsers do not support VBScript and will ignore any VBScript statements. You can however, use it as a model for building a script that interrogates for the version number of Internet Explorer. You might then redirect the visitor's browser to HTML pages that you have designed to support the version of the browser being used.

Interacting with Visitors

By default VBScripts execute in a top-down order. In other words, the first statement within the VBScript executes, then the second statement, and so on. Of course, there are exceptions to this rule. Functions and subroutines located in the HEAD section of your HTML pages are only executed when called by other VBScript statements. In other instances the implementation of If...Then...Else and Switch statements make the execution of some VBScript statements optional.

Browser events occur when things happen to your HTML pages. For example, when a HTML page loads the onLoad event fires and when it unloads (for example, the visitor either closes the browser or loads a new URL) the unLoad event fires. Other events occur when your visitor moves the mouse, clicks on a mouse button, or types at the keyboard. By adding logic to your VBScripts that react to browser events, you can significantly enhance the experience that visitors to your web site will have.

Setting Up Event Handlers

To deal with browser events, you need to add event handlers to your VBScripts. An *event handler* is a trap that recognizes when an event occurs. Event handlers are associated with specific events. Reference Table A.19 in Appendix A for a list of browser events and event handlers. Examples include the click event and the onClick event handler and

the `load` event and the `onLoad` event handler. You have probably noticed that event handlers are named after the event that executes them by appending `on` to the beginning of the event name.

Events are associated with specific objects. When an event is triggered its event handler automatically executes if one has been written for it.

There are several ways that you can define events. First, you can embed them directly within HTML tags as demonstrated here.

```
<BODY onLoad="window.status = 'Welcome to my web site!'">
```

In this case the `onLoad` event handler is triggered when the HTML page is loaded into the browser window. To get a little more fancy you can add multiple event handlers inside HTML tags.

```
<BODY onLoad="window.alert('Hello!')"
  onUnload="window.alert('Good Bye!')">
```

You can also set up event handlers by defining subroutines and functions named after the event which they are to execute. For example, the following VBScript subroutine is named `myButton_onMouseOver`. It automatically executes when the visitor uses the mouse to move the pointer over a button named `myButton`.

```
Sub myButton_onMouseOver
  window.status = "Hello world!"
End Sub
```

A third way to use event handlers in your VBScript is to set them up within a HTML `SCRIPT` tag as shown here.

```
<SCRIPT FOR="myButton" EVENT="onDblClick" LANGUAGE="VBScript"
  window.status="Hello World!"
</SCRIPT>
```

In this example, a VBScript is defined for a specific form button and will execute only when the visitor clicks the associated form button.

Working with Different Types of Events

Event handlers can be defined according to when they execute. These categories include

- ✪ Window and frame events
- ✪ Mouse events
- ✪ Keyboard events
- ✪ Error events
- ✪ Events commonly used with forms

A detailed list of these events is provided in Appendix A. The rest of this afternoon will be dedicated to demonstrating how to use event handlers associated with the first three categories of events handlers in the preceding list. The remaining two categories will be covered later this evening.

Window and Frame Event Handlers

Window and frame event handlers are triggered when events that affect the window and frame objects occur. These event handlers include

- ✪ **onLoad**. Executes when a HTML or image finishes loading
- ✪ **onResize**. Executes when the visitor resizes a frame or window
- ✪ **onUnload**. Executes when a visitor closes the browser window or frame or loads a different URL
- ✪ **onMove**. Executes when the visitor moves a frame or window

To use these event handlers place them inside the HTML BODY tag as demonstrated in the next two examples. The first example places the onLoad event handler in the BODY tag. It executes when the HTML page loads and calls the DisplayMsg() function. In addition, it passes the function an argument for processing by placing the argument inside the function's parentheses, in this case the argument is a name. Because the value being passed is text, it is also included inside a pair of quotation marks. Passing a number does not require the quotation marks.

The function receives the passed argument and assigns it to the variable named name, which is then displayed using the MsgBox() function.

```
<HTML>

  <HEAD>
    <TITLE>Script 3.16 - Example of embedding a VBScript statement ➡
        into HTML Tags</TITLE>

    <SCRIPT LANGUAGE="VBScript">
    <!-- Start hiding VBScript statements
      Function DisplayMsg(name)
        MsgBox("Hello and good morning " & name)
      End Function
    ' End hiding VBScript statements -->
    </SCRIPT>

  </HEAD>

  <BODY onLoad=DisplayMsg("Jerry")>
    <H3>Example of embedding a VBScript statement into HTML Tags!</H3>
  </BODY>

</HTML>
```

Figure 3.20 shows how the HTML page looks when loaded into Internet Explorer.

Figure 3.20

A HTML page that greets a visitor by name.

The second example demonstrates how to execute the onLoad(), onResize(), and onUnload() event handlers. Because all these event handlers must reside within the BODY tag, I have listed them one after the other with a blank space in-between each one.

```
<HTML>

  <HEAD>
    <TITLE>Script 3.17 - Working with Window events</TITLE>
  </HEAD>

  <BODY onLoad="window.alert('I load therefore I am!')"
    onResize="window.alert('What is wrong with the way I am?')"
    onUnload="window.alert('You killed me. What did I ever do to ➥
        you?')">
    <H3>Event demo!</H3>
  </BODY>

</HTML>
```

Figures 3.21through 3.23 show the various pop-up dialogs that appear when this script is executed.

Figure 3.21

This message appears when the HTML page is loaded into the browser.

Figure 3.22

The `onResize` event handler is used to display this pop-up dialog when the user resizes the browser window.

Figure 3.23

This pop-up dialog appears when the user closes the browser window thus triggering the `onUnload` event handler.

Mouse Event Handlers

Mouse events execute whenever the visitor does something with the mouse, such as clicking a form button or moving the pointer over an image. The following mouse event handlers are available to you.

○ **onMouseOver**. Executes when a visitor moves the pointer over an object

○ **onMouseOut**. Executes when a visitor moves the pointer off an object

○ **onMouseDown**. Executes when a visitor presses a mouse button

○ **onMouseUp**. Executes when a visitor releases a mouse button

○ **onMouseMove**. Executes when a visitor moves the mouse

○ **onMouseWheel**. Executes when a mouse wheel is rotated

○ **onClick**. Executes when a visitor clicks an object

○ **onDblClick**. Executed when a visitor double-clicks an object

The next VBScript example shows how you can incorporate the onMouseOver and onMouseOut event handlers into your scripts. In this example a HTML form is created that consists of a single button named myButton. Two subroutines have been defined in the HEAD section of the HTML page. The first function is named myButton_onMouseOver and automatically executes every time the visitor uses the mouse to move the pointer over the myButton button. Similarly, the myButton_onMouse-Out subroutine executes when the pointer is moved off the myButton button.

When the HTML page first executes the onLoad statement, which is embedded in the BODY tag, it places a text message in the Internet Explorer status bar. The VBScript statement in the mybutton_onMouseOver subroutine assigns a text message to the window object's status property, thus displaying the message in the Internet Explorer status bar. The statement in the myButton_onMouseOut subroutine replaces the text message with an empty string, thus clearing the status bar.

The trick that makes everything work is the assignment of the NAME attribute to the myButton button along with the appending of the appropriate event handler name to the name of the button when assigning a name to each subroutine.

```
<HTML>

  <HEAD>
    <TITLE>Script 3.18 - onMouseOver and onMouseOut events</TITLE>

    <SCRIPT LANGUAGE="VBScript">
    <!-- Start hiding VBScript statements
      Sub myButton_onMouseOver
        window.status = "Hello world!"
      End Sub
      Sub myButton_onMouseOut
        window.status = ""
      End Sub
    ' End hiding VBScript statements -->
    </SCRIPT>

  </HEAD>

  <BODY onLoad="window.status = 'This message is displayed on the IE
status bar'">
    <H3>Move the mouse over the button and keep an eye on the IE
Status bar</H3>
    <Form NAME="myForm">
     <INPUT NAME="myButton" TYPE="button" VALUE="Demonstrating mouse
events">
    </FORM>
  </BODY>

</HTML>
```

Figure 3.24 shows how the previous example looks when the page is loaded into Internet Explorer and the pointer is moved on top of the button.

This next example also demonstrates the onMouseOver and onMouseOut event handlers, as well as the onMouseDown and onMouseUp event handlers. Two links to web sites are located in the BODY section of the HTML

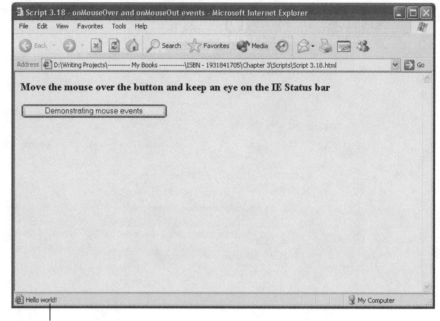

Figure 3.24

The onMouseOver and onMouseOut event handlers let you write code that reacts to user mouse clicks.

Status bar message

page. The links are named link1 and link2. A VBScript is embedded in the HEAD section of the HTML page that defines four functions. Two of these functions are used to provide event handlers for one link and the other two functions provide event handlers for the other link. Moving the pointer over and off the first link changes the foreground and background colors of the HTML page. Similarly, clicking the second link results in changing the background and foreground colors of the HTML page just before the specified web site is loaded.

```
<HTML>

  <HEAD>
    <TITLE>Script 3.19 - onMouseOver, onMouseOut, onMouseDown & ➡
         onMouseUp events</TITLE>

    <SCRIPT LANGUAGE="VBScript">
```

```
    <!-- Start hiding VBScript statements
       Function link1_onMouseOver()
         document.bgColor="red"
         document.fgColor="white"
       End Function
       Function link1_onMouseOut()
         document.bgColor="white"
         document.fgColor="black"
       End Function
       Function link2_onMouseDown()
         document.bgColor="blue"
         document.fgColor="white"
       End Function
       Function link2_onMouseUp()
         document.bgColor="white"
         document.fgColor="black"
       End Function
     ' End hiding VBScript statements -->
     </SCRIPT>

  </HEAD>

  <BODY>
   <H3>Testing mouse events!</H3>
   <A HREF="http://www.premierpressbooks.com" NAME="link1">Visit ➥
        my publisher</A>
   <A HREF="http://www.amazon.com" NAME="link2">Visit amazon.com</A>
  </BODY>

</HTML>
```

Figure 3.25 shows the HTML page created by the preceding example when it is first loaded.

The next example shows how you can implement onClick and onDblClick event handlers. A form is created with two buttons named button1 and button2. When you click the first button, the pop-up dialog shown in Figure 3.26 appears. A similar pop-up dialog appears when you double-click the second button.

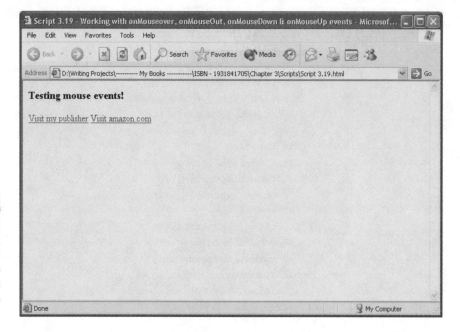

Figure 3.25

The background
and foreground
colors change when
the visitor moves
the pointer over the
first link or clicks
the second link.

```
<HTML>

  <HEAD>
    <TITLE>Script 3.20 - Working with onClick and onDblClick ➥
        events</TITLE>

    <SCRIPT LANGUAGE="VBScript">
    <!-- Start hiding VBScript statements
      Function button1_onClick()
        window.alert("You single clicked!")
      End Function
      Function button2_onDblClick()
        window.alert("You double clicked!")
      End Function
    ' End hiding VBScript statements -->
    </SCRIPT>

  </HEAD>

  <BODY>
   <H3>Testing mouse events!</H3>
```

```
  <FORM>
  <INPUT NAME="button1" TYPE="button" VALUE="Click on me!">
  <INPUT NAME="button2" TYPE="button" VALUE="Double click on ME">
  </FORM>
</BODY>

</HTML>
```

Figure 3.26

The `onClick` and `onDblClick` events allow VBScript to react to any mouse clicks.

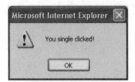

Keyboard Event Handlers

Mouse events execute whenever the visitor types on the keyboard. Three keyboard events are provided, which include

⚙ **onKeyDown.** Executes when a visitor presses on a key

⚙ **onKeyUp.** Executes when a visitor releases a key

⚙ **onKeyPress.** Executes when a visitor presses and releases a key

The following example demonstrates the use of the `onKeyDown` event handler. A HTML form is defined that contains a text entry field named `entryField`. A function in the HEAD section named `entryField_onKeyDown()` executes when the visitor gives focus to the text field (For example, places the cursor in the text field) and then presses a key.

```
<HTML>

  <HEAD>
    <TITLE>Script 3.21 - Working with the onKeyDown event</TITLE>

    <SCRIPT LANGUAGE="VBScript">
    <!-- Start hiding VBScript statements
      Function entryField_onKeyDown()
        window.alert("I am sorry to interrupt but what do you ➡
          think you are doing?")
```

```
     End Function
 ' End hiding VBScript statements -->
 </SCRIPT>

</HEAD>

<BODY>
 <H3>Testing keyboard events!</H3>
 <FORM>
   <INPUT NAME="entryField" TYPE="text" VALUE="">
 </FORM>
</BODY>

</HTML>
```

Figure 3.27 shows the pop-up dialog that is displayed when the visitor presses a keyboard key.

Figure 3.27

The `onKeyDown` event lets VBScript react to every user keystroke.

What's Next?

Okay, you've learned a lot about the inner workings of browsers and how VBScript is used to manipulate browser objects using their properties and methods. You've also learned about the challenges of writing scripts that will work in different versions of Internet Explorer. It's time to spend some quality time with your family and friends and put VBScript out of your mind for a while. When you return this evening we'll finish our discussion of using VBScript in web pages by looking at other ways you can use VBScript to interact with visitors to your web pages. You will also find out how to collect information from your visitors using forms, how to validate form data, and how to store and later retrieve information about your visitors using VBScript's cookies.

Web Page Tricks

- ✿ Learn how to handle errors within your VBScripts
- ✿ Learn new tricks for working with the Internet Explorer status bar
- ✿ Discover how to perform timed operations
- ✿ Spice up your web pages with rollover effects
- ✿ See how to control HTML frames using VBScripts
- ✿ Find out how to use VBScript to validate HTML Forms
- ✿ Learn how to bake VBScript cookies

ood evening! I hope that your break was restful and that you are
ready to get down to some serious fun. This afternoon you learned
a lot about browser object models and how to use object properties and methods to manipulate Internet Explorer and HTML pages.

This evening we'll expand your VBScript programming expertise by looking at some advanced scripting topics. These topics will include how to
add error-handling logic to your VBScripts and how to do some fancy
tricks with the Internet Explorer status bar. We'll also have some fun creating a VBScript clock and working with rollover controls.

We'll also learn how to write VBScripts that provide advanced control
over frames and forms. In addition, I'll show you how to capture and
store information about each person that visits your web site so that you
can greet them by name whenever they come back and visit again. Along
the way I'll introduce you to a number of VBScript functions that will
help make VBScripts easier to build and work with. So if you are ready,
let's get to it.

Managing VBScript Errors

This afternoon you learned a lot about how to work with browser events.
There is another browser event that I want to cover, the error event.

VBScripts are subject to two types of errors—syntax and runtime. *Syntax errors* occur as a result of a typo in your script or because you have not correctly followed the VBScript statement's syntax. *Runtime errors* occur for a number of different reasons. For example, a runtime error occurs if your VBScript attempts to manipulate a browser window that has already been closed by the user.

NOTE Refer to Appendix A, "VBScript Language Reference" for a complete list of VBScript syntax and runtime errors.

VBScript provides you with two options for dealing with errors.

- ✪ Tell your VBScripts to ignore them
- ✪ Add logic to your VBScripts to handle errors

TIP By default, Internet Explorer hides VBScript error messages from the user. This is appropriate because most users cannot make heads or tails of what VBScript error messages mean. However, as a VBScript programmer you may benefit from seeing them appear when you are writing and testing your own VBScripts. To set this up, open Internet Explorer and click Tools, Internet Options, select the Advanced property sheet and enable the Display a notification about every script error option as shown in Figure 4.1.

Ignoring Errors

To tell your VBScripts to ignore an error when one occurs, place the following statement in your scripts.

```
On Error Resume Next
```

Place this statement before any VBScript statements where errors are likely to occur. This statement tells VBScript to continue executing, starting with the next statement following the statement where the error occurred.

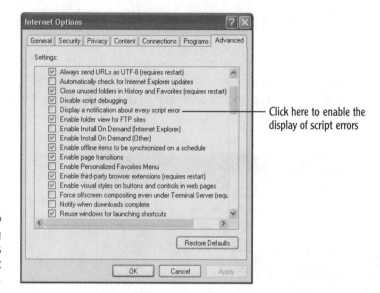

Figure 4.1

Configuring Internet Explorer's handling of script errors.

Click here to enable the display of script errors

The following example shows a simple VBScript that contains a VBScript error.

```
<HTML>
  <HEAD>
    <TITLE>Script 4.1 - An example of a VBScript run-time ➥
        error</TITLE>
  </HEAD>

  <BODY>
    <B>Error Demonstration</B><P>

    <SCRIPT LANGUAGE="VBScript">
    <!--
      document.write("This is line 1" & "<P>")
      document.write("This is line 2" & "<P>")
      document.writ("This is line 3" & "<P>")
      document.write("This is line 4" & "<P>")
      document.write("This is line 5" & "<P>")
    // -->
    </SCRIPT>

  </BODY>
</HTML>
```

The third line in the script, that follows, contains a typo.

```
document.writ("This is line 3" & "<P>")
```

Specifically, the `document` object's `write()` method is misspelled. If you load this example into Internet Explorer you'll get an error as shown in Figure 4.2.

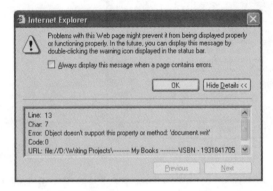

Figure 4.2

An error message indicating that the `document` object does not support a property or method named `writ()`.

The following script shows how adding the `On Error Resume Next` statement to the script allows it to continue executing after the error occurs.

```
<HTML>
  <HEAD>
    <TITLE>Script 4.2 - On Error Resume Next Example</TITLE>
  </HEAD>

  <BODY>
    <B>Error Demonstration</B><P>

    <SCRIPT LANGUAGE="VBScript">
    <!--
      On Error Resume Next
      document.write("This is line 1" & "<P>")
      document.write("This is line 2" & "<P>")
      document.writ("This is line 3" & "<P>")
      document.write("This is line 4" & "<P>")
      document.write("This is line 5" & "<P>")
```

```
    // -->
    </SCRIPT>

    </BODY>
</HTML>
```

Figure 4.3 shows the output created when this script is loaded into Internet Explorer. This example demonstrates how an error can be skipped without impacting the rest of the VBScript's execution. However, more often than not simply ignoring an error causes other errors to occur later in the script's execution. Therefore, use the On Error Resume Next statement to ignore VBScript errors with caution.

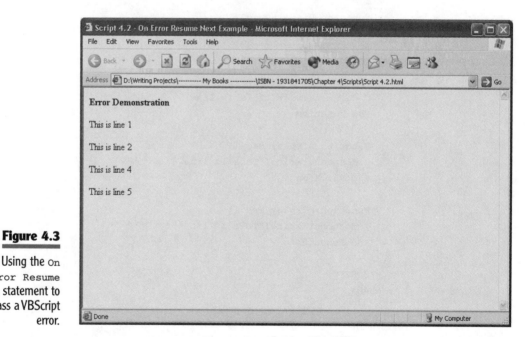

Error Demonstration

This is line 1

This is line 2

This is line 4

This is line 5

Figure 4.3

Using the On Error Resume Next statement to bypass a VBScript error.

When placed outside of a procedure at the beginning of a VBScript, the On Error Resume Next statement is global in scope, meaning that it will tell VBScript to ignore errors that occur anywhere in the script or in the procedures called by the script. However, when an On Error

Resume Next statement is placed inside a procedure, it is local in scope and when the procedure is exited its scope ends. For example, look at the following script.

```
<HTML>
  <HEAD>
    <TITLE>Script 4.3 - Managing error in procedures</TITLE>
    <SCRIPT LANGUAGE="VBScript">
    <!--
      Function Display_Msg1()
        On Error Resume Next
        document.write("This is line 1" & "<P>")
      End Function

      Function DisplayDMsg2()
        document.write("This is line 2" & "<P>")
      End Function

      Function Display_Msg3()
        document.writ("This is line 3" & "<P>")
      End Function

      Function Display_Msg4()
        document.write("This is line 4" & "<P>")
      End Function

      Function Display_Msg5()
        document.write("This is line 5" & "<P>")
      End Function
    // -->
    </SCRIPT>
  </HEAD>

  <BODY>
    <B>Error Demonstration</B><P>

    <SCRIPT LANGUAGE="VBScript">
    <!--
        Display_Msg1()
        Display_Msg2()
        Display_Msg3()
```

```
        Display_Msg4()
        Display_Msg5()
    // -->
    </SCRIPT>

    </BODY>
</HTML>
```

As you can see, a VBScript embedded in the BODY section of the HTML page makes calls to five VBScript functions. The first function that is called contains the On Error Resume Next statement. If an error occurs within this procedure it will be ignored. However, none of the other functions contain the On Error Resume Next statement. When the third function, which has an error, executes, the VBScript terminates and displays an error.

To prevent this error from terminating the script you could either move the On Error Resume Next statement to the beginning of the VBScript in the BODY section or place a copy of the statement inside each procedure.

The Err Object

As I have already mentioned, ignoring an error is not always a good option. A better way of dealing with errors is to add additional code to your script to handle them. To do this you'll need to use the properties and methods of the Err object.

TIP If you want to disable the effects of the On Error Resume Next statement at a certain point in your VBScript, then add the following statement at the appropriate location.

```
On Error Goto 0
```

The Err object contains information about the most recent error. You can get at this information by referencing the Err object's properties, which are listed here.

- **Number.** Retrieves or sets the error number associated with the error.
- **Description.** Retrieves or sets the message associated with the error.
- **Source.** Retrieves or sets the name of the object that caused the error.

The following example demonstrates how to handle an error by interrogating the value of the Err object's number property.

```
<HTML>

  <HEAD>
    <TITLE>Script 4.4 - Trapping VBScript errors</TITLE>
  </HEAD>

  <BODY>
    <H3>VBScript error handling example</H3>

    <SCRIPT LANGUAGE="VBScript">
    <!-- Start hiding VBScript statements
      Option Explicit
      On Error Resume Next

      MsgBox("Welcome to my web site")
      Document.bogusmethod()
      If Err > 0 then
        MsgBox "Error: " & Err.Number & " - " & Err.description
        Err.Clear
      End if

      Document.Write "This message will appear only if no errors" ➡
                 & " occurred or if errors were properly" ➡
                 & " handled!"

    ' End hiding VBScript statements -->
    </SCRIPT>

  </BODY>

</HTML>
```

As you can see the second statement in the VBScript is the `On Error Resume Next` statement. Then the script attempts to execute a document object method called `bogusmethod()`. However, this method does not exist so an error is generated. The following statements then handle the error.

```
If Err > 0 then
  MsgBox "Error: " & Err.Number & " - " & Err.description
  Err.Clear
End if
```

NOTE The `number` property is the `Err` object's default property. Therefore, the following statements are equivalent.

```
Err
Err.number
```

Here is what these statements do. First, the return code of the previous command (for example, `document.bogusmethod()`) is checked. If the error code is greater than zero (for example, an error has occurred), the `MsgBox()` function is used to display the `Err` object's `number`, `description` and `source` properties. Then the `Err` object's `clear()` method is executed. This method clears out the error information currently stored in the `Err` object's properties.

TIP A better use of the `Err` object's `description` property in this example might have been to assign it a more user friendly error message before displaying its contents, therefore making it easier for the user to understand.

Figure 4.4 shows the error message that is displayed by the VBScript. Figure 4.5 shows the output seen by the user when the script completes its execution.

Figure 4.4

Trapping a VBScript error and preventing it from stopping script execution.

Figure 4.5

The script continues executing even after experiencing an error.

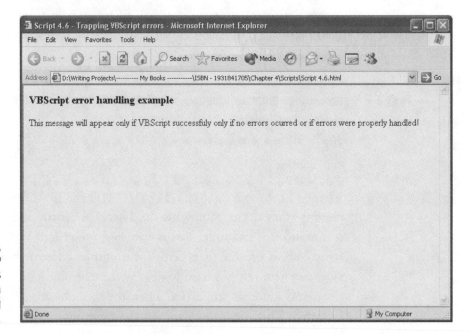

NOTE

The `Err` object's `clear()` method is automatically executed at the following times.

• When an `On Error Resume Next` statement is executed

• When an `Exit Sub` statement is executed

• When an `Exit Function` statement is executed

The `Exit Sub` and `Exit Function` statements are used within VBScript subroutines and functions as a way of ending their execution before the end of the subroutine or function is reached.

TIP

Another `Err` object method that you may find useful is the `raise()` method. You can use this method to generate a runtime error. This way you can test the error handling logic within your scripts to see if it is working as you anticipated. For example, adding the following statement to a VBScript produces a `For loop not initialized` runtime error.

```
Err.Raise(92)
```

Similarly, the following statements not only produce a runtime error, but also customize the `Err` object's `source` and `description` properties.

```
Err.Raise(92)
Err.Source= "New source text"
Err.Description= "New descriptive text"
```

Making Status Bar Enhancements

This afternoon you learned how to place messages in the browser status bar using the `window` object's `status` property. Now let's have a little more fun with the status bar by writing a pair of scripts that can post blinking and scrolling messages. You can use these two examples in your own VBScripts to draw attention to text in the status bar that otherwise might be ignored. However, use these techniques sparingly. Many users will tire of seeing an endless supply of blinking and scrolling messages on all your web pages.

The following VBScript demonstrates how you can place a blinking message on the browser status bar.

```
<HTML>

  <HEAD>
    <TITLE> Script 4.5 - A blinking status bar message example</TITLE>

    <SCRIPT LANGUAGE="VBScript">
    <!-- Start hiding VBScript statements
```

```
Option Explicit
Dim loopAgain
Dim msgTrigger
msgTrigger = "true"
window.status = " "

Function Msg_Blink()
  If msgTrigger = "true" Then
    window.status = "This message should be blinking in your ➥
                    status bar!"
    msgTrigger = "false"
  Else
    window.status = " "
    msgTrigger = "true"
  End If
  loopAgain = window.setTimeout("msg_Blink()",1000)
End Function

' End hiding VBScript statements -->
</SCRIPT>

</HEAD>

<BODY>
  <H3>Keep your eye on the Internet Explorer status bar</H3>
  <SCRIPT LANGUAGE="VBScript">
  <!-- Start hiding VBScript statements
    Msg_Blink()
  ' End hiding VBScript statements -->
  </SCRIPT>
</BODY>

</HTML>
```

In this example, the VBScript located in the BODY section starts things off by executing the Msg_Blink() function. This function checks the value of the msgTrigger variable each time it is called. If the variable's value equals true a message is written to the browser status bar and the variable's value is changed to false. Conversely, when the variable's value is found to be equal to false a blank string is written to the browser status bar and the variable's value is changed to true. The value of the variable thus switched between `true` and `false` with each execution of the `Msg_Blink()` function causing the function to post and then clear the text message on the browser's status bar.

The last statement in the function, shown here, creates a loop by calling the function again.

```
loopAgain = window.setTimeout("Msg_Blink()",1000)
```

This statement uses the `window` object's `setTimeout()` method to execute the `Msg_Blink()` function after waiting 1000 milliseconds (1 second).

Figure 4.6 shows the blinking message that appears on the Internet Explorer status bar when the HTML page is loaded into the browser.

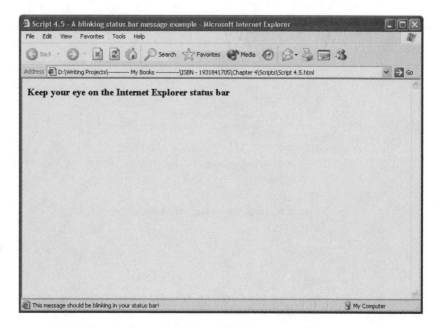

Figure 4.6

Here is the blinking message posted on the browser status bar.

This next example shows one way to create a scrolling message in the browser status bar. In this example, the status bar is cleared and then the `window` object's `setTimeout()` method is used to create a loop in the `Scroll_Msg()` function, which displays one character of the message at a time, every 200 milliseconds.

```
<HTML>

  <HEAD>
    <TITLE> Script 4.6 - A scrolling status bar message ➥
        example</TITLE>

    <SCRIPT LANGUAGE="VBScript">
    <!-- Start hiding VBScript statements

      Option Explicit
      Dim msg
      Dim loopAgain
      Dim i
      window.status = " "

      msg="Let me hypnotize you with this ➥
        message..................... "
      i = 1

      Function Scroll_Msg()

        window.status =  Left(msg, i)

        i = i + 1
        If i > Len(msg) Then
          i = 1
        End If
        loopAgain = window.setTimeout("Scroll_Msg()",200)
      End Function

    ' End hiding VBScript statements -->
    </SCRIPT>

  </HEAD>

  <BODY>
    <H3>Keep your eye on the Internet Explorer status bar</H3>
    <SCRIPT LANGUAGE="VBScript">
    <!-- Start hiding VBScript statements
      Scroll_Msg()
    ' End hiding VBScript statements -->
    </SCRIPT>
  </BODY>

</HTML>
```

The message that is displayed in the browser status bar is stored in a variable named `msg` as shown here.

```
msg="Let me hypnotize you with this message.....................   "
```

This example uses the `Left()` function and a variable named `i` to control which portion of the message is displayed during each iteration of the function. The `Left()` function displays all the characters in a string starting from the left side of the string up to the character position represented by `i`. The first time the function executes the value of `i` is equal to 1 and therefore only the first character of the message is displayed. The message itself is 60 characters long. When `i` becomes greater than 60 (for example, `If i > Len(msg) then`), the value of `i` is reset to 1 starting the whole process over again.

Figure 4.7 shows how the scrolling message appears when viewed in Internet Explorer.

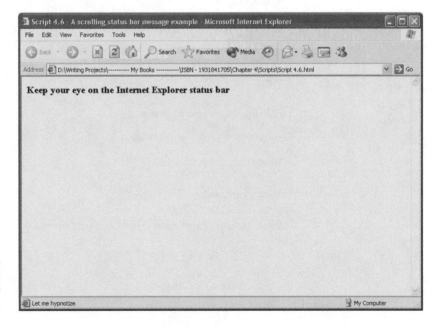

Figure 4.7

Adding a scrolling message to your web page.

Performing Timed Operations

Another neat trick that you may want to add to your web pages is a VBScript digital clock. As the following example shows, all that you need to set up one is a form with a text box, the `window` object's `setTimeout()` method, and the `Time()` function.

```
<HTML>

  <HEAD>
    <TITLE>Script 4.7 - A VBScript clock example</TITLE>
  </HEAD>

  <BODY>

    <SCRIPT LANGUAGE="VBScript">
    <!-- Start hiding VBScript statements

      Option Explicit
      Dim loopAgain

      Function Display_Clock()
        document.myForm.myClock.value = time()
        loopAgain = setTimeout("Display_Clock()",1000)
      End Function

    ' End hiding VBScript statements -->
    </SCRIPT>

  <BODY onLoad="Display_Clock()">

    <FORM NAME="myForm">
        <B>The time is: </B>
        <INPUT TYPE="text" NAME="myClock" SIZE="10">
    </FORM>

  </BODY>

</HTML>
```

The programming logic for this example is contained in a VBScript located in the HTML page's HEAD section in the form of a function named

`Display_Clock()`. This function is called by the `onLoad="Display_Clock()"` statement embedded in the `BODY` tag.

Once executed the function continues to execute itself every second by creating a loop using the `setTimeout()` method. During each execution of `Display_Clock()` the current system time, retrieved by calling the `Time()` function, is displayed in the form's text field as shown here.

```
document.myForm.myClock.value = time()
```

Figure 4.8 shows how the digital clock looks when this example is loaded into Internet Explorer.

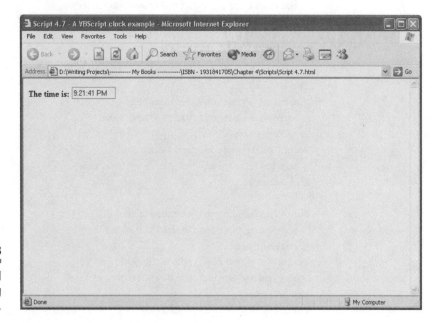

Figure 4.8

Creating a digital clock using VBScript.

Implementing Rollover Effects

One of the best visual effects that you can add to a web page is a rollover. A *rollover* is an image, button, or link that changes its appearance when you use the mouse to move the pointer over an object. Rollovers are most commonly used in creating menus to show the visitor which menu option is currently highlighted.

```
<HTML>
  <HEAD>
    <TITLE>Script 4.8 - Creating Button rollovers</TITLE>

    <SCRIPT LANGUAGE="VBScript">
    <!-- Start hiding VBScript statements
      Function myButton1_onMouseOver
        myForm.myButton1.VALUE="<<  NBC >>"
      End Function
      Function myButton1_onMouseOut
        myForm.myButton1.VALUE="NBC News"
      End Function
      Function myButton1_onClick
        window.location="http://www.nbc.com"
      End Function

      Function myButton2_onMouseOver
        myForm.myButton2.VALUE="<<  ABC >>"
      End Function
      Function myButton2_onMouseOut
        myForm.myButton2.VALUE="ABC News"
      End Function
      Function myButton2_onClick
        window.location="http://www.abc.com"
      End Function

      Function myButton3_onMouseOver
        myForm.myButton3.VALUE="<<  CBS >>"
      End Function
      Function myButton3_onMouseOut
        myForm.myButton3.VALUE="CBS News"
      End Function
      Function myButton3_onClick
        window.location="http://www.cbs.com"
      End Function

      Function myButton4_onMouseOver
        myForm.myButton4.VALUE="<< Email>>"
      End Function
      Function myButton4_onMouseOut
        myForm.myButton4.VALUE="Contact Us"
      End Function
```

```
    Function myButton4_onClick
      window.alert("Please feel free to email us at: ➥
        jlf04@yahoo.com")
    End Function

  ' End hiding VBScript statements -->
  </SCRIPT>
</HEAD>

<BODY>
  <B>Network News</B><P>
  <FORM NAME="myForm">
    <INPUT NAME="myButton1" TYPE="button" VALUE="NBC News"><P>
    <INPUT NAME="myButton2" TYPE="button" VALUE="ABC News"><P>
    <INPUT NAME="myButton3" TYPE="button" VALUE="CBS News"><P>
    <INPUT NAME="myButton4" TYPE="button" VALUE="Contact Us">
  </FORM>
  </BODY>
</HTML>
```

To make rollovers work you simply create procedures that react to the `MouseOver` and `MouseOut` events for a given object and use these procedures to trigger a change in the object's appearance. For example, the preceding HTML page consists of a form named `myForm` that has four buttons on it. Each of these buttons is defined with a default value that provides the button's label. In addition, a pair of functions has been written for each button. One function executes when the user moves the pointer over its associated button and the other function executes when the pointer is moved off the button.

By toggling the text assigned to the button's value these functions change the label that appears on the buttons.

NOTE Be careful when using buttons to create rollover effects. It is important that both versions of the text displayed on each button take up the same amount of space on the button. Otherwise, the rollover animation may look choppy.

Figure 4.9 shows how this example looks when the user moves the pointer over one of the form's buttons.

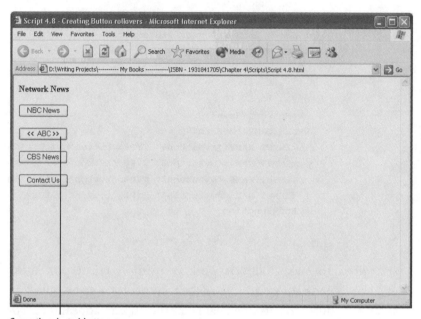

Figure 4.9

Creating button
rollovers.

Currently selected button

This next example shows how to create rollovers that change the colors of text links. This example is similar to the previous example in that it defines four links and a corresponding pair of functions for each link's MouseOver and MouseOut events. Instead of changing the text assigned to a button's label, these functions change the color of the text assigned to their associated link.

```
<HTML>
  <HEAD>
    <TITLE>Script 4.9 - A link rollover example</TITLE>

    <SCRIPT LANGUAGE="VBScript">
    <!-- Start hiding VBScript statements
      Function amazon_onMouseOver
        amazon.style.color="red"
      End Function
```

```
      Function amazon_onMouseOut
         amazon.style.color="blue"
      End Function

      Function bamm_onMouseOver
         bamm.style.color="red"
      End Function
      Function bamm_onMouseOut
         bamm.style.color="blue"
      End Function

      Function bn_onMouseOver
         bn.style.color="red"
      End Function
      Function bn_onMouseOut
         bn.style.color="blue"
      End Function

      Function borders_onMouseOver
         borders.style.color="red"
      End Function
      Function borders_onMouseOut
         borders.style.color="blue"
      End Function
      ' End hiding VBScript statements -->
      </SCRIPT>
   </HEAD>

   <BODY>
      <B>Select a link:</B><P>
      <A HREF="http://www.amazon.com" NAME="amazon"> amazon.com</A><P>
      <A HREF="http://www.bamm.com" NAME="bamm"> Books-A-Million</A><P>
      <A HREF="http://www.bn.com" NAME="bn"> Barnes & Noble</A><P>
      <A HREF="http://www.borders.com" NAME="borders"> Borders</A>
   </BODY>
</HTML>
```

Figure 4.10 shows how the preceding example looks when loaded into Internet Explorer. However, the image shown in this book really does not do this example justice so be sure that you take a minute to load the example and see how it works for yourself.

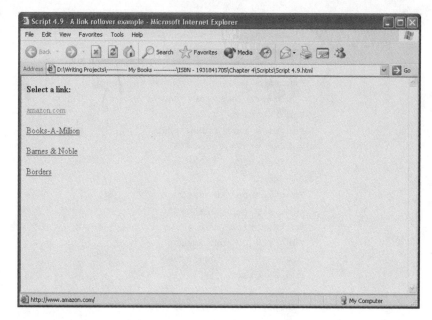

Figure 4.10

Turning text links
into rollovers.

Taking a Break

Time for a break. Why not take a half-hour to relax. When you return we'll pick back up by learning how to use VBScript to control HTML frames. We will also discuss how to use VBScript to control forms and validate their contents. Then we will wrap up the evening by learning how to store and retrieve information about the people that visit your web site using VBScript cookies.

Controlling Frames with VBScript

If your web site utilizes frames, then you'll be pleased to know that you can use VBScript to help control them. To VBScript a frame is just another window object. Therefore, you can use the same properties and methods associated with the window object when working with frames.

Frames are often used to divide a web page into multiple sections where one section provides a navigation frame and the remaining frames are used to deliver some sort of content.

The following example is made up of four HTML pages that show you how to use VBScript to control your frames. The first HTML page, shown here, defines how the frames for the web page will be set up. As you can see there is no VBScript, just plain old HTML.

```
<HTML>
  <HEAD>
    <TITLE>Script 4.10 - Frameset Page</TITLE>
  </HEAD>
  <FRAMESET COLS="175,*">
    <FRAME SRC="Script 4.11.html" NAME="left" SCROLLING="no" ➥
        FRAMEBORDER="1" NORESIZE>
    <FRAME SRC="Script 4.12.html" NAME="right" SCROLLING="auto" ➥
        FRAMEBORDER="1" NORESIZE>
    </FRAMESET>
  </FRAMESET>
</HTML>
```

The page is divided into two frames named `left` and `right`. The left frame will be used to build a navigation menu and will control the content that is displayed in the right frame. To add VBScript to your frames you need to understand how frames are organized within web pages. Each frame is listed in an indexed list or array called `frames[]`. Frames are added to the frames[] array in the order in which they appear on the page. The frame named `left` is the first frame in the `frames` array and can be referenced by either its name or by its index position within the `frames` array. Therefore, both of the following references are equivalent.

```
left
frames[0]
```

Frames are also referenced in relation to their location within the frameset. In this context the frameset statement is referred as the `top` or `parent`. The following statements both refer to the second frame in the frameset, which is also known by the name of `right`.

```
top.frame[1]
parent.frame[1]
```

The second script in this example provides navigation controls for the frame.

```
<HTML>
  <HEAD>
    <TITLE>Script 4.11 - Frame controls page</TITLE>
    <SCRIPT LANGUAGE="VBScript">
    <!--
      Function myButton1_onMouseOver
        myForm.myButton1.VALUE="<<   NBC >>"
      End Function
      Function myButton1_onMouseOut
        myForm.myButton1.VALUE="NBC News"
      End Function
      Function myButton1_onClick
        top.right.location="http://www.nbc.com"
      End Function
      Function myButton2_onMouseOver
        myForm.myButton2.VALUE="<<   ABC >>"
      End Function
      Function myButton2_onMouseOut
        myForm.myButton2.VALUE="ABC News"
      End Function
      Function myButton2_onClick
        top.right.location="http://www.abc.com"
      End Function
      Function myButton3_onMouseOver
        myForm.myButton3.VALUE="<<   CBS >>"
      End Function
      Function myButton3_onMouseOut
        myForm.myButton3.VALUE="CBS News"
      End Function
      Function myButton3_onClick
        top.right.location="http://www.cbs.com"
      End Function
      Function myButton4_onMouseOver
        myForm.myButton4.VALUE="<< Email>>"
      End Function
      Function myButton4_onMouseOut
        myForm.myButton4.VALUE="Contact Us"
      End Function
```

```
     Function myButton4_onClick
        top.right.location="Script 4.13.html"
     End Function
  // -->
  </SCRIPT>
</HEAD>
<BODY>
  <B>Network News</B><P>
  <FORM NAME="myForm">
    <INPUT NAME="myButton1" TYPE="button" VALUE="NBC News"><P>
    <INPUT NAME="myButton2" TYPE="button" VALUE="ABC News"><P>
    <INPUT NAME="myButton3" TYPE="button" VALUE="CBS News"><P>
    <INPUT NAME="myButton4" TYPE="button" VALUE="Contact Us">
  </FORM>
</BODY>
</HTML>
```

As you can see this script is very similar to an example that you looked at earlier this evening. Only now it has been adapted to suit its new role within a frameset. Four buttons are defined on a form in the HTML page's BODY section. Three of these buttons are labeled to identify the web sites of a number of new networks. The fourth button is used to display an HTML page that provides contact information for the web site.

Functions, serving as event handlers, are defined for each button in the HEAD section. The first two functions react to the mouse onMouseOver and onMouseOut events to create button rollovers. A third function executes whenever the user clicks on its associated button. In the case of the first three buttons the functions load the web pages of the NBC, CBS and ABC news networks. This task is accomplished as demonstrated here.

```
top.right.location="http://www.nbc.com"
```

In this case the location property (remember that all the window object's properties and methods apply to frames) of the second frame, referenced as top.right loads the specified URL.

The third HTML page in this example is just another HTML page that displays a welcome message. This page is loaded as the default page when the user first visits the web site.

```
<HTML>
  <HEAD>
    <TITLE>Script 4.12 - HTML page loaded into the right frame</TITLE>
  </HEAD>

  <BODY>
    <B>
      <FONT COLOR=red>
        <CENTER>
        <H3>Welcome to Network News Central!</H3>
        </CENTER>
      </FONT>
    </B>
  </BODY>
</HTML>
```

Figure 4.11 shows how this example looks when first loaded into Internet Explorer.

When the user clicks any of the first three buttons the URL for the associated news network is loaded. When the user clicks the fourth button

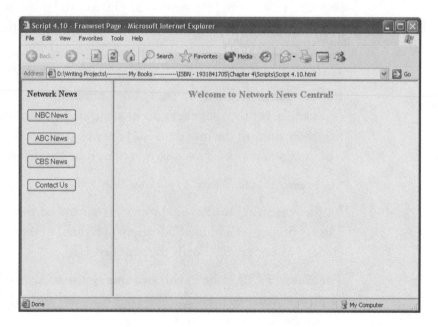

Figure 4.11

Using VBScript to control frames.

the following HTML page is loaded. This page provides a link to an email address where comments can be sent.

```html
<HTML>
  <HEAD>
    <TITLE>Script 4.13 - Displaying email information</TITLE>
  </HEAD>

  <BODY>
    <CENTER>
      <H3>Contact Information</H3>
      <FONT>
        You can email us at:
        <A HREF="mailto:jlf04@yahoo.com">jlf04@yahoo.com</P>
      </FONT>
    </CENTER>
  </BODY>
</HTML>
```

Figure 4.12 shows how the example looks after the user clicks on the fourth button.

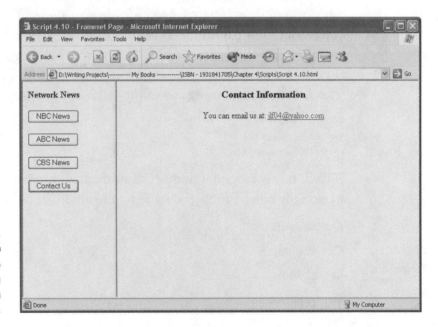

Figure 4.12

Using VBScript to load a custom HTML page into a frame.

Authenticating HTML Forms

You can add HTML forms to your web pages to collect information from the people that visit your web site. However, using just HTML you are unable to validate any of the information that the visitor might supply resulting in potentially useless data. This is where VBScript comes in handy. VBScript allows you to validate all the information on a form before letting a visitor submit it.

Internet Explorer creates a `forms[]` object or `array` object for every form contained on an HTML page. You can then access each form on the page by referencing its indexed position within the array. For example, `forms[0]` references the first form on an HTML page and `forms[1]` references the second form on the page. Alternatively, you can refer to forms by name if you added the NAME attribute to the FORM tag when you set up the form.

Each form has its own `elements[]` array, which contains a list of all the elements (the buttons, text boxes, checkboxes, and so on), located on the form. You can therefore refer to each element on a form using either its indexed location within the `elements[]` array or by its NAME attribute. For example, if you created a HTML page that has only one form named `myForm` that contains only a single button named `myButton`, you could reference the button using any of the following options.

```
myForm.myButton
myForm.element[0]
forms[0].elements[0]
```

HTML forms contain a number of properties. Some of these properties are actually objects in their own right and are listed here.

- ✿ `button`
- ✿ `checkbox`
- ✿ `hidden`
- ✿ `password`

- radio
- reset
- select
- submit
- text
- textarea

Besides these properties, there are several other form properties that will help you when working with forms including

- **name.** Created by a HTML tag's NAME attribute.
- **length.** Identifies the number of elements in the forms[] and elements[] arrays.
- **action.** Created by the <FORM> tag's ACTION attribute.
- **encoding.** Created by the <FORM> tag's ENCTYPE attribute.

The form object also has a number of methods. The two methods that you'll find yourself using most often are

- **submit().** Can be used to email the contents of a form.
- **reset().** Can be used to clear and reset the contents of a form back to their default values.

button

The button object is used to define a button. By itself a HTML button does not do much. However, when you add a little VBScript you can make all kinds of things happen. For example, the following HTML page contains a form with a button named myButton.

A VBScript has been defined in the HEAD section that contains a function named myButton_onClick(). As you can see, this function is set up as an event handler for the button's onClick event. Its purpose is to display a pop-up message when the user clicks the button.

```
<HTML>

  <HEAD>
    <TITLE>Script 4.14 - A form button example</TITLE>

    <SCRIPT LANGUAGE="VBScript">
    <!-- Start hiding VBScript statements

      Function myButton_onClick()
        window.alert("Hello and welcome to my web site!")
      End Function

    ' End hiding VBScript statements -->
    </SCRIPT>
  </HEAD>

  <BODY>
    <H3>Jerry Ford's Web Site!</H3><P>
    <FORM>
      <INPUT NAME="myButton" TYPE="button" VALUE="Click Here">
    </FORM>
  </BODY>

</HTML>
```

Figure 4.13 shows the output created when the user loads the HTML page and clicks the button.

Checkbox

Checkboxes are very simple form elements. A checkbox is either checked or it's not. The following example shows a HTML page where two check-boxes and a button have been defined. The checkboxes are named chkbx1 and chkbx2.

```
<HTML>

  <HEAD>
    <TITLE>Script 4.15 - A form checkbox example</TITLE>

    <SCRIPT LANGUAGE="VBScript">
    <!-- Start hiding VBScript statements
```

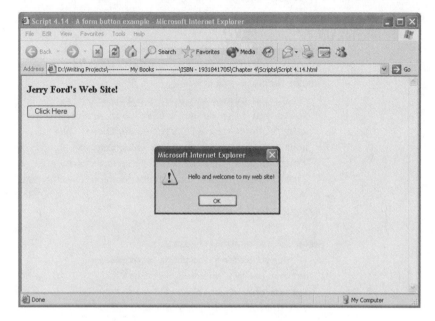

Figure 4.13

Using VBScript with form buttons.

```
Function myButton_onClick()
   If myForm.chkbx1.checked = "True" Then
     selection = "You selected the first option. "
   Else
     selection = "You did not select the first option. "
   End If
   If myForm.chkbx2.checked = "True" Then
     selection = selection & "You selected the second option."
   Else
     selection = selection & "You did not select the second ➥
                              option."
   End If
   MsgBox(selection)
End Function

' End hiding VBScript statements -->
</SCRIPT>

</HEAD>
```

```
<BODY>

  <H3>Jerry Ford's Web Site!</H3><P>

  <FORM NAME="myForm">
    <B>Please customize your purchase:</B><P>
    Would you like to supersize your order?
    <INPUT NAME="chkbx1" TYPE="checkbox"><BR>
    Would you like to receive notification when your order ships?
    <INPUT NAME="chkbx2" TYPE="checkbox"><P>
    <INPUT NAME="myButton" TYPE="button" VALUE="Click here when ➨
                                           done!">

  </FORM>

  <SCRIPT LANGUAGE="VBScript">
  <!-- Start hiding VBScript statements
    myForm.chkbx1.checked = "True"
    myForm.chkbx2.checked = "False"
  ' End hiding VBScript statements -->
  </SCRIPT>

</BODY>

</HTML>
```

A VBScript in the BODY section is used to set the initial default settings
for these checkboxes as shown here.

```
myForm.chkbx1.checked = "True"
myForm.chkbx2.checked = "False"
```

A function named myButton_onClick() is defined in the HEAD section.
When the visitor clicks the form's button, this function displays a pop-up
message specifying which options were selected. For example, the following statement validates the status of the first checkbox.

```
If myForm.chkbx1.checked = "True" Then
```

Figure 4.14 shows the output produced when the visitor loads this example and selects the first checkbox.

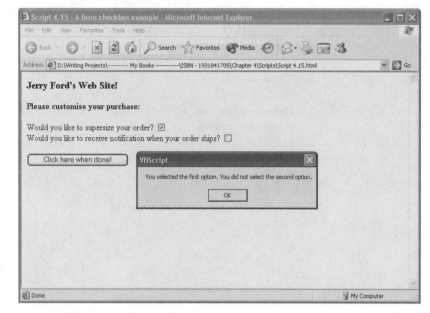

Figure 4.14

Using VBScript to validate `checkbox` selections.

Radio

Radio buttons are very similar to checkboxes except that the user is only allowed to select a single radio button from a group of radio buttons. To place radio buttons into a group you simply assign them the same name when defining them. In this example five radio buttons are defined, each of which has been assigned the name of `myRadio` (e.g., `NAME="myRadio"`).

```
<HTML>

  <HEAD>
    <TITLE>Script 4.16 -  Form Radio button example</TITLE>

    <SCRIPT LANGUAGE="VBScript">
    <!-- Start hiding VBScript statements
      Option Explicit
      Dim i
      Dim radioSelected
      radioSelected = "No"
```

```
Function myButton_onClick()
  For i = 0 To myForm.myRadio.length - 1
    If myForm.myRadio(i).Checked = "True" Then
      radioSelected = "Yes"
    End If
  Next
  If radioSelected = "Yes" Then
    MsgBox("Thanks for picking a color!")
  Else
    MsgBox("You must select a color!")
  End If
End Function
' End hiding VBScript statements -->
</SCRIPT>

</HEAD>

<BODY>

<FORM NAME="myForm">
  <H3>What color would you like to paint your car?</H3></P>
  Red <INPUT NAME="myRadio" TYPE="radio" VALUE="Red"><BR>
  Blue <INPUT NAME="myRadio" TYPE="radio" VALUE="Blue"><BR>
  Green <INPUT NAME="myRadio" TYPE="radio" VALUE="Green"><BR>
  Purple <INPUT NAME="myRadio" TYPE="radio" VALUE="Purple"><BR>
  Yellow <INPUT NAME="myRadio" TYPE="radio" VALUE="Yellow"><P>
  <INPUT NAME="myButton" TYPE="button" VALUE="Click here to ➡
      confirm your color selection">
</FORM>

</BODY>
</HTML>
```

Beneath the radio buttons a regular button named myButton has been defined. When the visitor clicks this button, the myButton_onClick() function executes. This function sets up a loop to process each radio option in the group to determine which one has been selected as shown here:

```
For i = 0 To myForm.myRadio.length - 1
```

During each iteration of the loop, the function looks for the selected radio option as shown here.

```
If myForm.myRadio(i).Checked = "True" Then
```

The function displays a pop-up message that either identifies the option that was selected or asks the visitor to try again. Figure 4.15 shows the output generated by the previous example when the visitor fails to make a selection.

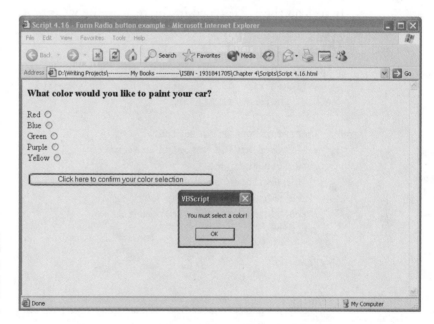

Figure 4.15

Using VBScript to verify that the visitor has selected a radio button.

NOTE

You can always preset a default radio option. However, in doing so you run the risk that the visitor may forget to make a selection leaving the default option selected resulting in an undesirable selection. Instead, it is often better to leave all the radio buttons cleared and force the visitor to make a selection. In the end it's really a question of interface design and personal preference as to whether or not you choose to set defaults when designing your HTML forms.

Text

This next script provides a quick example of how to use VBScript to capture the text that a visitor types into a form text field. The form is called myForm. The text field is named urlField and is automatically assigned a default value of http:// just to give the visitor a head start when typing in a URL. A subroutine name goButton_onClick() is set up in the HTML page's HEAD section. This subroutine executes when the user clicks the form's button and uses the window object's location property to load the URL typed in the text by the visitor.

```
<HTML>

  <HEAD>
    <TITLE>Script 4.17 - Working with the form text and ➥
        buttons</TITLE>

    <SCRIPT LANGUAGE="VBScript">
    <!-- Start hiding VBScript statements
      Sub goButton_onClick
       window.location=myForm.urlField.value
      End Sub
    ' End hiding VBScript statements -->
    </SCRIPT>

  </HEAD>

  <BODY>
    <H3>Type a URL and click on the Load URL button!</H3>
    <FORM NAME="myForm">
      <INPUT NAME="urlField" TYPE="text" VALUE="http://" size="35">
      <INPUT NAME="goButton" TYPE="button" VALUE="Load URL">
    </FORM>
  </BODY>

</HTML>
```

Figure 4.16 shows how the form appears when first loaded into the browser.

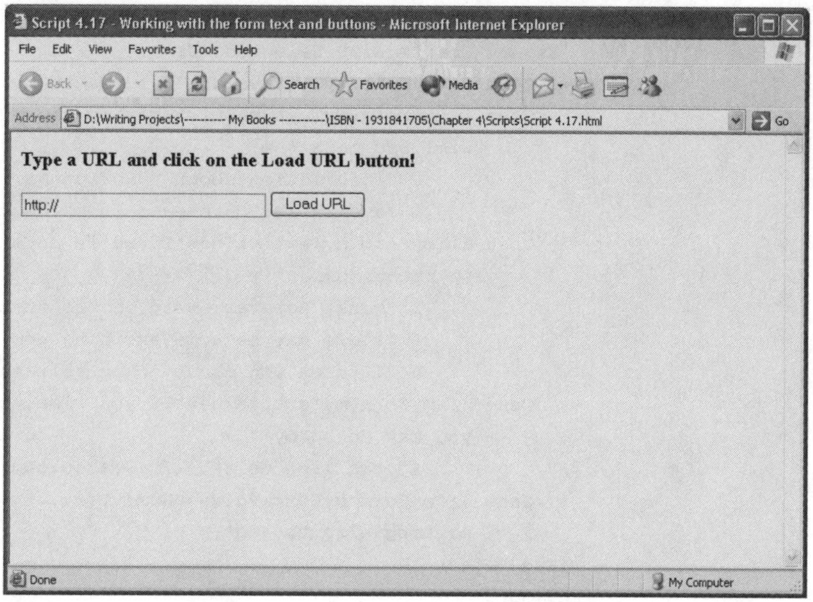

Figure 4.16

Using VBScript to access the contents of form's text field.

textarea

The `textarea` object is a close cousin to the `text` object except that it allows multiple lines of text to be typed. Instead of using the `textarea` object to collect information from the users the following example puts a twist on things by demonstrating how to use the `textarea` object to display predefined collections of text based on categories selected by the user.

```
<HTML>
  <HEAD>
    <TITLE>Script 4.18 - A example of the form textarea ➥
        element</TITLE>

    <SCRIPT LANGUAGE="VBScript">
    <!-- Start hiding VBScript statements

      Option Explicit
      Dim loadText
```

```
        Sub myList_OnChange()
          Select Case myList.Selectedindex
            Case 0: myForm.myText.value="Welcome to my web site!"
            Case 1: myForm.myText.value="This is the place where I ➥
                will add more " ➥
                    & "information about VBScript as it becomes " ➥
                    & "available. So please keep checking!"
            Case 2: myForm.myText.value="There is nothing new for me ➥
                to report this " ➥
                    & "week. However, word on the street says that " ➥
                    & "there may be some exciting new surprise " ➥
                    & "information about to be released!"
            Case 3: myForm.myText.value="If you wish to contact us ➥
                you may do so by " ➥
                    & "emailing us at jlf04@yahoo.com"
            Case 4: myForm.myText.value="Hum.......... I have ➥
                nothing else to add"
          End Select
        End Sub

    ' End hiding VBScript statements -->
    </SCRIPT>

</HEAD>

<BODY>
    <H3>Index</H3>
    <SELECT NAME=myList SIZE=6>
      <OPTION SELECTED>Welcome!
      <OPTION>VBScript Links
      <OPTION>What's New?
      <OPTION>Contact us
      <OPTION>Miscellaneous
    </SELECT>
    <p>
  <CENTER>
    <FORM NAME="myForm">
      <TEXTAREA COLS="80" ROWS="8" NAME="myText">Welcome to my ➥
          web site!</TEXTAREA>
    </FORM>
  </CENTER>
</BODY>
</HTML>
```

A SELECT object located in the body section determines the text that is displayed in the textarea field, which is defined in a form located in the BODY section.

Whenever the visitor clicks one of the options listed by the SELECT object the myList_OnChange() subroutine, located in the HEAD section, executes. Here a Select Case statement is used to set up a series of Case options corresponding to the SELECT object's entries as shown here.

```
Select Case myList.Selectedindex
```

This statement is followed by a number of Case statements. These statements supply text that is displayed in the textarea field as shown here.

```
Case 0: myForm.myText.value="Welcome to my web site!"
```

This statement shows the first Case option, which displays a welcome message in the textarea field by assigning a new value to the textarea field. Figure 4.17 shows how this example looks when the visitor selects the second option.

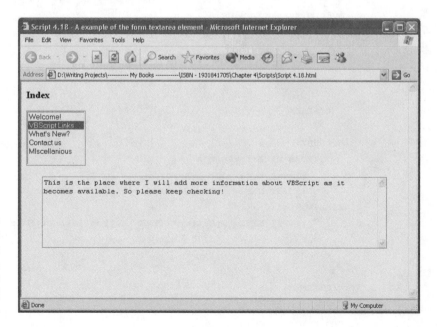

Figure 4.17

Using the textarea form object to display large amounts of text.

password

The password object is used to collect text input from the user while simultaneously masking the value of the typed characters. Otherwise, the password object works just like the text object. The following example shows a HTML page with a form that contains a password field and a button. The visitor is prompted to type in a password and then click the button. This executes the myButton_onClick() function, which then displays the characters that the visitor typed in the password field.

```
<HTML>

  <HEAD>
    <TITLE>Script 4.19 - A form password field example</TITLE>


    <SCRIPT LANGUAGE="VBScript">
    <!-- Start hiding VBScript statements

      Function myButton_onClick()
        MsgBox("The password that you typed is: " &
myForm.myPsswd.value)
      End Function

    ' End hiding VBScript statements -->
    </SCRIPT>

  </HEAD>

  <BODY>
    <FORM NAME="myForm">
      Please type your password:
      <INPUT NAME="myPsswd" TYPE="password" SIZE="10"
MAXLENGTH="10"><P>
        <INPUT NAME="myButton" TYPE="button" VALUE="Submit">
      </FORM>
    </BODY>

</HTML>
```

Figure 4.18 demonstrates how the example would look had the visitor typed a password of qwerty. As you can see, even though the text was masked when the visitor typed it into the password field, VBScript can still access and display its actual value.

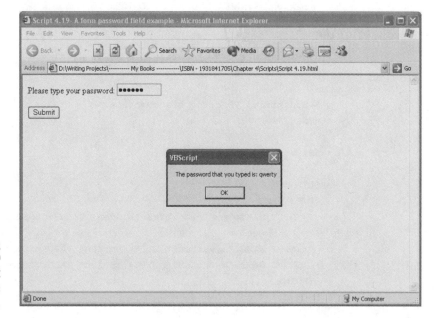

Figure 4.18

Masking text input using the password object.

hidden

The hidden object is very much like the text object in that you can assign and retrieve text information to and from it. The only difference is that the hidden field is never displayed on the HTML page. This means that you can store text in hidden fields based on much the same way that you store text in variables. However, because variables are easier to work with you probably won't use the hidden field often. The following example provides a quick look at how the hidden object works.

```
<HTML>

  <HEAD>
    <TITLE>Script 4.20- A form hidden field example</TITLE>
```

```
<SCRIPT LANGUAGE="VBScript">
<!-- Start hiding VBScript statements

  Function myButton1_onClick
   document.myForm.myField.value="I told you not to click the ➥
       other button!"
  End Function

  Function myButton2_onClick
   window.alert(document.myForm.myField.value)
  End Function

 ' End hiding VBScript statements -->
  </SCRIPT>

</HEAD>

<BODY>
  <FORM NAME="myForm">
    <INPUT NAME="myField" TYPE="hidden" VALUE="Nothing to see ➥
        here!">
    <INPUT NAME="myButton1" TYPE="button" VALUE="Do not click me!">
    <INPUT NAME="myButton2" TYPE="button" VALUE="Show Hidden">
  </FORM>
</BODY>

</HTML>
```

When the HTML page is first loaded, a value of Nothing to see here! is stored in this field as shown here.

```
<INPUT NAME="myField" TYPE="hidden" VALUE="Nothing to see here!">
```

This example presents the user with two buttons. One of the buttons instructs the user to click it. The other button displays the text stored by the hidden object. If the user clicks the first button, then the following statement is used to change the text stored by the hidden object.

```
document.myForm.myField.value="I told you not to click the other ➥
        button!"
```

If the user then clicks the second button, they will see the message displayed in Figure 4.19.

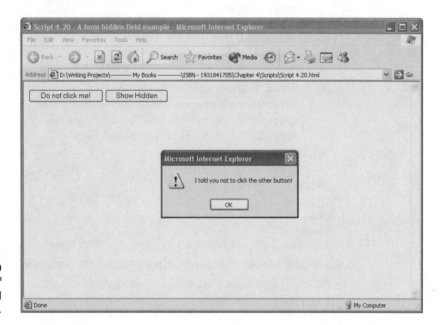

Figure 4.19

Hiding text using the `hidden` object.

SELECT

You have already seen the SELECT object used many times in this book. It can be used to display a drop-down or scrollable list of options from which the visitor can select. The following example demonstrates how to combine the SELECT object with VBScript to create a navigation control.

```
<HTML>

  <HEAD>
    <TITLE>Script 4.21 - A Creating a custom navigation tool with ➥
        the select element</TITLE>
  </HEAD>

  <BODY>
    <H3>Select an on-line bookstore</H3>

    <SCRIPT LANGUAGE="VBScript">
```

```
<!-- Start hiding VBScript statements
   Function myList_onChange()
     window.location=document.myForm.myList.value
   End Function
' End hiding VBScript statements -->
</SCRIPT>

<FORM NAME="myForm">
  <SELECT NAME="myList" size=1>
  <OPTION VALUE="http://www.amazon.com"> Amazon.com
  <OPTION VALUE="http://www.bn.com"> Barnes & Noble
  <OPTION VALUE="http://www.bamm.com"> Books-A-Million
  </SELECT>
</FORM>
</BODY>

</HTML>
```

The SELECT object is used to define a list of online bookstore web sites. When the user clicks one of the options, the following statement in the myList_onChange() function is executed.

```
window.location=document.myForm.myList.value
```

This statement sets the window object's location property to the specified URL thus forcing the browser to load the URL. Figure 4.20 shows how this example appears when loaded into Internet Explorer.

reset

The reset button automatically resets all form elements back to their original values. This can be helpful to a user who realizes that he has made a number of mistakes when filling out a form and that it would be easier just to start over again than to try to correct all the errors. By setting up a procedure that reacts to the reset button's onClick event you can intervene before the form is cleared. Another use of the reset button's onClick event might be to ask the user to try filling the form out again as demonstrated in the following example.

```
<HTML>

  <HEAD>
    <TITLE>Script 4.22 - A form reset example</TITLE>

    <SCRIPT LANGUAGE="VBScript">
    <!-- Start hiding VBScript statements

      Function myReset_onClick()
        MsgBox("The form has been reset. Please try again!")
      End Function
    ' End hiding VBScript statements -->
    </SCRIPT>

  </HEAD>

  <BODY>

    <FORM NAME="myForm">

      <H3>What color would you like to paint your car?</H3>
      Red <INPUT NAME="myRadio" TYPE="radio" VALUE="Red"><BR>
      Blue <INPUT NAME="myRadio" TYPE="radio" VALUE="Blue"><BR>
      Green <INPUT NAME="myRadio" TYPE="radio" VALUE="Green"><BR>
```

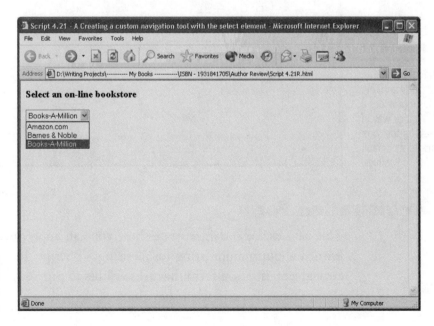

Figure 4.20

Creating a custom navigation control.

```
Purple <INPUT NAME="myRadio" TYPE="radio" VALUE="Purple" ➡
    Checked><BR>
Yellow <INPUT NAME="myRadio" TYPE="radio" VALUE="Yellow"><P>
<INPUT Name="myReset" TYPE="reset">

  </FORM>

  </BODY>

</HTML>
```

Figure 4.21 shows how this HTML page looks when loaded into Internet Explorer.

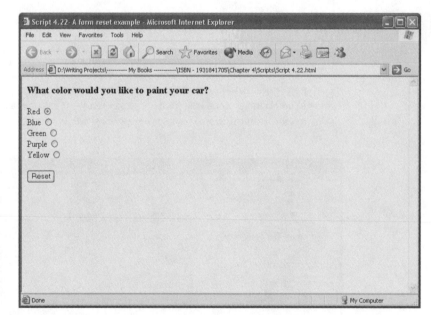

Figure 4.21

Adding a reset button to a HTML form provides a quick way of resetting the form back to its default values.

A Registration Form

This next example demonstrates how you can apply what you have just learned about manipulating forms using VBScript. In this example I've created a registration form that asks visitors to provide some information about themselves and what they think of the web site.

The form is defined using the following HTML statement.

```
<FORM NAME="myForm" ACTION="mailto:jlf04@yahoo.com"
ENCTYPE="text/plain">
```

This statement tells the browser to email the contents of the form to the specified email address as plain text when visitors click the submit button. The form itself consists of a collection of text fields, radio buttons, a SELECT drop-down list, and three buttons, two of which are the reset and submit buttons as shown in Figure 4.22.

```
<HTML>
  <HEAD>
    <TITLE>Script 4.23 - A form validation example</TITLE>

    <SCRIPT LANGUAGE="VBScript">
    <!-- Start hiding VBScript statements

      Option Explicit
      Dim radioSelected
      Dim i

      Function process_Order()
        If Len(document.myForm.firstName.value) < 1 Then
          window.alert("You must provide your first name.")
          Exit Function
        End If
        If Len(document.myForm.lastName.value) < 1 Then
          window.alert("You must provide your last name.")
          Exit Function
        End If
        If Len(document.myForm.emailAddress.value) < 1 Then
          window.alert("You must provide your email address.")
          Exit Function
        End If
        radioSelected = "No"
        For i = 0 To myForm.myRadio.length - 1
          If myForm.myRadio(i).Checked = "True" Then
            radioSelected = "Yes"
          End If
        Next
```

```
      If radioSelected = "No" Then
        window.alert("You must select a newsletter option.")
        Exit Function
      End If
      window.alert("Your registration form looks good. Click ➥
          on Submit!")
    End Function


  ' End hiding VBScript statements -->
  </SCRIPT>


</HEAD>


<BODY>
  <CENTER>
    <H3>Registration Page</H3>
  </CENTER>
  <B>Please fill out the following information to register at ➥
      our web site!</B>


  <FORM NAME="myForm" ACTION="mailto:jlf04@yahoo.com" ➥
      ENCTYPE="text/plain">
    <B>What is your first name:</B> <INPUT NAME="firstName" ➥
        TYPE="text" SIZE="10" MAXLENGTH="30"><P>
    <B>What is your last name: </B> <INPUT NAME="lastName" ➥
        TYPE="text" SIZE="10" MAXLENGTH="30"><P>
    <B>What is your email address:</B> <INPUT NAME="emailAddress" ➥
        TYPE="text" SIZE="20" MAXLENGTH="30"><P>
    <B>Select which of our newsletters you'd like to receive:</B><P>
    Weekly Update Newsletter: <INPUT NAME="myRadio" TYPE="radio" ➥
        VALUE="weekly"><BR>
    Monthly Recap Newsletter: <INPUT NAME="myRadio" TYPE="radio" ➥
        VALUE="monthly"><BR>
    No Newsletter: <INPUT NAME="myRadio" TYPE="radio" ➥
        VALUE="none"><BR>


    <P><B>What do you think of our web site?</B>
    <SELECT NAME="myList">
      <OPTION SELECTED VALUE="high">I like it a lot
      <OPTION VALUE="medium">Not bad
      <OPTION VALUE="low">Needs more work
    </SELECT></P>
```

```
      <B>Would you like to provide any additional information: ➥
         (Optional)</B><P>
      <TEXTAREA NAME="myTextarea" ROWS="5" COLS="50"></TEXTAREA><P>

      <INPUT NAME="myReset" TYPE="reset" VALUE="Clear the Form">
      <INPUT NAME="mySubmit" TYPE="submit" ➥
         VALUE="Submit Your Order" onClick="window.alert('Thanks ➥
         for registering with our web site!')">
      <INPUT NAME="mybutton" TYPE="button" ➥
         VALUE="Validate Your Order" onClick="process_Order()">
   </FORM>
  </BODY>
</HTML>
```

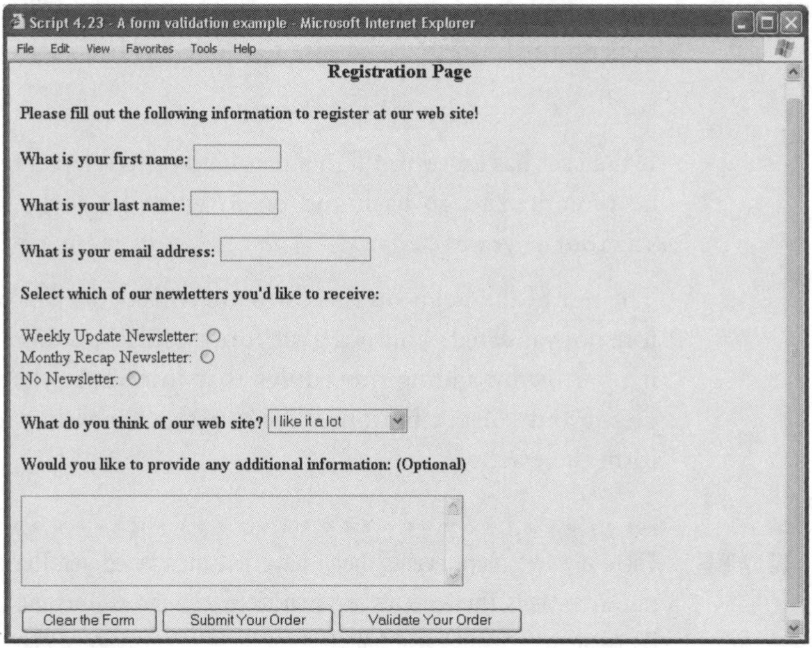

Figure 4.22

Building a registration form for your web site.

When the user clicks the button labeled Validate Your Order, a function called process_Order() is executed. This function validates the contents of the forms as shown in the statements that follow.

The following statement checks to see if the visitor typed in his or her first name.

```
If Len(document.myForm.firstName.value) < 1 Then
```

The following statement checks to see if the visitor typed in his or her last name.

```
If Len(document.myForm.lastName.value) < 1 Then
```

Likewise, this next statement checks to see if the visitor typed in his or her email address.

```
If Len(document.myForm.emailAddress.value) < 1 Then
```

Next, the following statement loops through the collection of radio buttons on the form to make sure that one has been selected.

```
For i = 0 To myForm.myRadio.length - 1
```

If the user has failed to fill in a text field or to select a radio button he will be prompted to go back and do so when he clicks the button labeled Validate your Order.

The rest of the fields on this form are considered optional and are therefore not validated. This is a basic form validation example. You could jazz it up a bit by adding procedures that intervene when visitors click the reset and submit buttons to be sure that the visitor really wants to perform these actions.

NOTE   There are two more events that I have not mentioned yet. These are the Reset and Submit events. These events are associated with the reset and submit form buttons. By creating VBScript event handlers for these events you can create warning messages that inform the visitor of the consequences of clicking these buttons. You could remove the onSubmit event handler in the previous example to invoke a form validation procedure that eliminates the need to depend on the visitor initiating the validation process.

You could also go to greater lengths to validate the information in the text fields. For example, you could use the `length()` function to make sure that the text typed in this field is of a certain minimum length or use the `InStr()` function to make sure that the user includes the @ character in his email address.

Baking VBScript Cookies

In this final example of the evening we are going to look at how to bake VBScript cookies. A cookie is a small piece of information that can be stored on the computers of the people that visit your web pages. Professional web sites use cookies all the time to record information about you and your activities when you visit their web sites. For example, any web site that greets you by name is using a cookie to identify you each time you visit the web site.

Cookie technology is extremely limited. You cannot use cookies to plant computer viruses or fill up a visitor's hard drive. However, they are perfect for storing small pieces of information, such as a visitor's name or preferred customization settings.

To store or retrieve a cookie you use the `document` object's `cookie` property. Cookies have a specific syntax that you must follow. To create a cookie, you must define your cookies as demonstrated here.

```
document.cookie = "name=" &  name & ";expires=" & exp_Date
```

The components of this statement can be broken down as follows.

- ✪ **"name="**. Identifies the information being stored in the cookie.
- ✪ **Name**. A variable, which contains the actual value being stored on the visitor's computer.
- ✪ **";expires="**. Provides a label for the cookie's expiration date (all cookies must have an expiration date).
- ✪ **exp_Date**. The value of the expiration date.

A cookie's expiration date must be formatted as demonstrated here:

```
Monday, 02-Feb-2002 12:45:00 GMT
```

The following statement shows how to retrieve this cookie when the visitor returns.

```
myCookie = document.cookie
```

Baking a Cookie

Let's take a look at a quick example that shows how to bake a complete VBScript cookie. In this example we'll create a script that prompts visitors to type their names. The script then builds a cookie containing the visitor's name and saves it on their computer.

```
<HTML>

  <HEAD>

    <TITLE>Script 4.24 - Baking a VBScript cookie</TITLE>

    <SCRIPT LANGUAGE="VBScript">
    <!-- Start hiding VBScript statements

    Function Bake_The_Cookie(name)
         exp_Date = Weekdayname(DatePart("w",Date())) & ", " _
                 & Date_Format(DatePart("d",Date())) & "-" _
                 & Monthname(DatePart("m",Date()),1) + 1) & "-" _
                 & DatePart("yyyy",Date()) _
                 & " 00:00:00 GMT"
        myCookie = "name=" & name & ";expires=" & exp_Date
        document.cookie = myCookie
        MsgBox(myCookie)
    End Function

        Function Date_Format(rawDate)
          If Len(rawDate) = 1 Then rawDate = "0" & rawDate
          date_Format = rawDate
        End Function

    ' End hiding VBScript statements -->
    </SCRIPT>
  </HEAD>
```

```
<BODY>

  <H3>Cookie Information Collector</H3>

  <FORM NAME="myForm">
    <B>What is your name? </B>
    <INPUT TYPE="text" NAME="visitorName">
    <INPUT NAME="myButton" TYPE="button" VALUE="Save Cookie" ➥
        onClick="Bake_The_Cookie(document.myForm.visitorName.value)">
  </FORM>

</BODY>

</HTML>
```

This script defines two functions in the HEAD section of the HTML page. The first function is called Bake_The_Cookie(). Its job is to bake the VBScript cookie. The second function is named Date_Format(). It is called by the Bake_The_Cookie() function and is used to format date values into a two-character format (for example, all date values must consist of two digits and if the day or month is a single digit this function adds a zero to the front of it).

A form named myForm is defined in the HTML page's BODY section. It contains a text field and a button. The user is prompted to type his or her name and then click the button. When this happens the onClick event associated with the button calls the Bake_The_Cookie() function passing it the visitor's name (for example, document.myForm.visitor-Name.value).

The Bake_The_Cookie() function does several things. First, it sets up the cookie's expiration date as shown here.

```
exp_Date = Weekdayname(DatePart("w",Date())) & ", " ➥
                & date_Format(DatePart("d",Date())) & "-" ➥
                & Monthname(DatePart("m",Date(),1) + 1) & "-" ➥
                & DatePart("yyyy",Date()) ➥
                & " 00:00:00 GMT"
```

The expiration date must be set up in a specific format as previously discussed. To accomplish this task the `Weekdayname()` function is used. This function retrieves a string containing the specified day of the week. The `Weekdayname()` function is passed a date which itself is retrieved using the `DatePart()` function. This function retrieves a specified part of a specified date. In this case the W in `DatePart("w",Date())` tells the `DatePart()` function to retrieve the weekday of the current date.

Next, the function calls on the `DatePart()` function again to retrieve the day of the week. This value is then passed to the `Date_Format()` function where it is padded with a zero if necessary. The `Monthname()` function is then called. It retrieves a string indicating a month value based on the value of the following expression.

```
DatePart("m",Date(),1) + 1
```

This expression calls on the `DatePart()` function to retrieve the numeric value of the month (as indicated by the letter m) and adds 1 to it. Adding 1 to this value creates a cookie whose expiration data is 1 month from the current date. Of course, you can change this value as necessary to extend the life of your own VBScript cookies.

Finally, the function retrieves the four-character value of the current year and appends the phrase " 00:00:00 GMT" to the end of it. This phrase sets the hour, minute, and second when the cookie expires.

The last thing that the `Bake_The_Cookie()` function does is store the cookie on the visitor's computer as shown here.

```
document.cookie = myCookie
```

The function then displays the complete cookie using the `MsgBox()` function so that you can see the final product as shown in Figure 4.23.

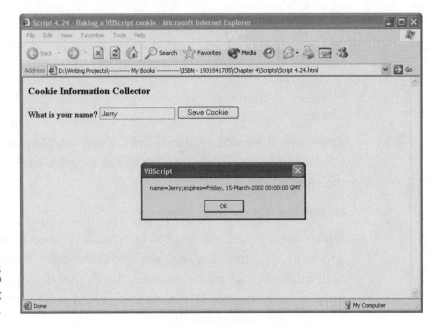

Figure 4.23

Baking your first
VBScript cookie.

Retrieving a Cookie

Okay, now that you know how to create and store a VBScript cookie let's look at an example that shows how to retrieve the cookie when the visitor later returns to your web page.

As this example shows, it's a lot easier to retrieve your cookie than it was to bake it in the first place.

```
<HTML>
  <HEAD>
    <TITLE>Script 4.25 - Reading your VBScript cookie</TITLE>
  </HEAD>
  <BODY>
    <SCRIPT LANGUAGE="VBScript">
    <!-- Start hiding VBScript statements

        If document.cookie <> "" Then
          MsgBox(document.cookie)
          MsgBox(Mid(document.cookie,6))
        Else
```

```
        window.alert("Your cookie was not found!")
      End If

  ' End hiding VBScript statements -->
  </SCRIPT>
 </BODY>
</HTML>
```

The script is located in the HTML page's BODY section. It begins by checking to see if the visitor already has a cookie from your web site as shown here.

```
If document.cookie <> "" Then
```

If a cookie is found, the MsgBox() function is used to display it. A second MsgBox() function uses the Mid() function to display the value assigned to the cookie (for example, the visitor's name). By changing the wording in the MsgBox() function you could easily turn the pop-up dialog into a customized greeting.

NOTE

You can only retrieve cookies that are created by your own web site. Each time a cookie is created an attribute known as a domain is added and is set equal to your Internet domain URL uniquely identifying you as its creator. This attribute is then used again when the visitor returns to your web site to make sure that your cookie does in fact belong to your web site.

Figure 4.24 shows the output of the first pop-up dialog for a visitor whose name is Jerry.

Adding a VBScript Cookie to Your HTML Page

Okay, now let's put everything that you have learned about cookies to work in a real life example. This example includes logic that first looks to see if a visitor already has one of your cookies. If they do, then the name stored in the cookie is used to display a customized greeting message. If the cookie is not found, the visitor is prompted to type his or her name.

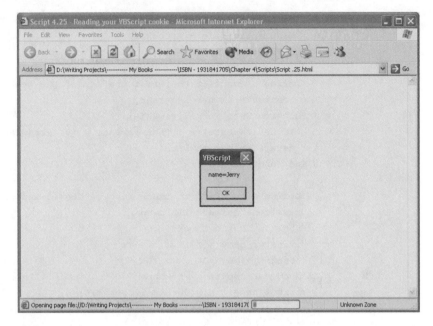

Figure 4.24

Retrieving your
cookie.

If the visitor chooses to provide a name, then it is baked into a cookie and
used to create a customized greeting. If the visitor chooses not to provide
a name, a generic greeting is displayed; however, then the next time the
visitor returns to your web page, he will again be prompted to identify
himself.

```
<HTML>
  <HEAD>
    <TITLE>Script 4.26 - Adding a VBScript cookie to your HTML ➥
        page</TITLE>

    <SCRIPT LANGUAGE="VBScript">
    <!-- Start hiding VBScript statements

      'Define a function to bake the VBScript cookie
      Function Bake_The_Cookie(name)
        exp_Date = Weekdayname(DatePart("w",Date())) & ", " ➥
                & Date_Format(DatePart("d",Date())) & "-" ➥
                & Monthname(DatePart("m",Date(),1) + 1) & "-" ➥
                & DatePart("yyyy",Date()) ➥
                & " 00:00:00 GMT"
```

```
      myCookie = "name=" & name & ";expires=" & exp_Date
      document.cookie = myCookie
   End Function


   'Define a function to format the day of the week as 2 ➥
      characters when necessary
   Function Date_Format(rawDate)
     If Len(rawDate) = 1 Then rawDate = "0" & rawDate
     date_Format = rawDate
   End Function


   'Define a function to check for the cookie and use it in the ➥
      welcome message if found
   Function Cookie_Check()
     visitor_name = ""
     cookie_name = ""
If document.cookie <> "" Then
   visitor_name = Mid(document.cookie,6)
       document.write("<H4>Hello " & visitor_name & ",</H4>")
Else
       input = window.prompt("Welcome to the Bookmall. What is ➥
          your name?","")
       //User did not click on cancel or leave the field blank ➥
          and click on OK
       If input <> "" Then
          Bake_The_Cookie(input)
          document.write("<H4>Welcome " & input & "," & "</H4>")
       Else
         document.write("<H4>Welcome.</H4>")
       End If
     End If
   End Function


   ' End hiding VBScript statements -->
   </SCRIPT>
</HEAD>
<BODY>
   <H3><CENTER>Welcome to my web site!</CENTER></H3>
   <SCRIPT LANGUAGE="VBScript">
   <!-- Start hiding VBScript statements
     Cookie_Check()
   ' End hiding VBScript statements -->
```

```
   </SCRIPT>
   I hope you do not mind but this web site uses cookies!
  </BODY>
</HTML>
```

This example consists of a VBScript located in the BODY section and three functions defined in a VBScript located in the HEAD section. As you may have noticed, you have already seen most of the code used in this example. The `Bake_the_Cookie()` function and the `Date_Format()` function are borrowed from the first cookie example that I showed you and are responsible for formatting and baking the cookie. The `Cookie_Check()` function, which is called by the VBScript located in the BODY section, is an adaptation of the previous cookie example and is responsible for retrieving your cookie and using it in a customized greeting. However, this time if your cookie is not found, the function calls the `Bake_The_Cookie()` function to prompt the visitor for his name so that a new cookie can be baked.

Figure 4.25 shows the custom greeting created for a user whose name is Jerry.

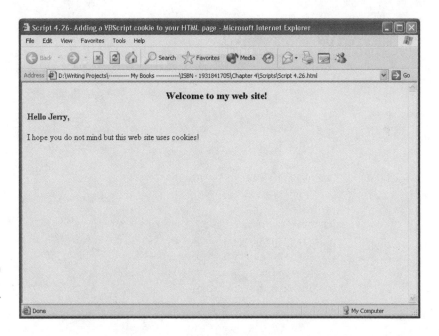

Figure 4.25

Using a cookie to greet your visitor by name.

What's Next?

Well, I think we have covered enough for this evening. You have learned a great deal since this afternoon about how to use VBScript to spice up your HTML pages. Let's call it a night and tomorrow morning we'll get started on learning how to use VBScript and the Windows Script Host or WSH to automate complex and repetitive tasks on your computer.

Working with the Windows Script Host

- ✪ Learn different ways that you can use VBScript and the WSH
- ✪ Examine the basic architecture of the Windows Script Host
- ✪ Review VBScript runtime objects and their methods and properties
- ✪ Learn the basics of XML and how to create Windows script files

Good morning! You spent most of yesterday learning how to apply your VBScript programming skills to web pages. Now it is time to switch gears and focus your attention on how to use VBScript and the Windows Script Host to automate tasks on your computer. We'll start the first part of this morning by going through a thorough review of the WSH and its components.

The second half of the morning will be dedicated to examining how the WSH uses XML to combine VBScript with other scripting languages to create Windows script files. We'll then wrap things up by taking a look at the WSH object model and how it can be used to expose the functionality of Windows operating systems to your VBScripts.

You'll find this morning's chapter a little different than its predecessors. We won't be spending a lot of time writing scripts. Instead we'll be performing an in- depth examination of WSH, its components, and how it works in order to lay the foundation for the rest of the day. So, if you're ready, let's get to it.

What Is the Windows Script Host?

The Windows Script Host (WSH) is Microsoft's advanced scripting environment. WSH allows you to write scripts using different scripting languages, including VBScript. In fact, the WSH even allows you to build scripts using multiple scripting languages and a little *Extensible Markup Language (XML)*. These scripts are known as Windows script files.

The Windows NT, 2000, and XP line of operating systems also support a built-in scripting language known as *Windows Shell scripting*. However, Windows Shell scripts are functionally limited when compared to the WSH. Windows shell scripts lack the ability to directly interact with the Windows desktop and registry. They also have less granular access to the Windows file systems and to resources on Windows-based networks. Windows 95, 98, and Me operating systems do not support Windows shell scripting. Instead, the users of these operating systems are left with simple batch files, which have only limited capabilities.

The WSH, on the other hand, provides every Microsoft operating system, starting with Windows 95, with robust and powerful scripting capabilities. The WSH also allows scripts to be developed using any WSH compatible scripting language. Microsoft provides the VBScript and JScript scripting languages with the WSH. However, other scripting languages are available from third-party developers that allow you to use the WSH with Perl, Python, and Rexx scripting languages.

Architecturally the WSH is composed of several components, including:

- ✪ **Scripting Hosts**. Either of two script-execution hosts. Execution hosts provide an environment in which scripts can be executed in much the same way that the browser provides an execution environment for VBScripts embedded in HTML pages.

- ✪ **Scripting Engines**. Script interpreters designed to process and execute programming statements written using a specific scripting language such as VBScript.

- ✪ **Object Models**. Provides access to collections of objects that expose the functionality of Windows operating systems and allow WSH scripts to programmatically interact with and manipulate Windows resources.

WSH scripts can be created using any editor that can save data as a plain text file. WSH scripts are composed of program statements belonging to one or more scripting languages. A WSH script composed entirely of VBScript would be saved as a plain text file with a `.vbs` file extension. Similarly, a WSH script composed entirely of JScript would be saved with a `.js` file extension.

WSH scripts that consist of scripts written using different script languages are known as Windows script files and have a `.wsf` file extension. Each scripting language has its own strengths and weaknesses. By creating Windows script files, you can develop scripts that leverage the best features of different scripting languages.

Different Things You Can Do with VBScript and the WSH

Before I get too deep into the bowels of how the WSH works, let's take a minute to look at some of the things that you can do with it. Of course, because this book is about VBScript, you'll be able to use VBScript to accomplish any of the tasks that I am about to mention.

The reason that the WSH exists is to provide you with a means of automating Windows tasks. It is particularly well suited for automating tasks that are repetitive. For example, if you need to delete all the files located in a given folder at the beginning of every day, then write a task to do it. If you need to create a large number of user accounts on your computer, don't do it by hand. That takes too long. Instead, write a script that processes a list of user names stored in a text file.

WSH is also great for automating complex tasks such as registry modifications. Humans can make errors and an error in working with the registry can be fatal to your computer. A well-written script, on the other hand, will not mistype a registry key or accidentally delete the wrong registry value. Best of all, you can share your scripts with others to empower them to safely make changes to their computer that otherwise you would never trust them to perform.

Perhaps you have some tasks that consume large amounts of computer resources and cause your computer to run too slowly when you are executing them. By leveraging the power of the Windows scheduling service, you can set up WSH scripts to perform tasks and then run them at night when you are away from your computer. For example, suppose that you wrote a script designed to process a large number of files at the end of each month. If you have thousands of files to process it could take hours for the script to run. Without a script it might take you all weekend to manually process the files. The script might cut down this time to just an hour. By scheduling the execution of your script to run at night when you aren't using your computer you won't be impacted when it runs. This allows you to be productive even when you are not at work.

There are tons of other examples of tasks that you might want to automate using VBScript and the WSH. These tasks include:

- Creating desktop shortcuts
- Managing files and folders
- Configuring the Windows Start menu
- Configuring the Windows Quick Launch bar
- Managing Windows services
- Managing Windows printers
- Collecting system information
- Creating reports
- Creating network drive mappings
- Scheduling after hours tasks
- Working with other Windows applications
- Managing Windows event logs

WSH Operating System Compatibility

Depending on which Windows operating system you use, you may already have the WSH installed and ready to go. However, unless you are

running Windows XP or have kept your other Windows operating systems updated, you may also have an older version of WSH.

Table 5.1 provides a summary of Windows operating systems and which version of WSH is supplied with each one. As you can see, any Windows operating system starting with Windows 95 or later can support the WSH. However, unless you are running Windows XP you'll probably want to upgrade to WSH 5.6.

NOTE   Functionally, WSH 2.0 and WSH 5.6 are equivalent. The main difference is that Microsoft has changed the version number. However, changes have occurred with VBScript and JScript, which are also at version 5.6. Because Microsoft packages WSH, VBScript, and JScript together, upgrading to WSH 5.6 is an easy way to upgrade your scripting languages as well.

TABLE 5.1 VERSIONS OF WSH SHIPPED WITH MICROSOFT OPERATING SYSTEMS

Operating System	Supports WSH	Supplied Version
Windows 3.X	No	Not Supported
Windows 95	Yes	None
Windows 98	Yes	WSH 1.0
Windows Me	Yes	WSH 2.0
Windows NT	Yes	WSH 1.0 (Installed by Service Pack 4)
Windows 2000	Yes	Wsh 2.0
Windows XP	Yes	WSH 5.6

You may visit **http://msdn.microsoft.com/scripting** and download the latest version of WSH to upgrade to the most current release level.

Examining How VBScript Fits into the WSH Architecture

Microsoft has designed the WSH in a modular fashion with functionality divided among a number of components as shown in Figure 5.1. This design allows Microsoft to upgrade individual components without having to overhaul the entire model. For example, it is possible to upgrade the VBScript without impacting the rest of the WSH components. In addition, because the WSH works with any WSH-compatible scripting engines, this architecture provides the capability to use different scripting engines, including JScript, Perl, Python, and Rexx.

NOTE Although Figure 5.1 was designed to depict VBScript's relationship to the WSH, any WSH-compatible scripting engine can be used. Refer to Friday Evening "Introducing VBScript," for information regarding where to find alternative scripting engines.

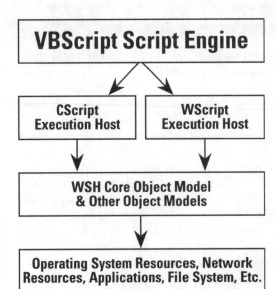

Figure 5.1

The WSH is composed of a number of components.

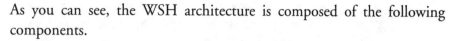

As you can see, the WSH architecture is composed of the following components.

- **Script Engine**. A WSH script engine, such as VBScript, interprets the script programming statements into machine-readable code so that the script can be executed by the computer.

- **CScript.exe**. A script execution host that provides support for scripts that do not implement graphical pop-up dialogs.

- **WScript.exe**. A script execution host that provides support for scripts that interact with the end user via graphical pop-up dialogs.

- **WSH Core Object Model**. The Core Object Model is implemented as an ActiveX control called WSH.OCX and provides access to objects that can be used to interact with and manipulate Windows resources.

The choice of the scripting engine is optional. Obviously this book addresses the development of scripts using the VBScript script engine. Scripts executed by the WSH are stored as plain text files. The script engine that is used to process the script is implied by the script's file extension. For example, VBScripts are saved with a .vbs file extension telling the WSH which script engine should be used to process them.

The WSH provides two script execution hosts that provide an environment in which the scripts actually execute. These execution hosts perform the same function as the browser does for scripts embedded inside HTML pages. You can use either execution host. The only difference between the two is that the WScript execution host provides the capability to display graphical pop-up dialogs.

The core object model provides access and control over an assortment of Windows and network resources, including:

- Files and folders
- Shortcuts
- Drives and printers
- The Windows registry

In addition, any scripts run using the WSH have the capability to execute any Windows command line command. Therefore, you can write scripts that can perform any tasks that you can do from the Windows command prompt. This includes using Windows NET commands such as NET STOP and NET START to control Windows services. In addition, this also means that if you have access to the Windows Resource kit you can execute any of its command line utilities from within your scripts.

NOTE WSH scripts execute using the authority of the person who runs them. Therefore, if you do not have the appropriate level of permissions on a computer to perform a certain task manually, your script will not be able to perform that task either.

One of the great things about the way that Microsoft has built the WSH is that it allows you to reference other object models. For example, to access files and folders within your WSH scripts you use the methods and properties of the `FileSystemObject`. We'll spend a lot of time looking at how to work with this object this afternoon.

You can also develop scripts that can interact with any Windows application that exposes its object model. For example, Microsoft Access, Excel, and Word all expose an object model, which allows you to write scripts that can directly interact with them. I'll also give you an example of how this works later this evening.

NOTE Of course, to work with any application that exposes its object model you must first have it installed on your computer.

Deciding Which WSH Execution Host to Use

As I have already stated, the WSH supports two separate execution hosts, CScript and WScript. CScript is designed to support the execution of scripts that produce character-based output or no output at all, making it the right choice for scripts that do not interact with the user and which can run as background tasks.

WScript on the other hand is best used to execute your scripts when you plan to ask the user questions and collect user input via graphical-based pop-up dialogs. However, if the people that will be executing your scripts are comfortable working with the Windows command prompt, you can just as easily set up your scripts to interact with the user that way.

In the end because both CScript and WScript provide the same basic functionality, the choice of which execution host to use really comes down to personal preference.

Selecting a Script Engine

Like the WSH execution hosts, the selection of a script engine comes down to personal preference. In other words, if you know VBScript, then write your scripts using VBScript and save them as plain text files with a .vbs file extension. If, on the other hand, you are a long time JavaScript programmer, then you'll probably want to use JScript.

NOTE   JScript is Microsoft's own implementation of Netscape's JavaScript language.

Functionally, all WSH-compatible script engines provide equivalent functionality although each language has is own unique strengths and weaknesses. For example, VBScript provides much better support arrays than Jscript, while JScript provides a more extensive collection of methods to call on.

NOTE   Microsoft usually includes a new release of the VBScript script engines with each new release of Internet Explorer. The new VBScript engine is automatically installed when you install or upgrade your copy of Internet Explorer. If you are not running the latest version of Internet Explorer you can go to **www.microsoft.com/windows/ie** and download it.

As you might expect, the WSH's support for VBScript and JScript is limited in that when executed by the WSH neither of these scripting languages can perform browser-related tasks, such as displaying forms or graphical effects. After all, these types of features are specific to the browser environment. In similar fashion, VBScripts and JScript embedded inside HTML pages are not able to access the local computer's file system or manipulate its resources.

NOTE The one exception to a script executing inside a HTML page's ability to affect the local computer is the use of cookie. Cookie technology does permit the storage of a small amount of text data on the local computer. This text data can later be retrieved by the web site that created it.

NOTE If you choose to create Windows script files, which allow you to develop automated tasks using more than one script language, each script in the Windows Script file will be submitted to the appropriate script engine. We'll go over how to create Windows Script files in more detail a little later in the morning.

Working with the WSH's Execution Hosts

Both the CScript and WScript execution hosts can be used to execute any WSH script. CScript is designed to process scripts that run as background tasks or which only require a character-based interface. WScript, on the other hand, is designed to execute scripts that interact with the user by displaying graphical pop-up dialogs.

The exact behavior of both of these script execution hosts depends on how they have been configured. Both have their own separate configuration settings. In fact, there are actually two ways to configure the WScript execution host. One way is from the Windows desktop and the other is from the Windows command prompt.

NOTE Yes, I said that the WScript execution host also supports command line execution. This means that you can run your scripts using WScript from both the desktop and from the Windows command prompt.

You can not only change the default manner in which the CScript and WScript execution hosts execute scripts, but you can also override their execution defaults on-the-fly with a few simple command line arguments, which I'll go over in a few minutes. Finally, you can also create .wsh files that specify customized execution settings for particular scripts.

CScript and WScript Command-Line Configuration

The command-line execution settings for CScript and WScript execution hosts are the same. The syntax for both of these execution hosts is outlined here.

```
cscript scriptname [//options] [arguments]
wscript scriptname [//options] [arguments]
```

Specify cscript to configure the CScript execution host or wscript to configure the WScript execution host. The scriptname parameter identifies the name of the script to be executed. //options is used to specify one or more optional parameters that define some aspect of the script's execution. arguments represent a list of one or more arguments that are to be passed to the script for processing.

Table 5.2 outlines the list of available //options arguments that can be used when configuring the CScript and WScript execution hosts.

Configuring CScript and WScript Command-Line Execution

Now that you have seen the configuration options for the WSH execution hosts let's put them to work in a few examples. First, let's look at how

TABLE 5.2 CSCRIPT AND WSCRIPT COMMAND-LINE OPTIONS

Option	Purpose
`//?`	Displays the command syntax of the CScript and WScript commands.
`//b`	Tells the execution host to run a script in batch mode, suppressing all errors and message output.
`//d`	Disables script debugging.
`//e:jscript | e:vbscript`	Specifies the script engine to be used to execute the script.
`//h:wscript | h:script`	Specifies the WSH execution host to be used to execute the script.
`//i`	Tells the execution host to run the script in interactive mode, which allows errors and message output to be displayed.
`//job:id`	Specifies a specific job within a Windows script file to be executed.
`//logo`	Causes the CScript or WScript logo to be display at the beginning of script execution.
`//nologo`	Prevents the CScript or WScript logo from being displayed at the beginning of script execution.
`//s`	Saves the specified options as the new default execution settings.
`//t:nn`	Sets a timeout value that is used to limit the amount of time that a script can execute. By default, scripts execute without a time limit.
`//x`	Disables script debugging.

we can run a script named `Script 5.1.vbs` from the Windows command prompt using the CScript execution host.

```
cscript "Script 5.1.vbs"
```

 NOTE The quotation marks enclosing the script name in the previous example are required because the name of the Windows script file contains a blank space.

To run this same script using the WScript execution host, type the following command and press Enter.

```
wscript "Script 5.1.vbs"
```

Scripts run using these commands are executed using the default settings of each execution host. Now let's rerun the script while overriding one of the execution host's default options. For example, you could use the following command to execute the script using the CScript execution host and give it a five-second execution time limit.

```
cscript "Script 5.1.vbs" //T:5
```

You can override more than one execution setting at a time by simply specifying additional options and preceding each of them with // characters as demonstrated here.

```
cscript "Script 5.1.vbs" //T:5 //nologo
```

Here I ran the script using the CScript execution host while imposing a five-second execution time limit and preventing the display of the CScript logo.

By default, WSH sets up the WScript execution host as the default execution host. You can change this behavior using the following command

```
cscript //H:cscript
```

Likewise, you can change the default execution host back to WScript as shown here.

```
wscript //H:wscript
```

So far the commands that I have shown you only change the way the execution host executes for the current execution of the script. However, if you prefer you can make the configuration changes permanent by adding the `//s` option as demonstrated here.

```
cscript //nologo //s
```

This example configures the CScript execution host so that it will no longer display its logo at the beginning of each script's execution. This configuration change remains in effect from this point on unless of course you later change the configuration setting for this execution host.

NOTE Changes made to an execution host only affect the user who makes them. Therefore, they will not impact any other user of the computer when he runs his own scripts.

Configuring WScript from the Windows Desktop

You can configure some of the WScript execution host's execution settings directly from the Windows desktop. Two configuration options are available. They include limiting the script execution time and specifying whether or not the WScript logo is displayed when using the WScript execution host at the Windows command prompt.

Use the following procedure to modify the default execution setting for the WScript execution host from the Windows desktop.

1. Click Start, Run and then type WScript and click OK. The Windows Script Host Settings dialog box appears, as shown in Figure 5.2.

2. There is no execution time limit by default. You can apply a time limit to all scripts processed by the WScript execution host by selecting Stop script after specified number of seconds and then typing a time limit in the seconds field.

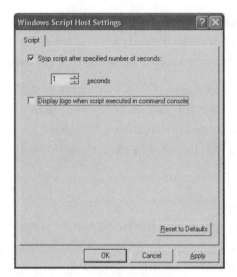

Figure 5.2

Configuring the
WScript execution
host from the
Windows desktop.

3. By default, the WScript logo is displayed when you use the
WScript execution host from the Windows command line. To
disable this, clear the Display logo when script executed in the
command console option.

4. Click OK.

That's it. From now on any time you run a script using the WScript execution hosts, these execution settings will be used, unless of course, you
override them.

Configuring How the Execution Host Processes Individual Scripts

Sometimes you may find that you have a script that you will always want
to execute with the WScript execution host using execution settings that
are different than the default execution settings. In this situation you can
create a Windows script host file for the script. To create a Windows
script host file, simply create a new text file with the appropriate configuration setting and save it with the same filename as the script with which

it is associated, only give the new filename an extension of .wsh. There-fore, if I have a script named Script 5.1.vbs, I would save its Win-dows script host file with a name of Script 5.1.wsh.

There are two ways to create a Windows script host file for a script. One is to let Windows do it for you and the other is to create it manually. I recommend against manually creating a Windows script host file because it's more work and it is too easy to mess things up with a typo.

You can use the following procedure to create a Windows script host file for any script.

1. Right-click the script for which you want to create the Windows script host file and select Properties. The Properties dialog box for the script appears.

2. Select the Script property sheet, as shown in Figure 5.3.

3. You can create a time limit for the script by selecting the Stop script after specified number of seconds option and typing in a number in the seconds field.

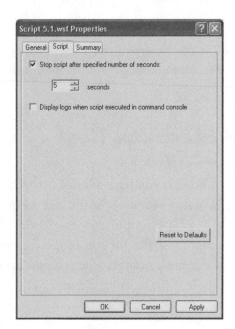

Figure 5.3

Creating a Windows script host file that governs how the WScript execution host will run the script.

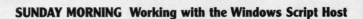

4. To disable the display of the logo message when the script is executed from the Windows command prompt, clear the Display logo when script executed in command console option.

5. Click OK.

You will notice that a new file with the same name as the script but with a `.wsh` file extension is created in the same location where the script resides.

NOTE

Be sure that if you later decide to move the script to a different location you also move its associated `.wsh` file. Otherwise the WScript execution host will start running the script using its default settings.

The contents of a typical Windows script host file are

```
[ScriptFile]
Path=D:\Script 5.1.wsf
[Options]
Timeout=5
DisplayLogo=0
```

`[ScriptFile]` identifies the file as a Windows script file. `Path` specifies the location of the script. `[Options]` identifies the beginning of the list of configuration settings. Finally, `Timeout` specifies an optional timeout setting and `DisplayLogo` determines whether the WScript logo will be displayed when the script is executed from the Windows command prompt.

NOTE

`DisplayLogo=0` disables the display of the logo and `DisplayLogo=1` enables its display.

When you run the script using the WScript execution host, it first looks to see if it can find a matching Windows script host file. If it does, it uses the configuration settings as specified in the file to process the script. If it does not find one, then it uses its default settings. Optionally, you can double-click a Windows script host file or type its name in at the Windows command prompt. This causes the WScript execution hosts to then look for the associated script and execute it.

Understanding the WSH Object Model

Now let's move on to a detailed examination of the WSH core object model. You are going to find a lot of good information here. However, the core object model is extensive and can be a bit overwhelming so don't be intimidated if it doesn't all sink in this morning. A lot of what I am going to show you now will make more sense this afternoon and evening as I begin to show you practical examples of how to incorporate the properties and methods of the object in the WSH core object model into your scripts.

TIP You might want to mark this section of your book so that you can come back to reference it in the future.

Perhaps the most important part of the WSH is its core object model. The WSH core object model provides your scripts with access to objects whose properties and methods can be used to manipulate the Windows operating systems. The WSH object model is made up of nine core objects, each of which provides access to a particular subset of Windows functionality.

NOTE The WSH Core Object Model does for your VBScripts on Windows operating systems what the DHTML and DOM objets models do for your VBScripts when you run them inside Windows Explorer. Only instead of exposing browser functionality, the WSH core object model exposes Windows functionality.

Figure 5.4 depicts each of the objects in the WSH core object model and shows its relationship to the others. The WScript object resides at the top or root of the core object model. This object is automatically initialized by the WSH at the start of script execution. Therefore, it is always available in your WSH scripts and does not even have to be formally defined by your script.

The WshShell and WshNetwork objects are created using the WSH `CreateObject()` method. The WScript, WshShell, and WshNetwork objects are exposed objects. This means that they are created and referenced directly within WSH scripts. The other objects in the WSH core object model are nonexposed objects that can only be instantiated by executing a method belonging to their parent object. Table 5.3 outlines the methods and the objects that are required to create an instance of a nonexposed object within your WSH scripts.

Table 5.4 provides a description of the Windows functionality that each of the objects in the WSH core object models provides. As you will see in a moment, the objects in the core object model provide an impressive number of properties and methods. In an effort to keep this material manageable, this table also identifies which properties and methods are associated with which WSH object. I will then list all the properties and methods separately.

Figure 5.4

The WSH Object Model provides your VBScripts with access to properties and methods that can be used to interact with and manipulate Windows operating systems and their resources.

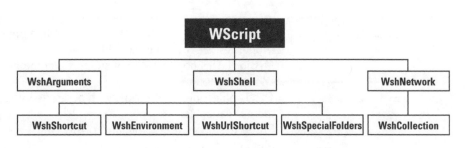

TABLE 5.3 WORKING WITH NONEXPOSED WSH OBJECTS

Object	Method Required to Create an Instance of Object
WshArguments	WScript.Arguments
WshCollection	WshNetwork.EnumNetworkDrives
WshShortcut	WshShell.CreateShortcut
Wsh.Environment	WshShell.Environment
WshUrlShortcut	WshShell.CreatShortcut
WshSpecialFolders	WshShell.SpecialFolders

TABLE 5.4 THE WSH OBJECT MODEL

Object Name	Description
WScript	This is the WSH root object. It provides access to the rest of the object in the WSH object model. Properties: Application, Arguments, FullName, Name, Path, ScriptFullName, ScriptName, StdErr, StdIn, StdOut, and Version. Methods: ConnectObject, CreateObject, DisconnectObject, Echo, GetObject, Quit, and Sleep.
WshArguments	This object provides access to command-line arguments. Properties: Count, Item, and Length. Methods: This object does not support any methods.
WshEnvironment	This is object provides scripts with access to Windows environmental variables. Properties: Count, Item, and Length. Methods: Remove.

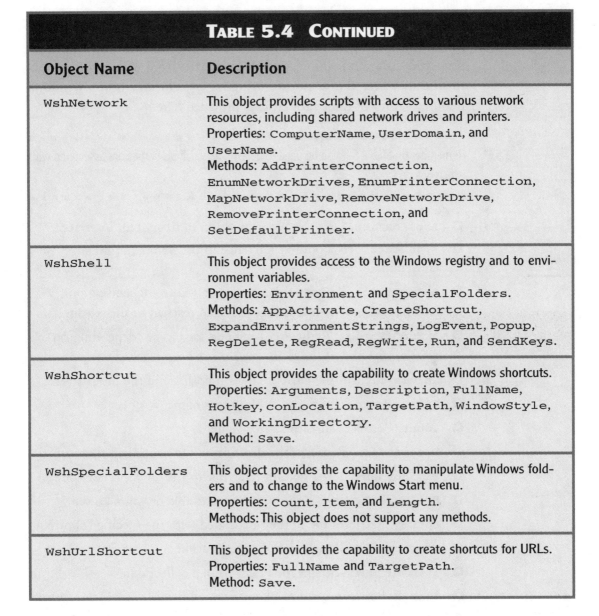

TABLE 5.4 CONTINUED	
Object Name	**Description**
`WshNetwork`	This object provides scripts with access to various network resources, including shared network drives and printers. Properties: `ComputerName`, `UserDomain`, and `UserName`. Methods: `AddPrinterConnection`, `EnumNetworkDrives`, `EnumPrinterConnection`, `MapNetworkDrive`, `RemoveNetworkDrive`, `RemovePrinterConnection`, and `SetDefaultPrinter`.
`WshShell`	This object provides access to the Windows registry and to environment variables. Properties: `Environment` and `SpecialFolders`. Methods: `AppActivate`, `CreateShortcut`, `ExpandEnvironmentStrings`, `LogEvent`, `Popup`, `RegDelete`, `RegRead`, `RegWrite`, `Run`, and `SendKeys`.
`WshShortcut`	This object provides the capability to create Windows shortcuts. Properties: `Arguments`, `Description`, `FullName`, `Hotkey`, `conLocation`, `TargetPath`, `WindowStyle`, and `WorkingDirectory`. Method: `Save`.
`WshSpecialFolders`	This object provides the capability to manipulate Windows folders and to change to the Windows Start menu. Properties: `Count`, `Item`, and `Length`. Methods: This object does not support any methods.
`WshUrlShortcut`	This object provides the capability to create shortcuts for URLs. Properties: `FullName` and `TargetPath`. Method: `Save`.

Examining WSH Core Object Properties

The objects that make up the WSH core object model expose dozens of properties. You can manipulate these properties from within your scripts to directly affect the Windows operating system and other Windows resources. A list of these properties is provided here.

 TIP   Remember that Table 5.4 can be used to determine which properties are associated with which object.

- ⚙ **Application**. Gets the WScript object's IDispatch interface.
- ⚙ **Arguments**. Sets a pointer reference to the WshArguments collection.
- ⚙ **AtEndOfLine**. Returns either true or false depending on whether the end-of-line maker has been reached in the stream.
- ⚙ **AtEndOfStream**. Returns either true or false depending on whether the end of the input stream has been reached.
- ⚙ **Column**. Returns the current column position in the input stream.
- ⚙ **ComputerName**. Retrieves a computer's name.
- ⚙ **Count**. Retrieves an enumerator value.
- ⚙ **Description**. Retrieves the description for a specified shortcut.
- ⚙ **Environment**. Sets a pointer reference to the WshEnvironment.
- ⚙ **FullName**. Retrieves a shortcut or executable program's path.
- ⚙ **HotKey**. Retrieves the hotkey associated with the specified shortcut.
- ⚙ **IconLocation**. Retrieves an icon's location.
- ⚙ **Item**. Retrieves the specified item from a collection.
- ⚙ **Length**. Retrieves a count of enumerated items.
- ⚙ **Line**. Returns the line number for the current line in the input stream.
- ⚙ **Name**. Returns a string representing the name of the WScript object.

- **Path**. Returns the location of the folder where the CScript or WScript execution hosts reside.

- **ScriptFullName**. Returns an executing script's path.

- **ScriptName**. Returns the name of the executing script.

- **SpecialFolders**. Provides access to the Windows Start menu and desktop folders.

- **StdErr**. Enables a script to write to the error output stream.

- **StdIn**. Enables read access to the input stream.

- **StdOut**. Enables write access to the output stream.

- **TargetPath**. Retrieves a shortcut's path to its associated object.

- **UserDomain**. Retrieves the domain name.

- **UserName**. Retrieves the currently logged on user's name.

- **Version**. Retrieves the WSH version number.

- **WindowStyle**. Retrieves a shortcut's window style.

- **WorkingDirectory**. Returns the working directory associated with the specified shortcut.

Examining WSH Core Object Methods

The objects in the WSH core object model also provide dozens of methods. You can execute these methods from within your scripts to manipulate these objects and their data. This provides your scripts direct control over the Windows operating system and its resources. A list of methods supported by the objects in the WSH core object model follows.

- **AddPrinterConnection**. Creates printer mappings.

- **AddWindowsPrinterConnection**. Creates a new printer connection.

- **AppActivate**. Activates the targeted application Window.

- **Close**. Terminates or ends an open data stream.

- **ConnectObject**. Establishes a connection to an object.

- **CreateObject**. Creates a new instance of an object.
- **CreateShortcut**. Creates a Windows shortcut.
- **DisconnectObject**. Terminates a connection with an object.
- **Echo**. Displays a text message.
- **EnumNetworkDrives**. Enables access to network drives.
- **EnumPrinterConnections**. Enables access to network printers.
- **ExpandEnvironmentStrings**. Retrieves a string representing the contents of the **Process** environmental variable.
- **GetObject**. Retrieves an **Automation** object.
- **GetResource**. Retrieves a resource's value as specified by the <resource> tag.
- **LogEvent**. Writes a message in the Windows event log.
- **MapNetworkDrive**. Creates a network drive mapping.
- **Popup**. Displays a text message in a pop-up dialog.
- **Quit**. Terminates or ends a script.
- **Read**. Retrieves a string of characters from the input stream.
- **ReadAll**. Retrieves the s string that is made up of the characters in the input stream.
- **ReadLine**. Retrieves a string containing an entire line of data from the input stream.
- **RegDelete**. Deletes a registry key or value.
- **RegRead**. Retrieves a registry key or value.
- **RegWrite**. Creates a registry key or value.
- **Remove**. Deletes the specified environmental variable.
- **RemoveNetworkDrive**. Deletes the connection to the specified network drive.
- **RemovePrinterConnection**. Deletes the connection to the specified network printer.
- **Run**. Starts a new process.

- **Save**. Saves a shortcut.
- **SendKeys**. Emulates keystrokes and sends typed data to a specified Window.
- **SetDefaultPrinter**. Establishes a default Windows printer.
- **Skip**. Skips x number of characters when reading from the input stream.
- **SkipLine**. Skips an entire line when reading from the input stream.
- **Sleep**. Pauses script execution for x number of seconds.
- **Write**. Places a string in the output stream.
- **WriteBlankLines**. Places a blank in the output stream.
- **WriteLine**. Places a string in the output stream.

Taking a Break

Okay, I think this is a good place to stop and take a 15-minute break. So, go stretch your legs for a while and maybe have a cup of coffee. When you return we'll go over the VBScript runtime object model and its methods and properties. You'll also learn how to use XML to create Windows script files.

Working with VBScript Runtime Objects

You know that the WSH provides your VBScripts with access to the WSH core object model, thus exposing large parts of the Windows objecting system. Now let's look at the VBScript runtime objects. These are objects that are only available when you use VBScript with the WSH. These objects provide properties and methods that expose the Windows file systems and allow your VBScripts to copy, move, and delete Windows files and folders and to read, write, and append to Windows files.

By incorporating the properties and methods of these objects into your VBScripts you can perform an assortment of nifty tricks, such as reading from and writing to log files and creating reports. You can also automate the administration and maintenance of these logs and reports. Table 5.5 lists each of the VBScript runtime objects and identifies its associated properties and methods.

TABLE 5.5 VBSCRIPT RUNTIME OBJECTS	
Object	**Description**
Dictionary	Stores data key, item pairs. Properties: CompareMode, Count, Item, Key. Methods: Add, Exists, Items, Keys, Remove, RemoveAll.
Drive	Provides access to disk drive properties. Properties: AvailableSpace, DriveLetter, DriveType, FileSystem, FreeSpace, IsReady, Path, RootFolder, SerialNumber, ShareName, TotalSize, VolumeName. Methods: This object does not support any methods.
Drives Collection	Provides access to various kinds of information regarding the drive's location on the computer. Properties: Count, Item. Methods: This object does not support any methods.
File	Provides access to file properties. Properties: Attributes, DateCreated, DateLastAccessed, DateLastModified, Drive, Name, ParentFolder, Path, ShortName, ShortPath, Size, Type. Methods: Copy, Delete, Move, OpenAsTextStream.
Files Collection	Provides access to all the files stored in a folder. Properties: Count, Item. Methods: This object does not support any methods.

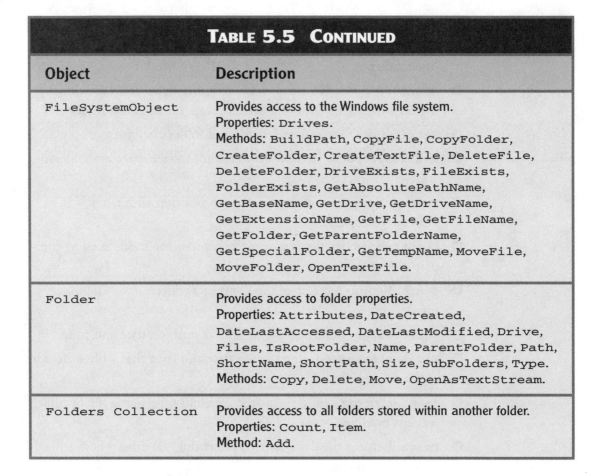

Object	Description
FileSystemObject	Provides access to the Windows file system. Properties: Drives. Methods: BuildPath, CopyFile, CopyFolder, CreateFolder, CreateTextFile, DeleteFile, DeleteFolder, DriveExists, FileExists, FolderExists, GetAbsolutePathName, GetBaseName, GetDrive, GetDriveName, GetExtensionName, GetFile, GetFileName, GetFolder, GetParentFolderName, GetSpecialFolder, GetTempName, MoveFile, MoveFolder, OpenTextFile.
Folder	Provides access to folder properties. Properties: Attributes, DateCreated, DateLastAccessed, DateLastModified, Drive, Files, IsRootFolder, Name, ParentFolder, Path, ShortName, ShortPath, Size, SubFolders, Type. Methods: Copy, Delete, Move, OpenAsTextStream.
Folders Collection	Provides access to all folders stored within another folder. Properties: Count, Item. Method: Add.

TABLE 5.5 CONTINUED

VBScript Runtime Properties

Like the objects in the WSH core object model, VBScript runtime objects provide an extensive supply of properties. You can use the properties to view or change numerous file system attributes. These properties are listed here.

TIP Remember that Table 5.5 can be used to determine which properties are associated with which VBScript runtime object.

- **AtEndOfLine**. Returns a value of either `true` or `false` depending on whether the file pointer precedes the `TextStream` file's end-of-line marker.

- **AtEndOfStream**. Returns a value of either `true` or `false` depending on whether the end of a `TextStream` file has been reached.

- **Attributes**. Retrieves or sets file and folder attributes.

- **AvailableSpace**. Retrieves the amount of free space available on a drive.

- **Column**. Retrieves the current column position within a `TextStream` file.

- **CompareMode**. Retrieves or sets the comparison mode used to compare a `Dictionary` object's string keys.

- **Count**. Returns a count of the items in a collection or Dictionary object.

- **DateCreated**. Returns a file or folder's creation date and time.

- **DateLastAccessed**. Returns the date and time that a file or folder was last accessed.

- **DateLastModified**. Returns the date and time that a file or folder was last modified.

- **Drive**. Returns the drive letter representing the drive where a file or folder is stored.

- **DriveLetter**. Returns a drive's drive letter.

- **Drives**. Creates a `Drives` collection representing the computer's `Drive` objects.

- **DriveType**. Returns a value indicating a drive's type.

- **Files**. Creates a `Files` collection representing the `File` objects stored inside a folder.

- **FileSystem**. Returns the file system type implemented on a drive.

- **FreeSpace**. Returns the amount of free space available to the user on a drive.

- **IsReady**. Returns a value of either `true` or `false` depending on whether a drive is available.

- **IsRootFolder**. Returns a value of either `true` or `false` identifying whether a folder is the root folder.

- **Item**. Retrieves or sets an item based on the specified `Dictionary` object key.

- **Key**. Sets a `Dictionary` object key.

- **Line**. Returns the current line number in the `TextStream` file.

- **Name**. Retrieves or sets a file or folder's name.

- **ParentFolder**. Retrieves a file or folder's parent folder object.

- **Path**. Retrieves the path associated with a file, folder, or drive.

- **RootFolder**. Retrieves the `Folder` object associated with the root folder on the specified drive.

- **SerialNumber**. Retrieves a disk volume's serial number.

- **ShareName**. Retrieves a network drive's share name.

- **ShortName**. Retrieves a file's or folder's 8.3 character short name.

- **ShortPath**. Retrieves the short path associated with a file's or folder's 8.3 character name.

- **Size**. Retrieves a file's or folder's byte size.

- **SubFolders**. Establishes a `Folders` collection consisting of all the folders located inside a specified folder.

- **TotalSize**. Returns the total number of bytes left on a drive.

- **Type**. Retrieves information about a file's or folder's type.

- **VolumeName**. Retrieves or sets a drive's volume name.

VBScript Runtime Methods

Well, if there are dozens of VBScript runtime properties, then it only seems right that there should be dozens of methods as well. By executing these methods in your VBScripts you can take complete control of the Windows file system.

NOTE This seems like a good place to mention that when you run a script it executes using the same level of permissions that you have on the computer. If you are running the script on a Windows 95, 98, or Me system you should have complete control over your environment. However, if you are using Windows NT, 2000, or XP you may not have the same level of access depending on how your account has been set up. Just remember, your scripts will not be able to perform any action on the computer that you yourself are not permitted to perform.

The methods that belong to the VBScript runtime objects are listed here.

VBScript Run-time Methods

- ✿ **Add (Dictionary).** Adds a key and item pair to a `Dictionary` object.

- ✿ **Add (Folders).** Adds a `Folder` to a collection.

- ✿ **BuildPath.** Appends a name to the path.

- ✿ **Close.** Closes an open `TextStream` file.

- ✿ **Copy.** Copies a file or folder.

- ✿ **CopyFile.** Copies one or more files.

- ✿ **CopyFolder.** Recursively copies a folder.

- ✿ **CreateFolder.** Creates a new folder.

- ✿ **CreateTextFile.** Creates a file and a `TextStream` object that can be used to read and write to the file.

- ✿ **Delete.** Deletes a file or folder.

- ✿ **DeleteFile.** Deletes a file.

- ✿ **DeleteFolder.** Deletes a folder's contents.

- ✿ **DriveExists.** Returns either `true` or `false` depending on the existence of a drive.

- ✿ **Exists.** Returns either `true` or `false` depending on whether a key exists in a `Dictionary` object.

- **FileExists**. Returns either `true` or `false` depending on whether a file can be found.

- **FolderExists**. Returns a value of `true` or `false` depending on whether a folder can be found.

- **GetAbsolutePathName**. Returns a complete path name.

- **GetBaseName**. Retrieves a filename less its file extension.

- **GetDrive**. Returns the `Drive` object associated with the drive in the specified path.

- **GetDriveName**. Retrieves the name of a drive.

- **GetExtensionName**. Retrieves a file's extension.

- **GetFile**. Retrieves a `File` object.

- **GetFileName**. Retrieves the last filename or folder of the specified path.

- **GetFileVersion**. Retrieves a file's version number.

- **GetFolder**. Retrieves the `Folder` object associated with the folder in the specified path.

- **GetParentFolderName**. Retrieves the name of the parent folder.

- **GetSpecialFolder**. Retrieves a special folder's name.

- **GetTempName**. Retrieves the name of a temporary file or folder.

- **Items**. Returns an array containing the items in a Dictionary object.

- **Keys**. Returns an array containing the keys in a Dictionary object.

- **Move**. Moves a file or folder.

- **MoveFile**. Moves one or more files.

- **MoveFolder**. Moves one or more folders.

- **OpenAsTextStream**. Opens a file and returns a `TextStream` object that can be used to reference the file.

- **OpenTextFile**. Opens a file and returns a `TextStream` object that can be used to reference the file.

- ✪ **Read**. Returns a string containing x number of characters from a TextStream file.
- ✪ **ReadAll**. Reads the whole TextStream file and returns its contents.
- ✪ **ReadLine**. Reads a line in a TextStream file.
- ✪ **Remove**. Deletes a Dictionary object's key, item pair.
- ✪ **Skip**. Skips x number of character positions when processing a TextStream file.
- ✪ **SkipLine**. Skips a line when processing a TextStream file.
- ✪ **Write**. Places a string in the TextStream file.
- ✪ **WriteBlankLines**. Writes x number of newline characters to the TextStream file.
- ✪ **WriteLine**. Writes a string in the TextStream file.

VBScript Runtime Constants

In addition to the collection of VBScript runtime objects, a new collection of VBScript runtime constants is also made available to any VBScript executed by the WSH.

NOTE　You will not see the constants when you are using VBScript to do your web page development.

The VBScript runtime constants provide access to a collection of values that are automatically made available to the scripts at execution time. These constants provide information about file, folder, and driver resources on the local computer. Table 5.6 provides a list of these constants.

TABLE 5.6 RUNTIME CONSTANTS	
Constant	**Description**
DriveType	Provides access to the following set of constants: Unknown: Undetermined drive type. Removable: Drive supporting removable media. Fixed: Includes any fixed disk drives on the computer. Remote: Shared network drives. CDROM: CD-ROM drives. RAMDisk: Logical drives created using memory.
File Attribute	Provides access to the following set of constants: Normal: A file without any set attributes. ReadOnly: A read-only file. Hidden: A hidden file. System: A system file. Directory: A folder. Archive: Identifies whether a file has changed since last backup. Alias: A shortcut. Compressed: A compressed file.
File Input/Output	Provides access to the following set of constants: ForReading: Opens a file for reading. ForWriting: Opens a file for reading and writing. ForAppending: Opens a file and allows data to be appended to the end of the file.
FileSystemObject	The following list describes the types of constants provided for by the VBScript FileSystemObject. DriveType: Identifies all available drive types. File Attribute: Identifies types of file attributes. File Input/Output: Identifies constants that can be used in file input/output operations. SpecialFolder: Identifies special folders.
SpecialFolder	Provides a reference to the following constants: WindowsFolder: Identifies the folder that contains Windows operating system files. SystemFolder: Identifies the System folder, which stores device drivers and library files. TemporaryFolder: Identifies the Windows Temp folder.

Using XML to Create Windows Script Files

As I have already stated, VBScript is not the only scripting language supported by the WSH. Microsoft also supplies JScript and there are third-party scripting engines available for Perl, Python, and Rexx. By using Windows script files you can combine the best features of any of these scripting languages into a single script.

For example, using Windows script files you can combine VBScript and JScript. The glue that allows you to bind these two different scripting languages or any other WSH compatible scripting language is the *Extensible Markup Language* or *XML*. XML is a markup language that allows you to identify components within a Windows script file. Specifically, XML allows you to identify each script embedded within the file and which script engine should be used to process it. The resulting Windows script file is then saved as a plain text file with a .wsf file extension.

XML looks a lot like HTML and has a similar syntax. Within Windows script files, XML uses tags to identify script components. However, unlike HTML, which is used to both structure and affect the presentation of a web page, XML is used within Windows script files only to provide information about the content of a document and not to define its appearance.

XML has strict rules for formatting documents. For example, unlike HTML, which sometimes allows the second tag in a pair of tags to be omitted without error, XML always requires the second tag. XML is case sensitive. In addition, the current XML 1.0 standard states that tags in all lowercase letters are preferred.

NOTE Like WSH VBScripts you can create Windows script files using any text editor that can save files as plain text including the Windows Notepad application. If you prefer you can also use the HomeSite editor to develop all your XML code. You'll find a link to the Macromedia web site where a trial copy of HomeSite can be downloaded at this book's companion web site at **www.premierpressbooks.com/downloads.asp**. There are also a number of excellent XML editors available. One that you might want to take a look at is XMLwriter available at **www.xmlwriter.net**.

XML Tags

Microsoft's implementation of XML within WSH only uses a partial set of XML tags. The following list describes the XML tags that you'll use when working with the WSH.

- **`<?job ?>`**. Enables or disables debugging and error handling for a job.
- **`<?XML ?>`**. Sets Windows script file's XML level.
- **`<comment> </comment>`**. Allows you to add XML comments.
- **`<job> </job>`**. Marks the beginning and end of a job inside a Windows script file.
- **`<package> </package>`**. Allows multiple jobs to be added to a Windows script file.
- **`<object> </object>`**. Sets up an object reference inside a Windows script file.
- **`<reference> </reference>`**. Sets up a reference to an external library.
- **`<resource> </resource >`**. Defines static data that any script within the Windows script file can reference.
- **`<script> </script>`**. Marks the beginning and end of a script within a Windows script file.

I'll go into greater detail about each of these XML tags as the morning continues.

The `<?job ?>` Tag

The XML tag is used to enable and disable debugging and error reporting of Windows script files. The `<?job ?>` tag does not have a matching closing tag. It is implemented using the following syntax.

```
<?job error="flag" debug="flag" ?>
```

When used, the `error` parameter is assigned a Boolean value of either `true` or `false`. Therefore `error="true"` enables error reporting while `error="false"` disables it. Similarly, the `debug` parameter is used to turn on and off debugging.

The following example shows how to use the `<?job ?>` tag to enable both error reporting and debugging.

```
<?job error="true" debug="true" ?>
```

NOTE The Windows script debugger is a tool provided by Microsoft that you can use to fix problems that may occur during the development of your scripts. Coverage of this tool is beyond the scope of this book. However, if you wish to learn more about it you can do so by visiting **msdn.microsoft.com/scripting**.

The `<?XML ?>` Tag

The `<?XML ?>` tag is used to identify what XML version the Windows script file was written for. This tag is optional. When present, it enforces a more strict interpretation of the XML statement in the Windows script file. When used, the `<?XML ?>` tag must be the first XML tag in the Windows script file.

The `<?XML ?>` tag uses the following syntax.

```
<?XML version="version" [standalone="DTDflag"] ?>
```

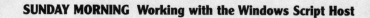

The `version` parameter is used to specify the version of XML for which the Windows script file was written. Its value is specified as X.X. Currently XML is still at version 1.0 although standards for version 2.0 are being proposed and debated. The `standalone` parameter specifies an external Document Type Definition. This option is not supported at the present time and if you choose to add it, then you must specify its value as being equal to `yes`.

The following example demonstrates how to write an `<?XML ?>` statement that specifies an XML version of 1.0 and which sets the `standalone` parameter to `yes`.

```
<?XML version="1.0" standalone="yes" ?>
```

The `<comment>` `</comment>` Tags

The `<comment>` `</comment>` tags allow you to document your XML statements by adding descriptive text. Of course, you can still add VBScript comments within your VBScripts thereby mitigating some of the advantages of this tag.

The syntax for the `<comment>` `</comment>` tags is shown here.

```
<comment>Descriptive text........ </comment>
```

The `<job>` `</job>` Tags

Every Windows script file must have a root XML element within which all other XML tags are located in a tree-like structure. Two pairs of XML tags can serve as root tags. One of them is the `<job>` `</job>` tags. These tags are used to identify individual jobs located within Windows script files.

NOTE The other pair of XML tags that can serve as root tags are the `<package>` `</package>` tags, which allow you to place more than one job in a Windows script file.

The `<job>` `</job>` tags have the following syntax.

```
<job [id=JobID]>
  . . .
</job>
```

The `id` parameter is used to assign an identifier to a particular job. Windows script files can contain more than one job. When a Windows script file contains a single job, this parameter is optional.

Within a Windows script file a job contains one or more scripts each of which may be written using a different scripting language. If you run a Windows script file that contains more than one job only the first job within the file is executed by default. However, by specifying a specific job's `id` you can specify which job will be executed.

The following example shows a Windows script file that contains a single job. The job contains two scripts, each of which has been written using a different scripting language. Because this is the only job in the Windows script file, I did not add the `ID` parameter to the first `<job>` tag.

```
<job>
<?job error="true" debug="true"?>
<comment>Script 5.1 - A Windows Script file with one job</comment>
<script language="VBScript">
   WScript.Echo "This message was displayed using VBScript."
 </script>
 <script language="JScript">
   WScript.Echo ("This message was displayed using JScript.")
 </script>
</job>
```

You may have also noticed the use of the `<comment>` `</comment>` tags in the script. You can see this script in action by saving it with a `.wsf` file extension and then double-clicking it to execute it.

The `<package>` `</package>` **Tags**

If you plan to place more than one job in a Windows script file, then you will be required to use the `<package>` `</package>` tags as the root element and then define the jobs within these tags. You can also use the `<package>` `</package>` tags within a Windows script file that only contains a single job, but it's not required.

TIP You might want to add these tags anyway just to be consistent and to make updating your Windows script files easier in the future.

NOTE Don't forget that when you use the `<package>` `</package>` tags in your Windows script files you'll also need to assign an `id` to each job inside the first `<job>` tag.

The syntax of the `<package>` `</package>` tags is

```
<package>
    . .
</package>
```

The following example shows how to create a Windows script file that contains two jobs. In this case, each job contains a single script.

```
<package>
  <comment>Script 5.2 - A Windows Script file with two jobs</comment>
  <job id="vbs_job">
    <script language="VBScript">
      WScript.Echo "This message was displayed using VBScript."
    </script>
  </job>
  <job id="js_job">
    <script language="JScript">
      WScript.Echo ("This message was displayed using JScript.")
    </script>
  </job>
</package>
```

The `<object>` `</object>` Tags

The `<object>` `</object>` tags are used to set up references to objects with Windows script files. The reference to these objects is limited to all scripts defined within the same job.

The syntax to use with the `<object>` `</object>` tags is shown here.

```
<object id="obj_ID" [classid="clsid:GUID" | progid="prog_ID"] />
```

The `id` parameter is used to assign the name by which the object can be referenced. The `classid` parameter specifies the class id of the registered object. The `progid` parameter is used to set a program `id`. You must specify either the *classid* or *progid* parameter.

The `<reference>` `</reference>` Tags

The `<reference>` `</reference>` tags are used to include references to external libraries that are exposed by objects that exist within other applications installed on your computer. External libraries are usually found inside the external object's executable program (.exe) or in a dynamic link library (.dll) that is provided with the application.

The WSH allows you to create new instances of external objects and execute their methods and properties. Unfortunately, the WSH does not provide access to any constants residing within the external object's library. However, by using the `<reference>` `</reference>` tags you can get around this problem and set up a reference to any constant value stored in an external object's library.

The syntax for the `<reference>` `</reference>` tags is

```
<reference [object="prog_ID" | guid="typelibGUID"] [version="version"] />
```

The `object` parameter references an external library using its program `id`. The `guid` parameter sets up a reference using the type library's `CLSID`. These two parameters are mutually exclusive meaning that you must use one or the other, but not both. The `version` parameter is optional. It can be added to specify the version number of the external library.

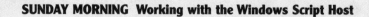

NOTE I won't go any further into an explanation of the `<reference> </reference>` tags. The use of external library references is an advanced programming technique, which is better left to other books. I mentioned these tags here only to give you an idea of what the tag does should you come across it sometime.

The `<resource>  </resource>` Tags

XML provides the `<resource>  </resource>` tags to simplify the creation of constants within Windows script files. The `<resource> </resource>` tags must be placed inside `<job> </job>` tags. This limits their scope to a particular job. Therefore, a constant defined using these tags can then be referenced by any script within a job in the Windows script file saving you the effort of redefining the same constant over and over again in each script in a given job. However, constants created by the `<resource> </resource>` tags in one are not available to scripts located in different jobs in the same Windows script file.

The syntax for the `<resource> </resource>` tags is

```
<resource id="resourceID">
   . . .
</resource>
```

The `id` parameter is used to provide an `id` by which the constant's value can be referenced. The `id` must be unique within the Windows script file.

For example, the following Windows script file shows one way that you can use the `<resource> </resource>` tags to create script constants. In this example, the constant that is defined is assigned an `id` of `PI`. A VBScript then displays the value assigned to the constant using the VBScript `MsgBox()` function and the WSH's `getResource()` method.

```
<job>
  <comment>Script 5.3 - Creating constants in Windows script ➥
       files</comment>
  <resource id="pi">
   3.14
```

```
    </resource>
    <script language="VBScript">
      MsgBox("The value of PI is: " & getResource("pi"))
    </script>
</job>
```

Figure 5.5 shows a pop-up dialog that is created when the Windows script file is executed.

Figure 5.5

Accessing constants from within your VBScripts that were created using the XML <resource> </resource> tags.

The `<script>` `</script>` Tags

By now you have seen the XML `<script>` `</script>` tags in action a number of times. As you have seen, they look and operate a lot like their HTML counterparts allowing you to specify the scripting engine that should be used to process each script within a Windows script file.

The syntax for the `<script>` `</script>` tags is outlined here.

```
<script language="script_language" [src="external_script"]>
  ...
</script>
```

The `language` parameter identifies the type of script that follows. The `src` parameter is optional and can be used to set up reference to an external script. When the `src` parameter is used, the external script is then called and executed just as if it had been embedded in the Windows script file.

For example, the following Windows script file contains a single job, which executes two VBScripts. The first VBScript is embedded inside the `<job>` `</job>` tags. The second script that is executed is actually an external script named `Script 5.5`.

```
<job>
  <comment>Script 5.4 - Calling an external VBScript from a Windows ➡
       script file</comment>
  <script language="VBScript">
    WScript.Echo ("This message was generated by an embedded ➡
       VBScript.")
  </script>
  <script language="VBScript" src="Script 5.5.vbs" />
</job>
```

Script 5.5 is a simple VBScript. Its contents are shown here.

```
' *********************************************
' * Script Name: Script 5.5.vbs              *
' * Author:   Jerry Ford                      *
' * Address: Richmond Virginia                *
' * Created: 02/28/02                         *
' *********************************************

' **** Perform script initialization here ****

Option Explicit
On error Resume Next

' ********* Main processing section **********
' Call a function that displays the user's name

DisplayMsg()

' ********** Procedures go here *************
' This function displays whatever name is passed to it

Function DisplayMsg()
  WScript.Echo ("This message was generated by an external VBScript.")
End Function
```

Executing Your Windows Script Files

Next let's take a look at various ways that we can execute Windows script files. I'll begin by outlining another Windows script file. In this example, the Windows script file is composed of three jobs. Therefore, I'll have to use the <package> </package> tags as the root element. Each job contains a single script.

```xml
<?xml version="1.0"?>
<package>
<comment>Script 5.6 - Windows Script file execution demo</comment>

  <job id="vbs_job1">
    <?job error="true" debug="true"?>
    <script language="VBScript">
      WScript.Echo "The first VBScript produced this message."
    </script>
  </job>

  <job id="js_job1">
    <?job error="true" debug="true"?>
    <script language="JScript">
      WScript.Echo ("The first JScript produced this message.")
    </script>
  </job>

  <job id="vbs_job2">
    <?job error="true" debug="true"?>
    <script language="VBScript">
      WScript.Echo "The second VBScript produced this message."
    </script>
  </job>

</package>
```

A Windows script file can be executed just like any VBScript file. For starters you can double-click it. You can also type in its name at the Windows command prompt. However, the exact behavior of a Windows script file depends on its contents. For example, if a Windows script file contains a single job, then that job will run. If the job contains a number of scripts, then each script will execute. If the Windows script file contains more than one job, then double-clicking it or typing in its name at that Windows command prompt will only cause the first job within the Windows script file to run.

You can also run a Windows script file from the command line by specifying the WSH script execution host that you want to process the script as part of the command. For example, to run the previous Windows script file using the CScript execution host you would type the following command at the Windows command prompt and press Enter.

```
cscript "Script 5.6.wsf"
```

Figure 5.6 shows the message that is displayed when the Windows script file is executed.

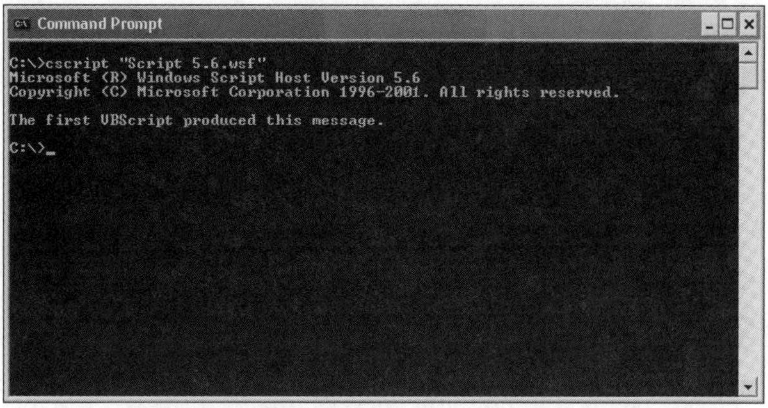

Figure 5.6

Executing a Windows script file using the WSH CScript.exe execution host.

Similarly, you would run the same script using the WScript execution host as shown.

```
wscript.exe "Script 5.6.wsf"
```

Figure 5.7 shows the message that is displayed when the Windows script file is executed.

However, only the first job within the Windows script file will be executed in both of these examples. You can alter the default behavior of Windows script files by specifying the job within the script that you want to run. You do this using the following syntax.

```
cscript.exe script_name //job:jobname
```

Figure 5.7

Executing a
Windows script file
using the WSH
WScript.exe
execution host
created using the
XMLtags.

or

```
wscript.exe script_name //job:jobname
```

For example, try typing the following command.

```
wscript "Script 5.6.wsf" //job:vbs_job2
```

As you see, this command runs the third script located in the third job in
the Windows script file.

Figure 5.8 shows the message that is displayed when the script is run this
time.

Figure 5.8

Specifying which
job you want to
execute in a
Windows script file.

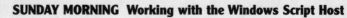

What's Next?

All right! Time to break for lunch and give your brain a break. When you return we will spend the rest of the day looking at different ways that you can automate tasks on your computer using VBScript and the WSH. You'll start this afternoon by learning how to manipulate the Windows file system and script tasks such as copying and moving files and reading and writing files. Finally, we'll finish up the book this evening by looking at how to script an assortment of tasks related to the operating system and desktop.

Working with Files and Folders

- ✪ Learn how to create text documents, reports, and logs
- ✪ Learn how to write scripts to perform file administration
- ✪ Learn how to programmatically work with Windows folders
- ✪ Find out how to schedule the execution of your file and folder administration scripts

Welcome back! This morning we covered a lot of material. This included a review of the WSH core object model and the properties and methods associated with each of its objects. In addition, you learned about VBScript runtime objects that are only available when you use the WSH to execute your VBScripts.

This afternoon we are going to expand on your understanding of the VBScript runtime objects. We'll look at a number of examples that demonstrate how these objects can provide your scripts with the capability to access and manipulate the contents of Windows drives, folders, and files.

By the time this afternoon is over you'll know how to write VBScripts that can display disk, folder, and file properties, that can read and write to files, and that can perform file and folder administration. And if that's not enough, I will also show you how to use the Windows Task Scheduler to set up an automated schedule so that you can run your scripts even when you are away from your computer.

Creating a WSH VBScript Template

Before I jump into this afternoon's work I thought it best to take a little time to talk about the importance of coming up with a good VBScript template that you can use when writing scripts that you'll run using the WSH.

Take a look at the following VBScript example. As you can see it is very straightforward. First it sets up error recovery, then defines a variable and calls a function that displays the contents of the variable. Now take a look at the example again only this time look at all its other parts. By this I mean, of course, the comments.

```
' *********************************************
' * Script Name: Template.vbs              *
' * Author: Jerry Ford                      *
' * Address: Richmond Virginia              *
' * Created: 02/28/02                       *
' *********************************************


' **** Perform script initialization here ****

Option Explicit

On Error Resume Next

Dim welcomeMsg
welcomeMsg = "Good day and welcome to my VBScript template!"

' ******** Main processing section *********

' Call a function that displays the user's name

Display_Msg(welcomeMsg)

' ********** Procedures go here ************

' This function displays whatever name is passed to it

Function Display_Msg(msg)

  WScript.Echo msg

End Function
```

Look at the first six lines in the script. They are used to provide some basic script documentation, including the name of the script, its author, author contact information, and the script's creation date. You could eas-

ily expand this section to include a description or any other information that you might think is helpful.

More comments are then used to divide the rest of the scripts up into three sections. The first section is used to contain any statements that setup or initialize the script's execution environment. This includes things such as:

- The Option Explicit statement
- The On Error Resume Next statement
- The declaration of variables
- The initial assignment of variable values

The next section in the script is called the Main processing section. This is where the controlling logic of the script is placed. Script statements located in this section may make calls to functions or subroutines located in the script's final section. By placing all your procedures in a single location you make them easier to find and modify.

Creating your own script template and using it to create all your VBScripts will help you to write structured scripts that are easy to read and maintain. Anyone else that follows behind you will always know where to find the script's initialization statements, main processing logic, and its procedures. In addition, you just might thank yourself a few years down the road if you find the need to come back and modify your own scripts long after you have written them.

Accessing the Windows File System

The WSH core object model does not provide the capability to interact with or manipulate the Windows file system. In other words, it does not give you a way to work with drives, folders, or even files. Instead, Microsoft puts this functionality into the VBScript runtime objects, which we covered this morning.

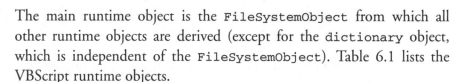

The main runtime object is the `FileSystemObject` from which all other runtime objects are derived (except for the `dictionary` object, which is independent of the `FileSystemObject`). Table 6.1 lists the VBScript runtime objects.

To use the `FileSystemObject` within your VBScripts you must first establish an instance of it. You can do this using the `WScript` object's `CreateObject()` method and by referencing it as `Scripting.FileSystemObject`. This is demonstrated in the following example.

```
Set fsoObject = WScript.CreateObject ("Scripting.FileSystemObject")
```

Here `fsoObject` is just the name that I assigned to a variable that can now be used by the rest of the script to reference the properties and methods of the `FileSystemObject`. With this instance of the `File-SystemObject` now established the script is read to interact with the Windows file system.

Let's put this previous `FileSystemObject` example to work in a few quick examples to see how it really works.

TABLE 6.1   OBJECTS AND COLLECTIONS EXPOSED BY THE `FileSystemObject`

Object	Access Provided
`Drive`	Disk drive properties
`Drives Collection`	System drive information
`File`	File properties
`Files Collection`	All files contained in the specified folder
`Folder`	Folder properties
`Folders Collection`	All folders contained in the specified folder

NOTE Windows NT, 2000, or XP operating system can use either the FAT or NTFS file systems. When the NTFS file system is being used advanced security permissions can be applied to the Windows File system. These advanced security permissions are not applied when FAT is used on these operating systems. Nor does Windows 95, 98, or Me support advanced security. Remember that if you are running your scripts on Windows NT, 2000, or XP and NTFS is being used as the file system, you must also be sure that you have appropriate security permissions to perform any task for which you want to write a script.

Displaying Drive Free Space

This first example demonstrates how to use a number of methods and properties of the VBScript runtime objects to access drive information. Specifically the example shown here displays the amount of free space on a computer's C: and D: drives.

```
' ***********************************************
' * Script Name: Script 6.1.vbs                 *
' * Author: Jerry Ford                          *
' * Address: Richmond Virginia                  *
' * Created: 02/28/02                           *
' ***********************************************

' **** Perform script initialization here ****

Option Explicit

On Error Resume Next

dim fsoObject, drive1, drive2

set fsoObject = WScript.CreateObject("Scripting.FileSystemObject")

set drive1 = fsoObject.GetDrive(fsoObject.GetDriveName("c:"))
set drive2 = fsoObject.GetDrive(fsoObject.GetDriveName("d:"))
```

```
' ********* Main processing section **********

' Call a function that displays drive information

Display_Msg()

' ********** Procedures go here *************

' This function displays the amount of free space on drive 1 and drive
2

Function Display_Msg()

  WScript.Echo( "Free Space on drive 1 is: " _
    & FormatNumber(drive1.FreeSpace / 1024 , 0) & " KB")
  WScript.Echo( "Free Space on drive 2 is: " _
    & FormatNumber(drive2.FreeSpace / 1024 , 0) & " KB")

End Function
```

The script begins by defining three variables. The first variable is fsoObject. It will be used to create an instance of the FileSystemObject as
discussed earlier. The next two variables will be used to set up references
to the computer's C: and D: drives.

The two statements that set up the values of these two variables for the
computer's drives probably look a little complex to you at first. So let's
take a moment and break them down. First, the GetDriveName()
method of the FileSystemObject is used by appending it to the variable fsoObject (for example, fsoObject.GetDriveName()). Remember that the fsoObject variable provides the script with a reference to
the FileSystemObject and its properties and methods. The Get-
DriveName() method returns the name of the drive associated with the
specified driver letter (that is, C: or D:). Next, the FileSystemObject
object's GetDrive() method is used to retrieve the Drive object associated with the specified drive name. The reason that we need to establish
a reference to the Drive object is because we are going to want to use its
Freespace property a little later in the script.

After executing the statements in the script's initialization section, the VBScript statement in the main processing section executes. There is only one VBScript statement in this section and it calls a function named `Display_Msg()`. The function then executes. Its job is to display the amount of free space on each drive. This is accomplished by taking the amount of free space left on a given drive as contained by the `Drive` object's `FreeSpace` property and dividing it by 1024 (1 kilobyte or 1 KB). The results are then formatted using the `Drive` object's `FormatNumber()` method, which in this case formats the number with zero trailing decimal spaces (that is, as whole number).

When I ran this script on my computer, I got the following results.

```
C:\>CScript "Script 6.1.vbs"
Microsoft (R) Windows Script Host Version 5.6
Copyright (C) Microsoft Corporation 1996-2001. All rights reserved.


Free Space on drive 1 is: 158,112 KB
Free Space on drive 2 is: 16,792 KB


C:\>
```

Examining File System Types

Let's look at another example of how to work with the methods and properties of the VBScript runtime objects. This time we'll write a VBScript example that displays the type of file system that the computer's C: and D: drives have been formatted with.

```
' **********************************************
' * Script Name: Script 6.2.vbs                *
' * Author: Jerry Ford                          *
' * Address: Richmond Virginia                  *
' * Created: 02/28/02                           *
' **********************************************


' **** Perform script initialization here ****

Option Explicit
```

```
On Error Resume Next

dim fsoObject, drive1, drive2

set fsoObject = WScript.CreateObject("Scripting.FileSystemObject")

set drive1 = fsoObject.GetDrive("C:")
set drive2 = fsoObject.GetDrive("D:")

' ********* Main processing section **********

' Call a function that displays drive information

Display_Msg()

' *********** Procedures go here *************

' This function displays the file system used to format drive 1 and
drive 2

Function Display_Msg()

  WScript.Echo("The file system used on drive 1 is: " &
drive1.FileSystem)
  WScript.Echo("The file system used on drive 2 is: " &
drive2.FileSystem)

End Function
```

As you can see this VBScript is similar to the previous example. The same variables are defined in the initialization section. In addition, the same instance of the `FileSystemObject` is set up and once again its `Get-Drive()` method is used to retrieve `Drive` object references to each drive on the computer.

Next, a single VBScript statement in the main processing section calls a function that displays a file system type for each drive. This is accomplished by using `Drive` object's `FileSystem` property.

When I ran this script on my computer I received the following results.

```
C:\>CScript "Script 6.2.vbs"
Microsoft (R) Windows Script Host Version 5.6
Copyright (C) Microsoft Corporation 1996-2001. All rights reserved.

The file system used on drive 1 is: FAT
The file system used on drive 2 is: NTFS

C:\>
```

Examining File Properties

Let's look at one final example before we rush off and begin to master the art of reading from and writing to text files. This example starts off like the previous two examples by defining its variables and instantiating an instance of the FileSystemObject. This time the FileSystemObject object's GetFile() method is used. This method is used to retrieve the File object associated with the specified file, which in this example is c:\winzip.log.

Again, a VBScript statement in the main processing section calls on a function named Display_Msg(). The function contains a number of WScript.Echo statements each of which displays a different property associated with the File object.

```
' ***********************************************
' * Script Name: Script 6.3.vbs               *
' * Author: Jerry Ford                         *
' * Address: Richmond Virginia                 *
' * Created: 02/03/02                          *
' ***********************************************

' **** Perform script initialization here ****

Option Explicit

On Error Resume Next

dim fsoObject, targetFile

set fsoObject = WScript.CreateObject("Scripting.FileSystemObject")
```

```
set targetFile = fsoObject.GetFile("c:\winzip.log")

' ********* Main processing section **********

' Call a function that displays drive information

Display_Msg()

' ********** Procedures go here *************

' This function displays file properties

Function Display_Msg()

  WScript.Echo("File properties of c:\winzip.log")
  WScript.Echo("----------------------------------")
  WScript.Echo("Created on:     " & targetFile.DateCreated)
  WScript.Echo("Last Modified: " & targetFile.DateLastModified)
  WScript.Echo("Last Accessed: " & targetFile.DateLastAccessed)
  WScript.Echo("File Name:      " & targetFile.Name)
  WScript.Echo("File Path:      " & targetFile.Path)
  WScript.Echo("File Type:      " & targetFile.Type)
  WScript.Echo("File Size:      " & targetFile.Size)

End Function
```

The following output was displayed when I ran this script.

```
C:\>CScript "Script 6.3.vbs"
Microsoft (R) Windows Script Host Version 5.6
Copyright (C) Microsoft Corporation 1996-2001. All rights reserved.

File properties of c:\winzip.log
----------------------------------
Created on:    2/3/2002 11:23:36 PM
Last Modified: 3/9/2002 10:38:52 AM
Last Accessed: 3/9/2002
File Name:     winzip.log
File Path:     C:\winzip.log
File Type:     Text Document
File Size:     79555

C:\>
```

Creating Documents, Reports, and Logs

By this point you should have a fairly good understanding of what the VBScript runtime objects are and what they can do. Now let's look at how you can use them to generate reports, logs, and other types of text documents.

To work with files and their contents you must first establish an instance of the `FileSystemObject` within your VBScript as shown here.

```
set fsoObject = WScript.CreateObject("Scripting.FileSystemObject")
```

Next, you should always check to see if the file that you want to work with already exists. If it does, you can open it. If it does not already exist, you can create it and then open it. You can check to see if a file exists using the `FileSystemObject` object's `FileExists` property as shown here.

```
If (fsoObject.FileExists("C:\myfile.txt")) Then
```

You must open a file before you can work with it. You can use the `FileSystemObject` object's `OpenTextFile()` method to open files. To use this method you need to supply a few pieces of information including the following.

- ✿ The name and path of the file to be opened
- ✿ Whether you want the file to be opened for reading, writing, or appending
- ✿ Whether to create the file if it does not exist

Table 6.2 defines constants that are used to tell the `OpenTextFile()` method what you want to do once the file is opened.

Table 6.3 defines two options that govern what the `OpenTextFile()` method should do when the file to be opened does and does not exist.

Now, using the information provided in Tables 6.2 and 6.3 you are ready to open a file.

TABLE 6.2 `OpenTextFile()` CONSTANTS		
Constant	**Description**	**Value**
`ForReading`	Opens a file for reading	1
`ForWriting`	Opens a file for writing	2
`ForAppending`	Opens a file for appending	8

TABLE 6.3 `OpenTextFile()` FILE CREATION OPTIONS	
Value	**Description**
`True`	Open the file if it exists, otherwise create and open it
`False`	Open the file if it exists, otherwise do not create it

Opening and Closing Files

It is very important that you correctly specify the type of operation that you are opening a file for (reading, writing, or appending). If you open a file to write to it and the file exists, then the file will be reinitialized. In other words, any data that is already in the file is lost and the file pointer is placed at the beginning of the new file (in the first row and column of the file).

By appending to a file, you are able to preserve its contents and add to it. In other words, the file is opened and the file pointer is placed at the end of the file in the last row and column position.

The file pointer is used to identify where the next character of data will be placed with a file. In a newly initialized file, the pointer would automatically be positioned in the upper-left corner (row 0, column 0). If one new character of information were added, the pointer would be moved

over one position to column 1 in row 0. If a carriage return were added (indicating an end-of-line marker), then the file pointer would move to column 0 row 1. Knowing the location of the file pointer and how it is moved around is important, especially if you will be writing to or reading from files that have fixed record formats with data fields starting and ending in specified column positions.

Okay, enough about the file pointer. Let's look at an example that ties together everything that we have talked about. In this example, I've written a VBScript that opens a file named myFile.txt, which resides in the root directory of my C: drive. If the file already exists, then the script opens it but if it does not already exist it will be created and opened.

```
' **********************************************
' * Script Name: Script 6.4.vbs                *
' * Author: Jerry Ford                         *
' * Address: Richmond Virginia                 *
' * Created: 02/13/02                          *
' **********************************************


' **** Perform script initialization here ****

Option Explicit

On Error Resume Next

Dim fsoObject, open_File, target_File

Set fsoObject = WScript.CreateObject("Scripting.FileSystemObject")

target_File = "C:\myFile.txt"

' ********* Main processing section **********

' Call a function that displays drive information

Open_My_File()

open_File.WriteLine "This line of data should be written to the text
file."
```

```
        Close_My_File()

        ' *********** Procedures go here *************

        ' This function opens a file

        Function Open_My_File()

          If (fsoObject.FileExists(target_File)) Then
            Set open_File = fsoObject.OpenTextFile(target_File, 8)
          Else
            Set open_File = fsoObject.OpenTextFile(target_File, 2, "True")
          End If

        End Function

        ' This function closes a file

        Function Close_My_File()

          open_File.Close()

        End Function
```

The file is opened using the forWriting constant (with a value of 2) if it already exists. If the file does not exist, then the forAppending constant (with a value of 8) is specified to open the file and place the file pointer at the end of the file.

If you take at look at the script's main processing section you will see the following statement between a pair of function calls, which open and close the file.

```
open_File.WriteLine "This line of data should be written to the text
file."
```

This statement writes one line of data to the file and executes a carriage return placing the file pointer in the first column of the following line. I'll talk more about the use of this and other methods that are used to write data to files in just a bit.

The last statement in the main processing section calls a function that executes the following statement.

```
open_File.Close()
```

This statement executed the `FileSystemObject` object's `close()` method i to close the opened file. You must remember to close any file that you open before allowing your script to end. Failing to do so may cause an error the next time that you open the file because the end-of-file marker will not have been created.

 NOTE You cannot mix and match different file operations at the same time. In other words, you cannot switch between reading and writing to a file. You must first open the file, perform one type of operation, and then close it before your can perform a different operation.

Run this script and open the `myFile.txt` file and you'll see the following line of data.

```
This line of data should be written to the text file.
```

Run the VBScript a couple more times and open the file again and this time you'll see the output shown in Figure 6.1.

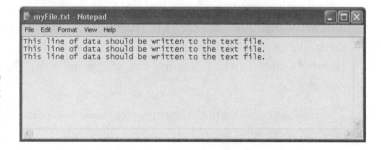

Figure 6.1

Creating a text file and writing and appending data to it.

Writing to Files

As you just learned, you should always check for the existence of a file before creating it. Once opened, you have several different ways in which you can write text data to your files.

One option is to write a specific number of characters at a time. This technique is best used when you need to write carefully formatted data to your files such as when you write reports with data that appears in columns.

Another option for writing to a file is to write an entire line of data at a time. This technique is best used when your documents are more free-formed and is probably the option that you'll use most often, especially if you plan to create log files in which you record error messages and other types of event information as your scripts execute.

Finally, you might want to add blank lines to your files. Blank lines are especially useful for formatting your documents to improve their presentation and make them easier to read.

Adding Characters to a File

You can write a specific number of characters to a file at a time using the `FileSystemObject` object's `Write()` method. This method does not automatically append a carriage return at the end of each write operation. Therefore, the next time a write operation occurs additional text is inserted immediately following the text written by the previous write operation.

The following example demonstrates how you can use the `Write()` method to append text to an existing file.

```
Set fsoObject = WScript.CreateObject("Scripting.FileSystemObject")
Set open_file = fsoObject.OpenTextFile("c:\myfile.txt", 8)
open_file.Write("Welcome to ")
open_file.Write("my VBScript!")
open_file.Close()
```

As you can see even though two separate write operations occurred, the text for both write operations was placed on the same line.

Adding a Line to a File

By replacing the `Write()` method with the `FileSystemObject` object's `WriteLine()` method in the previous example, you can change the previous script to write data to the file a line at a time.

```
Set fsoObject = WScript.CreateObject("Scripting.FileSystemObject")
Set open_file = fsoObject.OpenTextFile("c:\myfile.txt", 8)
open_file.WriteLine("Welcome to my VBScript!")
open_file.Close()
```

The `WriteLine()` method automatically adds a carriage return to the end of each line returning the file pointer to the first column of the next line.

Adding Blank Lines to a File

If you want to format your text files with blank lines to create better looking reports or make them easier to read you can use the `FileSystemObject` object's `WriteBlankLines()` method. When executed, this method writes a blank line to the file and executes a carriage return.

The following example demonstrates how to use the `WriteBlankLines()` method to format the data in a small report.

```
Set fsoObject = WScript.CreateObject("Scripting.FileSystemObject")
Set myCDrive = fsoObject.GetDrive("C:")
Set open_file = fsoObject.OpenTextFile("c:\myfile.txt", 8)

open_file.WriteLine("------------------------------")
open_file.WriteBlankLines(1)
open_file.WriteLine("      My C: Drive Report      ")
open_file.WriteBlankLines(1)
open_file.WriteLine("------------------------------")

open_file.WriteBlankLines(2)
```

```
open_file.WriteLine("File System - " & myCDrive.FileSystem)
open_file.WriteLine("Total Size  - " & myCDrive.TotalSize)
open_file.WriteLine("Free Space  - " & myCDrive.AvailableSpace)

open_file.Close()
```

As you can see from the previous example, you can specify the number of blank lines that the `WriteBlankLines()` method will write to the file. In addition to using the `WriteLine()` and `WriteBlankLines()` methods to write the text in the report, this script also uses the `FileSystem-Object` object's `GetDrive()` method. The `GetDrive()` method is then used to create an instance of the `Drive` object with a reference to the computer's `C:` drive so that the `Drive` object's properties could be used to retrieve information about the drive.

Figure 6.2 shows the report that was generated by this example.

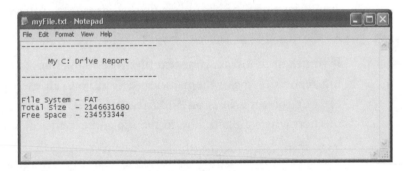

Figure 6.2

A sample report that has been formatted using blank lines.

Reading from Files

Reading the contents of a file is handled in much the same way as writing to it. First, be sure that the file exists. If it does, then your script may open it. The next thing your script should do is use the `TextStream` object's `AtEndOfStream` property to find out if the file has any data in it. After all, there is no point to trying to read an empty file. In fact, you should check the value of the `AtEndOfStream` property just before each read operation to be sure that your script has not reached the end of file marker (e.g., the end of the file).

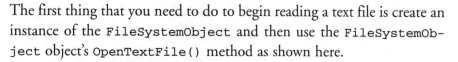

The first thing that you need to do to begin reading a text file is create an instance of the `FileSystemObject` and then use the `FileSystemObject` object's `OpenTextFile()` method as shown here.

```
Set fsoObject = CreateObject("Scripting.FileSystemObject")
Set open_file = fsoObject.OpenTextFile("c:\myfile.txt", 1)
```

As you can see the `forReading` constant has been specified. Next you could set up a loop that runs until the `AtEndOfStream` property has a value of `true` (the end of the file is reached). During each iteration of the loop your script should read a line of text using the `FileSystemObject` object's `ReadLine()` method as shown here.

```
Do while False = open_file.AtEndOfStream
  WScript.Echo(open_file.ReadLine())
Loop
```

The preceding VBScript statements will process every line in the file, terminating when the end of file marker is reached. After your script is done reading the file, it can close it as shown here.

```
open_file.Close
```

If you put these lines of code together and ran them as a script using the CScript execution host you'd see output similar to the following.

```
C:\>CScript test.vbs
Microsoft (R) Windows Script Host Version 5.6
Copyright (C) Microsoft Corporation 1996-2001. All rights reserved.


-----------------------------

     My C: Drive Report


-----------------------------



File System - FAT
Total Size  - 2146631680
Free Space  - 234553344

C:\>
```

In this example we read an entire file by reading it one line at a time. There are a number of other techniques for reading files. These include

- Skipping lines when reading a file
- Reading a specified number of characters from a file
- Reading an entire file in one operation

Skipping Portions of a File

If a file has headers or other information that you are not interested in reading you can always skip them and read only the portion of the file that interests you. For example, the file that we have been working with contains a five-line header followed by two blank lines after which the data in the report begins.

You can use either of the following methods, both of which belong to the FileSystemObject, to skip text in a file.

- **Skip()**. Skip a specific number of characters
- **SkipLine()**. Skips a line

The Skip() method lets you supply a number indicating how many characters should be skipped. For example, the following statement would skip 25 characters in a file referenced as open_file.

```
open_file.Skip(25)
```

Unfortunately, the SkipLine() method does not allow you to pass it a number, indicating how many lines to skip. If you want to skip more than one line, you can wrap the method up inside a loop as demonstrated here.

```
For i = 1 to 7
open_file.SkipLine()
Next
```

Here the first seven lines of the file referenced as open_file would be skipped.

Reading Formatted Data

If your file has been formatted to contain fixed length data, then you have the option of reading it by character instead of by line. To do so you will use the `FileSystemObject` object's `Read()` method.

The following example demonstrates how to use this method. Here a reference is set up for a file named `myfile.txt`. Then a `For` loop is set up to skip the first seven lines of the file using the `SkipLine()` method. Next the `Skip()` method is used to skip the first fourteen characters on the eighth line. Finally the next four characters, beginning with the twenty-third character are read and then displayed. Then the file is closed.

```
Set fsoObject = CreateObject("Scripting.FileSystemObject")
Set open_file = fsoObject.OpenTextFile("c:\myfile.txt", 1)
For i = 1 to 7
  open_file.SkipLine()
Next

open_file.Skip(14)
WScript.Echo("The file system in use on this drive is: " &
open_file.Read(4))
open_file.Close
```

If you run this example you should see the type of file system with which your primary hard drive has been formatted as shown in Figure 6.3.

Figure 6.3

Reading a formatted report.

Reading Entire Files

Another way in which you can read files is to read the entire file all at once using the `FileSystemObject` object's `ReadAll()` method as demonstrated in the following example.

```
Set fsoObject = CreateObject("Scripting.FileSystemObject")
Set open_file = fsoObject.OpenTextFile("c:\myfile.txt", 1)

read_rpt = open_file.ReadAll()

open_file.Close()

MsgBox(read_rpt)
```

In this example, the entire file is read using a single statement, which assigns the data read by the `ReadAll()` method to a variable named `read_rpt`. The file is then closed and the value of `read_rpt` displayed using the VBScript `MsgBox()` function.

As you can see from Figure 6.4, using the `ReadAll()` method in this manner makes it very easy to display large amounts of information using a pop-up dialog.

Figure 6.4

Reading an entire file all at once.

Taking a Break

Mastering the art of reading and writing text documents, reports, and logs takes time. However, with what you have learned this afternoon you should be well on your way. Let's take a 15-minute break and when you come back we'll pick back up by looking at how to write scripts that can be used to automate the administration of your files and folders. Then as a wrap-up for the afternoon I'll show you how you can use the Windows Task Scheduler to automate the execution of your scripts.

Performing File and Folder Administration

Managing your files and folders can involve a lot of work. Using VBScript and the WSH you can automate much of this work. For example, typical file and folder tasks involve copying or moving files and folders from one location to another in order to create backups or better organize them. Administration may also include deleting files once they have been processed or after they have reached a certain age.

You can use methods belonging to the `FileSystemObject` to manage one or more files or folders at a time. `FileSystemObject` methods for handling files include

- **`CopyFile()`.** Copies one or more files.
- **`MoveFile()`.** Moves one or more files to a different location.
- **`DeleteFile()`.** Delete one or more files.
- **`FileExists()`.** Provides verification of whether a file contains data.

The `FileSystemObject` also provides a number of methods that you can use to manage Windows folders, including

- **`CopyFolder()`.** Copies one or more folders.
- **`MoveFolder()`.** Moves one or more folders to a different location.
- **`DeleteFolder()`.** Deletes one or more folders.
- **`FolderExists()`.** Provides verification of whether a folder exists.
- **`CreateFolder()`.** Creates a new folder.

Alternatively, you can also use the `File` and `Folder` objects to manage your files and folders instead of the `FileSystemObject`. These two objects share many of the same methods, including

- **`Copy()`.** Copies a file or folder to the specified location.
- **`Delete()`.** Removes the specified file or folder.
- **`Move()`.** Moves a file or folder to the specified location.

NOTE Because the `File` and `Folder` objects use the same methods it is easy to make a mistake when using them. For example, if you have a file and a folder with the same or a similar name it is easy to delete accidentally the entire folder when you only wanted to delete a file. Use these objects with care.

Next, let's take a look at examples that demonstrate how you can use the `FileSystemObject`, `File`, and `Folder` objects and their methods to manage your file.

Managing Files and Folders with the `FileSystemObject` Object

As you have already seen this afternoon the `FileSystemObject` is actually fairly easy to work with. All that you have to do is establish an instance of it and you can start using its properties and methods. In the sections that follow you'll see examples of how to use this object to create, copy, move, and delete files and folders.

TIP I strongly recommend that you check for the existence of a file or folder before you attempt to do anything to it. You can do so using the `FileSystemObject` object's `FileExists` and `FolderExists` properties.

Copying Files

Using the `FileSystemObject` object's `CopyFile()` method you can copy one or more files. For example, you might want to copy all the files in the folder on your computer to a network drive at the end of each day. I'll show you how to work with network drives this evening. For now let's just focus on how the `CopyFile()` method works.

The first step in copying a file is to set up an instance of the `FileSystemObject`. Then you can execute its `CopyFile()` method as shown here.

```
Set fsoObject = CreateObject("Scripting.FileSystemObject")
fsoObject.CopyFile("c:\myfile.txt", "d:\myDocs\myfile.txt")
```

In this example, a file named `myFile.txt` is copied from the root folder on the `C:` drive to a folder named `myDocs` located on the computer's `D:` drive. You can modify this example to copy more than one file using wildcard characters as shown in the next example. Here all files in the root directly with a filename of `myFile` are copied to the destination folder regardless of their file extension.

```
Set fsoObject = CreateObject("Scripting.FileSystemObject")
fsoObject.CopyFile("c:\myfile.*", "d:\myDocs")
```

 NOTE Wildcard characters include the `?` and `*` characters. Wildcard characters allow you to identify files and folders using pattern matching. The `?` character is used to specify a single character match whereas the `*` character is used to match up against an unlimited number of characters. For example, if you specified `tes?.txt` then any four-character filename that started with the letters `tes` and had a `.txt` file extension would match. Likewise, if you specified `test.*` then any file with a filename of `test` would match regardless of its file extension.

The `CopyFile()` method supports an additional parameter that allows you to tell it what to do if you try to copy a file to an another folder where a file of the same name already exists. This parameter can be set to a value of `true` or `false`. Setting it to `true` will cause any matching files to be overridden. Setting it equal to `false` will prevent this from happening. Let's look at a couple examples.

The first example prevents files with duplicate file names from being overridden.

```
Set fsoObject = CreateObject("Scripting.FileSystemObject")
fsoObject.CopyFile("c:\*.txt", "d:\myDocs", "False")
```

The second example allows files with duplicate names to be overridden.

```
Set fsoObject = CreateObject("Scripting.FileSystemObject")
fsoObject.CopyFile("c:\*.txt", "c:\myDocs", "True")
```

Moving Files

Moving files is similar to copying them except that instead of leaving the original file in place and placing a duplicate copy in the destination location, the original file is moved leaving only one copy of the file. You can move one or more files using the `FileSystemObject` object's `MoveFile()` method.

For example, you can move all files with a `.txt` file extension found in the root of the `C:` drive to a `myDocs` folder on the `D:` drive using the following VBScript statements.

```
Set fsoObject = CreateObject("Scripting.FileSystemObject")
fsoObject.MoveFile("c:\*.txt", "c:\myDocs")
```

Deleting Files

You can use the `FileSystemObject` object's `DeleteFile()` method to delete one or more files. For example, you might want to write a script that cleans out a folder at the end of each day or that deletes files after reading and processing them. You can delete one or more files as demonstrated here.

```
Set fsoObject = CreateObject("Scripting.FileSystemObject")
fsoObject.DeleteFile("c:\*.txt")
```

Here all files that have a `.txt` file extension located in the root of the `C:` drive will be deleted.

Creating a Folder

Working with folders is similar to working with files. You can use the `FolderExists()` method of the `FileSystemObject` to determine if a folder exists. If the folder does not exist, you can create it using the `FileSystemObject` object's `CreateFolder()` method as demonstrated here.

```
Set fsoObject = CreateObject("Scripting.FileSystemObject")
If (fsoObject.FolderExists("d:\myDocs") = false) Then
Set myFolder = fsoObject.CreateFolder("d:\myDocs")
End If
```

The first thing that this example does is check to see if a folder named myDocs already exists on the computer's D: drive. If it does not exist, then the folder is created. Otherwise nothing happens.

NOTE You cannot use the CreateFolder() method to overwrite a folder that already exists. If you try, your script will get an error. You can, however, use the DeleteFolder() method to remove the folder and all its contents and then use the CreateFolder() method to create it again.

Copying Folders

Copying a folder is pretty much the same as copying a file. The folder and all its contents are copied to a new location leaving the original copy still in place. You can copy folders using the FileSystemObject object's CopyFolder() method.

Take a look at the following example. It copies a folder named myDocs located on the computer's D: drive to its C: drive.

```
Set fsoObject = CreateObject("Scripting.FileSystemObject")
fsoObject.CopyFolder("d:\myDocs", "c:\myDocs")
```

As you can see the CopyFolder() methods requires two arguments, the source and destination folder names, including their complete paths. By changing the name assigned to the destination folder, you can rename the folder as part of the copy operation as demonstrated here.

```
Set fsoObject = CreateObject("Scripting.FileSystemObject")
fsoObject.CopyFolder("d:\myDocs", "c:\myNewDocs")
```

If the destination folder already exists, then the contents of the source folder are copied into it alongside its current contents. The CopyFolder() method supports an additional third parameter that allows you to tell it what to do if the destination folder contains files with duplicate filenames of those found in the source folder. This parameter is set to either a value of true or false. Setting it to true causes any matching files to

be overridden. Setting it to `false` prevents this from happening. Let's look at a couple examples.

The first example prevents files with duplicate filenames from being overridden.

```
Set fsoObject = CreateObject("Scripting.FileSystemObject")
fsoObject.CopyFolder("d:\myDocs", "c:\myDocs", "False")
```

The second example allows files with duplicate names to be overridden in the destination folder.

```
Set fsoObject = CreateObject("Scripting.FileSystemObject")
fsoObject.CopyFolder("d:\myDocs", "c:\myDocs", "True")
```

Moving Folders

Moving a folder works pretty much the same as copying one except that moving the folder leaves you with only the one copy. You can move folders using the `FileSystemObject` object's `MoveFolder()` method. This method moves a folder and all its contents, including subfolders, to a new destination.

For example, the following VBScript statements move a folder called `myDocs` from the computer's `D:` drive to its `C:` drive.

```
Set fsoObject = CreateObject("Scripting.FileSystemObject")
fsoObject.MoveFolder("d:\mydocs", "c:\myDocs")
```

If a folder with the same name already exists at the root of the computer's `D:` drive, then the contents of the source folder will be copied into the existing destination along side its current contents.

· ·

NOTE   Unlike the `CopyFolder()` the `MoveFolder()` method does not provide an overwrite option that allows your script to overwrite any files in the destination folder that have duplicate filenames.

· ·

Deleting Folders

You can delete one or more folders using the `FileSystemObject` object's `DeleteFolder()` method. This method deletes a folder and all its contents, including subfolders. For example, the following VBScript statements can be used to delete a folder named `myDocs` located on a computer's `D:` drive.

```
Set fsoObject = CreateObject("Scripting.FileSystemObject")
fsoObject.DeleteFolder("c:\myDocs")
```

 NOTE Use the `DeleteFolder()` method with care! It will not only delete a folder but anything stored in the folder. Also if you use wildcard characters in your scripts it is easy to accidentally delete more folders than you might mean to.

Managing Files with the File Object

The `File` Object allows you to work with one file at a time as opposed to the `FileSystemObject`, which lets you manage multiple files. Using the `File` object instead of the `FileSystemObject` requires a little more work. You still have to create an instance of the `FileSystemObject` to interact with the file system. You also need to use the `FileSystemObject` object's `GetFile()` method to retrieve a `File` object that represents the file that your script will be managing. Once these two things are set up you can execute any of the `File` object's methods.

Copying a File

Using the `File` object's `Copy()` method you can copy a file from one location to another. This method does not support the use of wildcard characters and cannot therefore be used to copy multiple files.

The following example demonstrates how to use the `File` object's `Copy()` method to copy a file named `myFile.txt` from the `myDocs` folder on the computer's `D:` drive to the root of the `C:` drive.

```
Set fsoObject = CreateObject("Scripting.FileSystemObject")
Set source_file = fsoObject.GetFile("d:\myDocs\myFile.txt")
source_file.Copy("c:\")
```

In this example, the `FileSystemObject` object's `GetFile()` method is used to establish a reference to the file that is to be copied. Then the `Copy()` method is used to set the destination where the file is to be copied.

Moving a File

As you probably expect by now, moving a file using the `File` object's `Move()` method works almost exactly like copying it using the `Copy()` method. For example, the following VBScript statements demonstrate how to move a file from one location to another.

```
Set fsoObject = CreateObject("Scripting.FileSystemObject")
Set source_file = fsoObject.GetFile("d:\myDocs\myFile.txt")
source_file.Move("c:\")
```

Deleting a File

You can delete an individual file using the `File` Object's `Delete()` method. Like the `File` object's other methods, the `Delete()` method does not support wildcard characters limiting it to being able to delete just one file at a time.

Take a look at the following example. Here a file named `myFile.txt` is deleted from a folder named `myDocs` located on the computer's `D:` drive.

```
Set fsoObject = CreateObject("Scripting.FileSystemObject")
Set source_file = fsoObject.GetFile("d:\myDocs\myFile.txt")
source_file.Delete()
```

Managing Folders with the Folder Object

The `Folder` object is similar to the `File` object only it works with one folder at a time instead of one file at a time. Like the `File` object, it requires a little more work to set up than does simply using the `File-`

`SystemObject`. First, you'll need to instantiate the `FileSystemObject`. Then you must use the `FileSystemObject` object's `GetFolder()` method to retrieve a `Folder` object that represents the folder that your script will be working with. Once these two things are set up you can execute any of the `Folder` object's methods.

Copying a Folder

Like the `File` object, the `Folder` object supports the `Copy()` method. Because it doesn't support wildcard characters it is useful only when you want to work with a single folder at a time. The `Copy()` method copies the folder and all its contents, including any subfolders, to a new location.

TIP

If you need to copy multiple folders at once you will be better off using the `File-SystemObject` object's `CopyFolder()` method.

For example, the following VBScript statements demonstrate how to use the `Copy()` method. In this case a folder named `myDocs` is copied from the root of the computer's `D:` drive to the root of the computer's `C:` drive.

```
Set fsoObject = CreateObject("Scripting.FileSystemObject")
Set source_folder = fsoObject.GetFolder("d:\myDocs")
source_folder.Copy("c:\")
```

Moving a Folder

The `Folder` object's `Move()` method lets you move a folder from one location to another. This method recursively copies a folder and all its contents. Because it does not support wildcard characters, this method can only move one folder at a time, as opposed to the `FileSystemObject` object's `MoveFolder()` method, which can move any number of folders in a single operation.

The following example demonstrates how to use this method to move a folder. In this case the folder is named `myDocs` and it is moved from the computer's `D:` drive to its `C:` drive.

```
Set fsoObject = CreateObject("Scripting.FileSystemObject")
Set source_folder = fsoObject.GetFolder("d:\myDocs")
source_folder.Move("c:\")
```

Deleting a Folder

You can delete a folder using the `Folder` object's `Delete()` method. Wildcard character matching is not supported so it only works with one folder at a time. If you need to delete more than one folder you can use the `FileSystemObject` object's `DeleteFolder()` method, discussed earlier in this chapter.

This method deletes the specified folder and all its contents, including subfolders. Its use is demonstrated here.

```
Set fsoObject = CreateObject("Scripting.FileSystemObject")
Set source_folder = fsoObject.GetFolder("d:\myDocs")
source_folder.Delete()
```

Scheduling File and Folder Administration

Okay, so now you know the basics of file and folder administration. But let's face it—even after you have written VBScripts that perform all your administrative needs, it is still an inconvenience to have to sit and run them. This is where the Windows Task Scheduler comes in handy. The Task Scheduler runs as a background service on Windows XP. As long as it is up and running you can use it to schedule the execution of any VBScript to run at any time, even when you are not logged on to your computer. This way you can schedule the execution of your file and folder administration scripts, or any other scripts for that matter, to occur after hours when you are not using your computer. This will make you more productive and efficient.

Windows XP lets you schedule the execution of tasks using either of two methods as outlined here.

- ✪ **From the command prompt using the AT command**. A Windows command that you can use to set up the execution of scripts from the command line by specifying the script and its execution schedule in the form of command arguments.
- ✪ **Using the Scheduled Task Wizard**. A graphical interface located in the Scheduled Tasks folder, which guides you through the process of scheduling your VBScripts.

Setting Up the Task Scheduler Service

When you are logged on to your computer and manually initiating the execution of your scripts, these scripts are processed using whatever level of permissions have been set for you on the computer. Therefore unless you have the required level of permission to manually perform a particular task, your scripts will not be able to automate the task either.

When you are working on a computer running the Windows 95, 98, or Me operating system, security permissions are not much of a concern because these operating systems do not impose stringent security controls. However, if you are working on a computer running Windows NT, 2000, or XP and you have not been given administrative level access, security permissions become a concern. The best way to find out if you have the right set of security permissions to script a task is to try and perform the task manually. If you can complete all the steps required to perform the task, then chances are that your scripts will not have any problems either, unless you run the Windows Task Scheduler.

 NOTE If you are unable to perform a task manually, contact your system administrator and find out if he or she can assign additional security permission to your account.

When you use the Task Scheduler to run your scripts, the scripts run using the security permission assigned to the Task Scheduler. By default the Task Scheduler uses the security permissions assigned the Local System account. However, these provide only limited access and will probably not be sufficient to run most VBScripts. To fix this situation you'll need to create a new user account and assign it an appropriate level of security permission so that it can run your tasks.

The first step in setting up the Windows Task Scheduler is to be sure that it is running. The procedure for performing this task on a Windows XP system follows.

1. Click Start and then Control Panel. The Windows XP Control Panel appears.

2. Click the Performance and Maintenance link. This opens the Performance and Maintenance dialog.

3. Click the Administrative Tools link.

4. Double-click the Services icon. This opens the Services console as shown in Figure 6.5.

5. Scroll down until you see the Task Scheduler service and select it.

6. Be sure that its status is listed as Started. If it's not, then click the Start the service option, which will be displayed on the left side of the dialog.

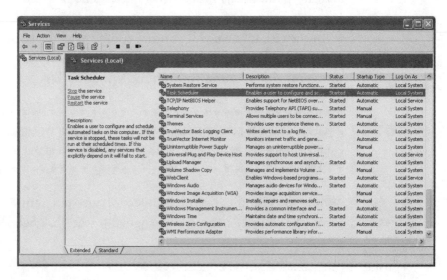

Figure 6.5

Windows XP uses services that run as background programs to provide much of its functionality.

NOTE

If the Task Scheduler service is running, then you will not see the Start the service option on the left side of the dialog. Instead you will see the following options as depicted in Figure 6.5.

• Stop the service

• Pause the service

• Restart the service

After you have the Task Scheduler service up and running you'll need to configure it to use an account other than the Local System account. This other account should be set up with sufficient security permissions to be able to run your VBScripts. Once you have created a new account and assigned it a password, use the following procedure to configure the Task Scheduler to use it.

1. From the Services console scroll down until you can see the Task Scheduler service.

2. Double-click on it. The Task Scheduler Properties dialog appears as shown in Figure 6.6.

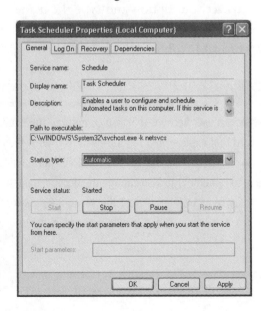

Figure 6.6

Configuring the Task Scheduler service.

3. Be sure that the Automatic option has been selected from the Start-up Type drop-down list and then select the Log On Property Sheet as shown in Figure 6.7.

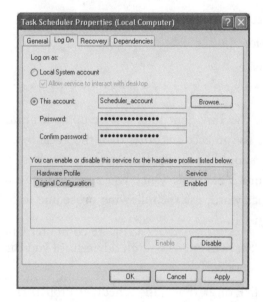

Figure 6.7

Specifying an alternative user account to be used by the Task Scheduler service.

4. Select the This account option and type the name of the new user account. Next type the password that was assigned to this account in the Password and Confirm Password fields.

5. Click OK.

TIP

Check to see whether the user account that you configured the Windows Task Scheduler to use has a password that expires on a regular basis. If it does then you might want to investigate changing the account so that its password will not have to be changed. Otherwise you will have to remember to also change the account's password as specified for the Task Scheduler service as well every time the account's password changes.

Scheduling VBScript Execution from the Windows Command Prompt

Now that you have started and configured the Task Scheduler you are ready to begin scheduling the execution of your VBScripts. One way to schedule your scripts is from the Windows command prompt using the AT command. The AT command allows you to add, delete, and view scheduled tasks.

The AT command's syntax is shown here.

Syntax

```
at [\\computername] [[id] [/delete] | /delete [/yes]]
at [\\computername] time [/interactive] [/every:date[,...] |
/next:date[,...]] command
```

- ✿ **None.** Displays a list of scheduled tasks.
- ✿ **\\\computername.** Specifies a remote computer where the task is to be executed.
- ✿ *Id.* Identifies the ID number assigned to a scheduled task.
- ✿ **/delete.** Terminates a scheduled command.
- ✿ **/yes.** Requires a confirmation.
- ✿ *Time.* Sets the time to execute the task expressed as *hh:mm* on a 24-hour clock.
- ✿ **/interactive.** Permits interaction with the desktop and the logged on user.
- ✿ **/every:*date*[,...].**Sets a schedule for task execution based on specified days of the week or month. Dates are specified as M, T, W, Th, F, S, Su or 1–31. Separate multiple using commas.
- ✿ **/next:*date*[,...].** Executes the task on the next occurrence of the specified day (M, T, W, Th, F, S, Su) or date (1 - 31).
- ✿ *Command.* Specifies the task, application or script to execute.

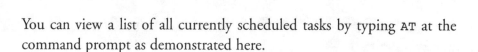

You can view a list of all currently scheduled tasks by typing AT at the command prompt as demonstrated here.

```
C:\>at
There are no entries in the list.
```

However, in this example no tasks have been scheduled. The next example shows the AT command again, only this time three VBScripts have been scheduled for execution.

```
C:\>at
Status ID    Day                   Time           Command Line
-----------------------------------------------------------------------
---------
         1   Each M W F            11:30 PM       cmd /c "Script
6.1.vbs"
         2   Each T Th             11:30 PM       cmd /c "Script
6.2.vbs"
         3   Each M T W Th F S Su  9:30 AM        cmd /c "Script
6.3.vbs"
```

The first script is named Script 6.1.vbs and is scheduled to execute every Monday, Wednesday, and Friday at 11:30 P.M. Similarly the second script is scheduled to execute every Tuesday and Thursday at the same time. The third script is scheduled to run every day of the week at 9:30 A.M.

You can also use the AT command to schedule new tasks. For example, to schedule the execution of another VBScript to run every Monday at 1 P.M. you would type.

```
at 13:00 /every:M cmd /c "Script 6.4"
```

You can delete a scheduled task by specifying its ID. Windows automatically assigns IDs to every scheduled task. You can find out the ID assigned to a given task by using the AT command to display the list of

scheduled tasks. For example, to delete the third scheduled job with ID 3 you would type.

```
at 3 /delete
```

If you leave off the ID specification you will delete every scheduled job as demonstrated here.

```
at /delete
```

 NOTE If you are working on a network and you have the appropriate level of security permissions to schedule jobs on a remote computer you can do so by specifying two back-slashes followed by the name of the network computer as demonstrated here.

```
\\ComputerA 12:00 /every:F cmd /c "Script 6.5.vbs"
```

Here a script named `Script 6.5.vbs` is set up to execute every Friday at noon on a computer whose name is `ComputerA`.

Using the Scheduled Tasks Wizard

If you prefer working from the Windows desktop instead of the command prompt you can use the Scheduled Task wizard to schedule your scripts. You will find the Scheduled Task wizard in the Scheduled Tasks folder that you can open by clicking Start, Control Panel, Performance and Maintenance, and then Scheduled Tasks as shown in Figure 6.8.

The Scheduled Tasks Folder will display an icon for every currently scheduled task. In addition, you will see the same information about each scheduled task that is available using the AT command. When you select a task a list of commands appears in the Folder Tasks area on the left side of the dialog as shown in Figure 6.9. From this list you can click the Delete this item option to delete the scheduled task.

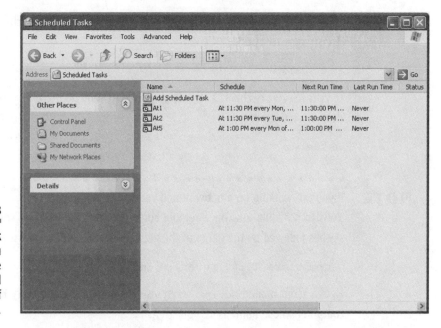

Figure 6.8

The Scheduled Task wizard allows you to visually manage the scheduling and administration of your VBScripts.

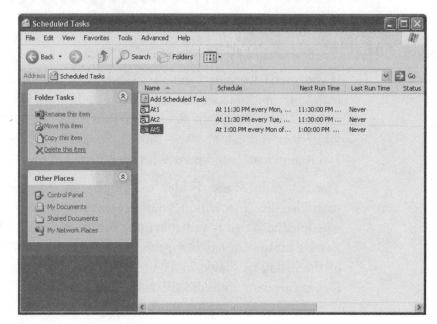

Figure 6.9

Deleting a scheduled task using the Scheduled Tasks folder.

Now let's take a look at how to use the Task Scheduler. The steps involved are outlined in the following procedure.

1. Open the Scheduled Tasks folder and double-click the Add Scheduled Task icon.

2. The Scheduled Task Wizard appears. Click Next.

3. You are prompted to select a program for which you would like to set up a schedule from a list of Windows applications that is displayed as shown in Figure 6.10. Click on Browse.

Figure 6.10

You can set up the scheduled execution of any Windows application.

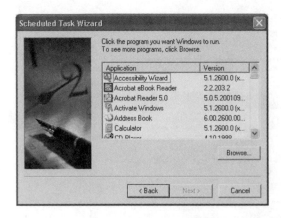

4. The Select Program to Schedule dialog appears as shown in Figure 6.11. Locate your script, select it and click Open.

5. The Scheduled Task wizard next prompts you to supply a name for the scheduled task and to supply information about when the task should be run as shown in Figure 6.12. Click Next to continue.

6. The dialog that you'll see next depends on which scheduling option you just selected. For example, Figure 6.13 shows the dialog that appears if you selected to run the task weekly. In this case the task has been set up to execute every Wednesday at 10:00 A.M. for the next year. Click Next to continue.

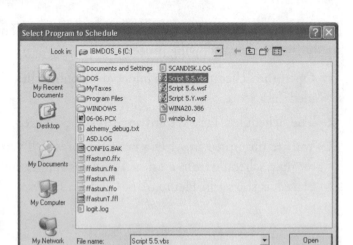

Figure 6.11

Select the VBScript
for which you want
to create an
automated
execution schedule.

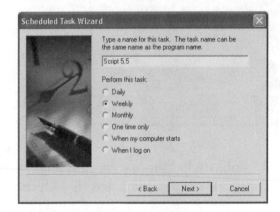

Figure 6.12

Name your
scheduled task and
select its schedule.

7. Next you are prompted to supply an account name and password
as shown in Figure 6.14. The Task Scheduler runs this script using
the security permissions assigned to this account. Click Next.

8. The wizard announces that it has successfully completed the setup
of your scheduled task. Click Finish. The new scheduled task now
appears in the Scheduled Tasks folder.

Figure 6.13

Setting up a weekly execution schedule.

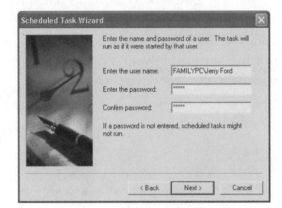

Figure 6.14

Supply an account whose security permissions should be used to execute the VBScript

Scheduled Tasks Limitations

Scripts that are executed via the Task Scheduler do not have access to the same resources as they do when you manually run them. Depending on what your scripts are designed to do, you may have to add some extra programming logic to them to allow them to work when executed by the Task Scheduler.

In particular, if your scripts will be performing file and folder administration on network drives for which you have created drive mappings on your computer, (for example, network drives to which you have assigned drive letters) your drive mappings will not be available to the scheduled scripts.

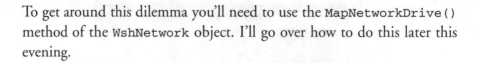

To get around this dilemma you'll need to use the `MapNetworkDrive()` method of the `WshNetwork` object. I'll go over how to do this later this evening.

What's Next?

You now have all the building blocks that you need to develop VBScripts that can automate the management of all your files and folders. I think it's time to call it an afternoon. Go get something to eat and forget about VBScript for a while. When you return we'll begin the weekend's final chapter where you will learn how to develop VBScripts to perform a host of helpful chores. The list of things you will learn to do includes creating shortcuts, modifying the Windows Start Menu, changing the Windows Quick Launch bar, integrating your VBScripts with Windows applications, and working with network resources.

SUNDAY EVENING

Desktop, Computer, and Network Automation

- ✪ Learn how to programmatically create and customize shortcuts
- ✪ Find out how to run Windows utilities and interact with Windows applications
- ✪ See how to execute Windows Control Panel utilities
- ✪ Learn how to wrap VBScript code around Windows commands
- ✪ Learn how to write messages to the Windows application event log
- ✪ Find out how to configure Windows by changing registry settings
- ✪ Learn how to set up mappings to network drives

Welcome to this weekend's final chapter. You should be feeling pretty good about yourself by now. Not only have you learned VBScript but you have also learned how to apply it to your web page development and computer automation. This is no small chore. Let's wrap up the book tonight by finishing up our coverage of VBScript and the WSH.

Tonight's material covers a number of activities and helps you to leverage the knowledge that you picked up last night. You'll learn how to create shortcuts and how to use them to configure the Windows XP Start menu and Quick Launch bar. You will also learn a number of ways that you can integrate your VBScripts with Windows and its applications. I will also go over some of the tricks required to work with Windows event logs and the registry.

As a final wrap of the evening I'll show you how to leverage the power of the Windows command line from within your VBScripts to create user accounts, manage Windows services and even automate network tasks. This is a lot to learn in a single evening so we'll have to pick up the pace a bit as we sprint for the finish line.

The Darker Side of VBScript

I thought that I'd start off this evening with a quick diversion. You may have heard in the past that VBScript has been associated with computer viruses. It has been used to create a number of computer viruses known as worms. A *worm* is a software program that sneaks its way onto a computer and then performs a destructive action. VBScript is often used to create these types of programs because of its power and ease of use.

Basically, the way this works is someone who knows VBScript writes a script, attaches it to an email and sends it off. The attachment (that is, the script) is given a clever name to get the recipient to open it. When the recipient opens it, Windows identifies it as a VBScript because of its `.vbs` file extension and automatically submits it to one of the WSH execution hosts where it is then run. The first things these programs usually do are access Outlook Express and send copies of themselves to everyone in the recipient's address list. Then the script finishes by wreaking whatever havoc it was designed to do.

The `ILOVEYOU` virus is a classic example of a VBScript worm. It appeared in early 2000 with a title of `I Love You` and a VBScript attachment with a name of `Love-Letter-For_You.txt.vbs`. At first glance the attachment looked like a text file with a three-character `.txt` file extension; however, the file's real file extension was `.vbs`. After sending copies of itself to everyone in your email address book the `ILOVEYOU` worm searched your computer for passwords, which were sent back to its creator. It then replaced a number of files with copies of itself, including any files that ended with one of the following file extensions: `.vbs`, `.vbe`, `.js`, `.wsh`, `.jpeg`, `.jpg`. This way you'd accidentally re-execute the worm any time you tried to open one of these files.

VBScript's ease of use and scripting power can easily be turned against any Microsoft user that has the WSH installed on his or her computer. To combat this dilemma, some people have uninstalled the WSH. Obviously this is not a good solution. Recently many antivirus programs and some personal firewall products have begun to look for and isolate VBScript file attachments on all incoming email to give the user a chance to verify their origin before opening them.

The bottom line is that VBScript is a programming tool that can be used to accomplish just about any task and just because a few people have chosen to misuse it does not make VBScript any less viable for solving your computing needs.

Taking Control of the Windows Desktop

Let's start off the evening by looking at several ways that you can programmatically administer the Windows desktop environment. For example, creating shortcuts on the Windows desktop allows you quick access to your favorite applications. However, if you do not like a cluttered desktop you can write a script to add menu items to the Windows Start menu instead. Another option is to use the Windows Quick Launch bar. The Quick Launch bar is the toolbar located just to the right of the Start button on the Windows taskbar and its purpose is to provide quick single-click access to Windows applications.

 NOTE Other ways to take control of the Windows desktop include writing scripts that change its appearance or making configuration changes, such as configuring the Windows screensaver. I'll go over these other desktop management techniques later in the evening when I talk about configuring Windows from the Windows registry.

Understanding How Shortcuts Work

A shortcut is a link to a Windows object. These objects can include Windows applications, files, folders, drives, and printers. Like most computer users you probably have a collection of shortcuts on your desktop. Manually creating a typical shortcut is not too difficult, but what if you have a bunch of them and also work on a number of computers. Maybe you have a desktop computer at work and a laptop at home. To keep things standardized you could write a VBScript that populates your desktop on each computer with a standard collection of shortcuts. This way if you purchase a new computer tomorrow all that you'll have to do is run the script and let it repopulate all your shortcuts for you.

As I already stated, a shortcut is just a link to another Windows object. For example, Figure 7.1 shows a shortcut for WordPad, the free word processor distributed with Windows operating systems.

Figure 7.1

A shortcut to the
WordPad word
processing
application.

You can identify a shortcut icon by the small black arrow in the lower-left corner of its icon. In addition to its icon, a shortcut contains a number of properties, the most important of which are the path and name of the object that it represents. Other shortcut properties that you may find yourself working with are listed in Table 7.1.

	TABLE 7.1 SHORTCUT PROPERTIES
Property	**Description**
Target	Specifies the complete path and filename of the Windows object.
Start in	Specifies the application's default working directory.
Shortcut key	Specifies a keyboard keystroke sequence that can be used to open the shortcut.
Run	Specifies whether the application will be opened in a normal window or in one that is maximized or minimized.
Comment	Specifies an optional shortcut description.
Icon filename	Identifies the icon used to represent the shortcut.

You can view a shortcut's properties by right-clicking it, clicking Properties, and then selecting the Shortcut property sheet as demonstrated in Figure 7.2.

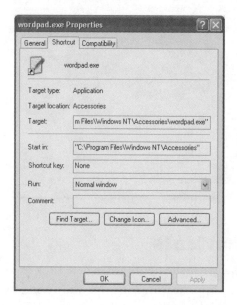

Figure 7.2

The Shortcut property sheet for a WordPad shortcut.

Shortcuts are also used to manage a number of Windows resources, including the Windows Start menu and the Quick Launch bar. Windows operating systems use folders as the organizational structure for managing both of these resources as well as the desktop. To add a shortcut to the Windows desktop all that you have to do is create it and place it in the following folder (where *xxxxxxxx* is your user name).

```
C:\Documents and Settings\xxxxxxxx\Desktop
```

For example, Figure 7.3 shows the folder that contains all the shortcuts on my Windows desktop.

Figure 7.3

By placing shortcuts into the correct folder you can configure a number of Windows resources, including the Windows desktop.

Creating Desktop Shortcuts

Now that you know what shortcuts are, where they reside, and what their properties are, let's try creating one on the Windows desktop using VBScript.

To create a desktop shortcut you'll need to establish an instance of the WshShell object as shown here.

```
Set wshObject = WScript.CreateObject("WScript.Shell")
```

Next, you need to set up a reference to the Windows desktop. You can do this using the Windows Desktop special folder. You can do this using the WScript object's SpecialFolders property as shown here.

```
desktopFolder = wshObject.SpecialFolders("Desktop")
```

Now you can define the shortcut. You do this by using the WScript object's CreateShortCut() method as shown here.

```
Set myShortcut = wshObject.CreateShortcut(desktopFolder &
"\\Notepad.lnk")
```

As you can see this VBScript statement concatenated the destination folder to `\\WordPad.lnk` which is the name being assigned to the shortcut. To create a shortcut you must use the `WshShortcut` object's `TargetPath` property to specify the location of the object that the shortcut is to represent.

```
myShortcut.TargetPath = "%windir%\Notepad.exe"
```

NOTE `%windir%` is a Windows environment variable that specifies the location of the folder where the Windows system files are stored. On Windows 95, 98, Me and XP operating systems this folder is named `c:\Windows` by default. On Windows NT and 2000 this folder is `c:\Winnt`. However, this folder can be changed during installation. By referencing it as `%windir%` you can always locate it without knowing its actual name.

All that's left to do is to save the shortcut using the `WshShortcut` object's `Save()` method as shown here.

```
myShortcut.Save()
```

Put all these statements together and you end up with the following script, which when executed places a link to the Notepad application on the Windows desktop.

```
Set wshObject = WScript.CreateObject("WScript.Shell")
desktopFolder = wshObject.SpecialFolders("Desktop")
Set myShortcut = wshObject.CreateShortcut(desktopFolder &
"\\Notepad.lnk")
myShortcut.TargetPath = "%windir%\Notepad.exe"
myShortcut.Save()
```

NOTE The Desktop special folder is one of a number of special folders that you can use in your VBScripts. Other special folders include

- **Desktop**. This folder represents your Windows desktop.
- **Programs**. This folder represents the Programs menu, which is located on the Windows Start menu.
- **StartMenu**. This folder represents the Windows Start menu.

Adding a shortcut to any of these folders will add it to the Windows resource that the special folder represents. Changes made to these special folders affect only the user that runs the script that changes them. In other words, if you make a change to the Desktop special folder it only affects your desktop and not the desktop for any other users that may share your computer. However, if you add a shortcut to any of the following special folders it affects the desktop of every user of the computer.

- **AllUsersDesktop**. This folder represents the desktop of every user of the computer.

- **AllUsersStartMenu**. This folder represents the Start menu of every user of the computer.

- **AllUsersPrograms**. This folder represents the Programs menu of every user of the computer.

Adding Shortcuts to Windows Folders

Although special folders make the placement of shortcuts easy, there may be a time when you just want to put a shortcut inside a regular Windows folder. For example, if you find that your desktop is becoming too cluttered with shortcuts, you might want to create a folder and move all your desktop shortcuts into that folder and then place a shortcut to that folder on the Windows desktop. This way all your shortcuts are still handy but your desktop remains uncluttered.

The following example demonstrates how to create a shortcut for the Notepad application inside a folder named myFolder located on the computer's C: drive.

```
Set fsoObject = CreateObject("Scripting.FileSystemObject")
Set trgtFolder = fsoObject.GetFolder("c:\myFolder")
Set wshObject = WScript.CreateObject("WScript.Shell")
Set myShortcut = wshObject.CreateShortcut(trgtFolder & ➥
        "\\Notepad.lnk")
myShortcut.TargetPath = "%windir%\notepad.exe"
myShortcut.Save()
```

The first thing this script does is instantiate the `FileSystemObject`. It then uses the object's `GetFolder()` method to retrieve a reference to the folder where the shortcut is to be saved. Next, an instance of the `WshShell` object is created in order to use its `CreateShortcut()` method. The shortcut is then created and saved.

Removing Your Shortcuts

If you do not need a shortcut any more you should delete it. Deleting a shortcut is just as easy as creating one. For example, the following script deletes a shortcut named `notepad.lnk` from the Windows desktop.

```
Set wshObject = WScript.CreateObject("WScript.Shell")
trgtFolder = wshObject.SpecialFolders("Desktop")
Set fsoObject = CreateObject("Scripting.FileSystemObject")
Set myShortcut = fsoObject.GetFile(trgtFolder & "\\notepad.lnk")
myShortcut.Delete
```

In similar fashion, the following VBScript deletes a shortcut stored in a regular Windows folder using the `FileSystemObject` object's `DeleteFile()` method. For example, the following statements delete a shortcut stored in a folder named `myFolder` on the computer's `C:` drive.

```
Set fsoObject = CreateObject("Scripting.FileSystemObject")
fsoObject.DeleteFile("c:\myFolder\notepad.lnk")
```

Defining Shortcut Properties

The `WshShortcut` object provides access to a number of properties that you manipulate and thus specify the shortcut settings. Table 7.2 lists these properties. Of these, only the `TargetPath` property is required.

For example, the following VBScript creates a shortcut for the Windows Notepad application on the Windows desktop.

```
Set wshObject = WScript.CreateObject("WScript.Shell")
trgtFolder = wshObject.SpecialFolders("Desktop")
Set myShortcut = wshObject.CreateShortcut(trgtFolder + ➥
        "\\Text_doc.lnk")
```

```
myShortcut.TargetPath = "%windir%\Notepad.exe"
myShortcut.Arguments = "c:\myJournal.txt"
myShortcut.Description = "The daily activity log of Jerry Ford"
myShortcut.Hotkey = "CTRL+Alt+J"
myShortcut.Save
```

Besides the `WshShortcut` object's `TargetPath` property, a number of the object's other properties have been set. As a result the shortcut can be opened by pressing the `Ctrl` + `Alt` + `J` keys at the same time. A file on the `C:` drive named `myJournal.txt` will always be loaded. Finally, if you move the pointer over the shortcut, its description will appear after a few moments.

TABLE 7.2 WSHSHORTCUT PROPERTIES

Property	Description
Arguments	Specifies arguments to be passed to the application.
Description	Specifies a comment.
Hotkey	Specifies a keystroke sequence that can be used to open the shortcut.
IconLocation	Specifies the icon to be displayed.
TargetPath	Specifies the complete path and filename of the object represented by the shortcut.
WindowStyle	Specifies the window style to be used when the application is started from the shortcut (normal, minimized, or maximized).
WorkingDirectory	Specifies the application's default working directory as well as the default location where any output will be saved.

Configuring the Windows Start Menu

The Windows Start menu is managed as a collection of special folders. Therefore by adding shortcuts to the appropriate special folder, you can modify its menu entries. Examples of special folders that you might want to modify include the `Startmenu` and `Programs` special folders. Alternatively, you could modify the `AllUsersStartMenu` and `AllUsersPrograms` special folders to modify the Start menu and Programs menu for every user of the computer.

For example, the following VBScript can be used to add a new menu entry for the Notepad application on your Start menu.

```
Set wshObject = WScript.CreateObject("WScript.Shell")
trgtFolder = wshObject.SpecialFolders("StartMenu")
Set myShortcut = wshObject.CreateShortcut(trgtFolder & ➥
        "\\notepad.lnk")
myShortcut.TargetPath = "%windir%\notepad.exe"
myShortcut.Save
```

Figure 7.4 shows how the Windows XP Start menu appears after the Notepad shortcut has been added.

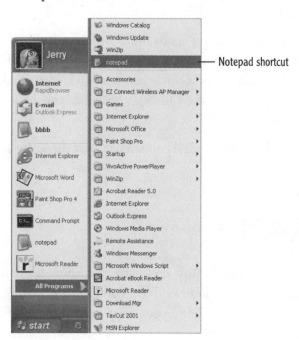

Notepad shortcut

Figure 7.4

Configuring the Windows Start menu by adding a shortcut.

Customizing the Quick Launch Bar

The Windows Quick Launch bar is a toolbar located on the Windows Task bar. It provides single click access to Windows applications and utilities. It is available by default on the Windows 98, Me, 2000, and XP operating systems. By default you'll find shortcuts on it for Internet Explorer, Outlook Express and the Windows Desktop.

Like the Start menu, you can modify the Quick Launch bar by adding shortcuts to the appropriate folder, in this case the folder is the AppData folder.

The following example demonstrates how to add a shortcut for the Notepad application to the Quick Launch bar.

```
Set wshObject = WScript.CreateObject("WScript.Shell")
quickAccessBar = wshObject.SpecialFolders("AppData")
appdataPath = quickAccessBar + "\Microsoft\Internet Explorer\Quick ➡
        Launch"
Set myShortcut = wshObject.CreateShortcut(appdataPath + ➡
        "\\notepad.lnk")
myShortcut.TargetPath = "%windir%\notepad.exe "
myShortcut.Save
```

As you can see the script is not much different from the one we just used to modify the Windows Start menu. The one major difference is the way that the location of the Quick Launch bar is identified. Here you must specify a reference to the Quick Launch bar and its location within the appdata special folder.

Figure 7.5 shows the Quick Launch bar after the script has been executed.

Figure 7.5

Adding a shortcut to the Windows Quick Launch bar.

That's pretty much it. You now have the know-how to create shortcuts and store them in Windows folders and special folders, allowing you to programmatically configure your Start menu and Program menu as well as the Windows Desktop and Quick Launch bar. Now let's turn our attention to examining different ways that we can integrate VBScript and the WSH with various Windows utilities and applications.

Integrating the WSH with Windows Utilities and Applications

Thanks to its integration with the WSH, you can write VBScripts that can start Windows utilities, Control Panel applets, and applications. In fact, you can use VBScript to load documents into most Windows utilities and applications and even populate documents with new data. This provides you with the capability to generate some really impressive scripts.

For example, you could write a VBScript that creates new user accounts based on data collected from the user, using pop-up dialogs. Or you might create new accounts based on information stored in a text-input file that the user can create. (I'll show you how to use VBScript to create new user accounts in just a little while.) However, if the user provides invalid data the script might fail. In that event the script could simply display an error and quit or it could offer to start the User Accounts applet, shown in Figure 7.6, so that the user can manually create the new accounts. This way no one can say you didn't try your best to help out the user.

Using Windows utilities, Control Panel applets, and applications in this manner not only gives your VBScripts a more graphical feel, but it also allows you to leverage the power already provided by Windows with minimal effort.

Starting Windows Utilities

Let's begin by looking at how to launch Windows utilities from within your VBScripts. To do so you need to use the WScript object's `CreateObject()` method as shown here.

```
Set shellApp = CreateObject("Shell.Application")
```

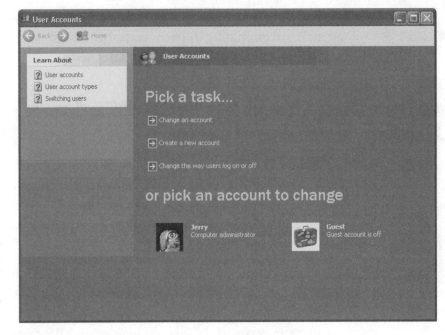

Figure 7.6

You can open any Windows Control Panel applet from within your VBScripts.

Then you can open the Windows utility.

```
shellApp.FileRun
```

Figure 7.7 shows the Windows Run utility, which is started by this example.

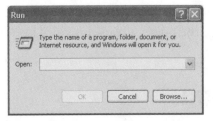

Figure 7.7

Launching the Windows Run utility from within your VBScripts.

Examples of other Windows utilities that you can open include

○ **FileRun**. The Windows Run utility.

○ **ShutdownWindows**. The Windows XP Turn Off Computer utility.

○ **FindFiles**. The Windows Search Results utility.

○ **FindComputer**. The Windows Search Results utility (with the computer's options automatically selected).

○ **SetTime**. The Windows Date and Time properties dialog.

○ **Help**. The Windows Help and Support Center.

Calling these utilities from within your VBScripts can be very handy. For example, suppose you wrote a script that prompted the user to type a filename, which the script would then process in some manner. If the user typed an invalid filename your script could display an error message and quit. Alternatively, it could instead display a pop-up dialog offering to run the Windows Search Results utility so that the user could search for the correct file and then rerun your script.

Another way that you could leverage the power of these utilities is to give the user a script that he could keep on his desktop to provide quick access to a given utility. For example, the following script runs the Windows XP Turn Off Computer utility. Double-clicking this script saves the user the trouble of having to navigate the Start menu to run the utility.

```
' **********************************************
' * Script Name: Script 7.1.vbs              *
' * Author: Jerry Ford                       *
' * Address: Richmond Virginia               *
' * Created: 03/17/02                        *
' **********************************************

' **** Perform script initialization here ****

Option Explicit

On Error Resume Next

Dim shellApp, answer
Set shellApp = CreateObject("Shell.Application")

' ********* Main processing section *********
```

```
' Verify that the user wants to open the Turn Off Computer dialog

answer = MsgBox("The Turn Off Computer dialog will be opened.", ➥
        1, "Turn off Computer Script!")
If answer = 1 then    ' User clicked on OK
  Initiate_Logoff()
End if


' *********** Procedures go here *************


' Open the Windows Turn Off Computer dialog

Function Initiate_Logoff()
  shellApp.ShutdownWindows
End Function
```

Starting Control Panel Utilities

Another powerful collection of Windows utilities, commonly referred to as applets, can be found on the Windows Control Panel. On the Windows XP operating system, the Windows Control Panel utilities are stored in the `C:\Windows\System32` folder as files with a `.cpl` file extension. Table 7.3 outlines the default CPL files that you will find in a Windows XP Home Edition or Windows XP Professional installation.

NOTE You may find other `.cpl` files in `C:\Windows\System32` depending on whether you have installed any applications that add their own Control Panel utilities.

If you are running another Windows operating system you can do a search on `*.cpl` to locate the Control Panel utilities on your computer. You can then double-click them to find out what they are.

The following example shows how to open the User Accounts applet that I mentioned earlier.

```
' **********************************************
' * Script Name: Script 7.2.vbs                *
' * Author: Jerry Ford                         *
```

TABLE 7.3 CONTROL PANEL UTILITIES

CPL File	Description
access.cpl	Accessibility Options
appwiz.cpl	Add or Remove Programs
desk.cpl	Display Properties
findfast.cpl	Find Fast
hdwwiz.cpl	Add Hardware Wizard
inetcpl.cpl	Internet Properties
intl.cpl	Regional and Languages Options
joy.cpl	Game Controllers
main.cpl	Mouse Properties
mmsys.cpl	Sounds and Audio Devices Properties
ncpa.cpl	Network Connections
nusrmgr.cpl	User Accounts
odbccp32.cpl	ODBC Data Source Administrator
powercfg.cpl	Power Options Properties
sysdm.cpl	System Properties
telephon.cpl	Phone and Modem Property Options (Dial Rules property sheet)
timedate.cpl	Date and Time Properties

```
' * Address: Richmond Virginia          *
' * Created: 03/23/02                    *
' ********************************************

' **** Perform script initialization here ****

Option Explicit

On Error Resume Next

Dim shellApp, answer
Set shellApp = CreateObject("Shell.Application")

' ********* Main processing section *********

answer = MsgBox("Click on OK to manually create user accounts?", 1)
If answer = 1 then    ' User clicked on OK
  Open_Control_Panel_File()
End if

' *********** Procedures go here *************

' Open the Windows Turn Off Computer dialog

Function Open_Control_Panel_File()
  shellApp.ControlPanelItem("nusrmgr.cpl")
End Function
```

As you can see this example is straightforward. First, it asks the user if they want to open the applet, and then does so using the following statement.

```
shellApp.ControlPanelItem("nusrmgr.cpl")
```

Here the WshShell object's ControlPanelItem() method is executed and the name of the Control Panel applet is processed as an argument.

Working with Windows Applications

Besides Windows utilities and Control Panel applets you can integrate Windows applications into your VBScripts using the WshShell object's Run() method. This command's syntax follows.

```
WScript.Run(command, [WindowStyle], [WaitonReturn])
```

Command identifies the Windows application, command, or utility to be run. *WindowStyle* is optional and is used to specify the window style in which the application, command, or utility will be opened. Table 7.4 provides a description of the possible window styles. *WaitonReturn* is an optional value of `True` or `False` and is added to specify whether the script waits or continues its execution after executing the `Run` method. By default the script will continue its execution.

TABLE 7.4 WINDOWS STYLE OPTIONS	
Style	**Description**
0	Window is hidden and the application runs in the background
1	Opens the application in a new window or restores a minimized or maximized window to its previous size
2	Minimizes the window
3	Maximizes the window
4	Displays a window without affecting the currently active window
5	Activates and displays a window taking focus away from the currently active window
6	Minimizes the window and gives focus to the most recently used window
7	Opens the window in a minimized state without taking focus away from the currently active window
8	Displays the window using default settings without affecting the currently active window
9	Opens the application in a new window or restores a minimized or maximized window to its previous size
10	Uses the Windows settings of the calling window to determine the settings for the new window

All that you have to do to use the `Run()` method within your VBScripts is to establish an instance of the `WshShell` object and execute the method. For example, the following statements can be used to start the Windows Notepad application.

```
Set wshObject = WScript.CreateObject("WScript.Shell")
wshObject.Run("notepad")
```

You can add the name of a file as an argument to the `Run()` method and instruct it to not only open the Notepad application but to also load the specified file as shown here.

```
Set wshObject = WScript.CreateObject("WScript.Shell")
wshObject.Run("notepad c:\errorlog.txt")
```

You can use this technique to perform all kinds of cool tricks. For example, suppose you wrote a script that created a text report. You could design the script, write the report to a file, and then display a pop-up message stating that it is ready to be viewed or you could start Notepad and automatically load the report for the user.

Let's look at another example using the Windows `WordPad` application this time. Only now instead of loading a text document, let's open an empty document and have VBScript type some text into it, creating a report on-the-fly.

```
' **********************************************
' * Script Name: Script 7.3.vbs                *
' * Author: Jerry Ford                          *
' * Address: Richmond Virginia                  *
' * Created: 03/24/02                           *
' **********************************************

' **** Perform script initialization here ****

Option Explicit

On Error Resume Next

Dim wshObject

Set wshObject = WScript.CreateObject("WScript.Shell")
```

```
' ********* Main processing section **********

' Start the WordPad application

wshObject.Run "WordPad"

' Call a function that will write a text message

Write_Text()

' *********** Procedures go here *************

' Open WordPad and write some text

Function Write_Text()

  ' Pause script execution to give Windows enough time to load WordPad
  WScript.Sleep 500

  ' Write a few lines of text
  wshObject.SendKeys "Hello. This is an example of how to use ➥
        VBScript and the WSH to open "
  wshObject.SendKeys "WordPad and add a few lines of text. Of ➥
        course, this is not the limit to "
  wshObject.SendKeys "the amount of text that can be written."

End Function
```

As you can see this script introduced a new WshShell object method called SendKeys(). This method does just what its name implies by sending or typing keystrokes to the specified application.

You may have also noticed the use of the WScript object's Sleep() method. This method was used to pause the script's execution for 500 milliseconds to give Windows enough time to open the application before the script tries to write to it.

Figure 7.8 shows how the WordPad document appears when this script is executed.

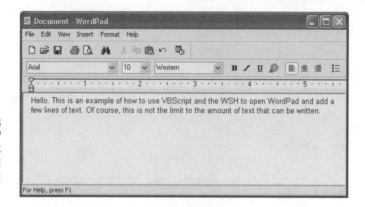

Figure 7.8

Adding dynamic
text to a WordPad
document using
VBScript.

You can use the Run(), Sleep(), and SendKeys() methods to integrate
your VBScripts with more than just Windows word processing applications. For example, the follow VBScript starts the Windows calculator
application and uses it to compute the value of 100 divided by 5.

```
Set wshObject = WScript.CreateObject("WScript.Shell")

wshObject.Run "Calc"

WScript.Sleep 500
wshObject.SendKeys "100" & "{/}"
wshObject.SendKeys "5"
wshObject.SendKeys "~"
```

NOTE In case it is not evident, I thought I'd point out that the ~ character in the previous example is used to represent the Equals button on the calculator. Also the / character had
to be placed inside the {} characters in order to have it correctly interpreted as a divi-
sion operation.

Figure 7.9 shows the result displayed by the calculator application after
this script has been executed.

Figure 7.9

An example of how VBScript and the WSH can be used to interact with the Windows calculator application.

Integrating with Applications Using Their Object Models

Besides using methods provided by the WSH object model to work with Windows applications, you can work with other applications using their own custom object models (provided that they expose an object model). Microsoft Word is an example of one such application.

If you have Microsoft Word installed on your computer, then you can write a VBScript and instruct it to open and access an instance of Microsoft Word and its object model as shown here.

```
Set myWordDoc = WScript.CreateObject("Word.Application")
```

Once instantiated, you can use the myWordDoc object to access any of the Word object model's methods and properties. The following VBScript example shows how to start Word, create a new document, write to it, print and save it, close the document, and exit Word.

```
' ***********************************************
' * Script Name: Script 7.4.vbs              *
' * Author:  Jerry Ford                       *
' * Address: Richmond Virginia                *
' * Created: 03/28/01                         *
' ***********************************************

' **** Perform script initialization here ****

Option Explicit

Dim myWordDoc
```

```vbscript
'Instantiate an instance of Microsoft Word
Set myWordDoc = WScript.CreateObject("Word.Application")

' ********* Main processing section **********

' Call a function that demonstrates how to work with the Word ➥
        object model

Word_Demo()

' *********** Procedures go here *************

'Create, print and save the Word document

Function Word_Demo()

  ' Makes Word visible
  myWordDoc.Visible = TRUE

  ' Create a new document
  myWordDoc.Documents.Add()

  ' Add a line of text
  myWordDoc.Selection.Typetext("This is the first paragraph!")

  ' Add a paragraph marker
  myWordDoc.Selection.TypeParagraph

  ' Add a line of text
  myWordDoc.Selection.Typetext("This is the second paragraph!")

  ' Print the document
  myWordDoc.Printout()

  ' Save the document
  myWordDoc.ActiveDocument.SaveAs("c:\myReport.doc")

  ' Wait long enough for the document to print before continuing
  WScript.Sleep 1000

  ' Close the document
  myWordDoc.ActiveDocument.Close()

  ' Exit Word
  myWordDoc.Quit()

End Function
```

In this example the script first opens Microsoft Word, then it creates a text document and submits it to be printed before saving it as `myreport.doc` and finally closing Microsoft Word.

TIP   You can use the Word example as a template for creating reports that automatically print themselves. This way, the reports will be printed and waiting for you in your printer's output bin when you want them.

Other Computer Automation Tasks

You can also use VBScript and the WSH to interact with two other critical Windows resources. These are the Windows application event log and the registry. Windows event logs are used by the operating system and its applications to record the events that report on the operation of the computer. These logs provide a historical record of what has happened on the computer and can also assist in debugging problems and auditing user activities.

The Windows registry is an internal database that stores critical configuration information for virtually every aspect of your computer. By learning how to configure the registry from within your scripts, you can develop scripts that can configure just about any Windows setting.

Writing to Windows Event Logs

If you work on a computer running Windows NT, 2000, or XP, then you have access to a collection of three logs that are automatically generated and managed by the operating system and its applications. These logs include

- **Application log**. Logs events generated by Windows applications.
- **Security log**. Logs events related to security and audit events.
- **System log**. Logs events recorded by the operating system.

NOTE

● ●

To log an event in the Windows application event log, an application must be designed to do so. If you are using old versions of software programs they may not generate events.

● ●

You can view the contents of these logs using the Windows Event Viewer Console as shown in Figure 7.10.

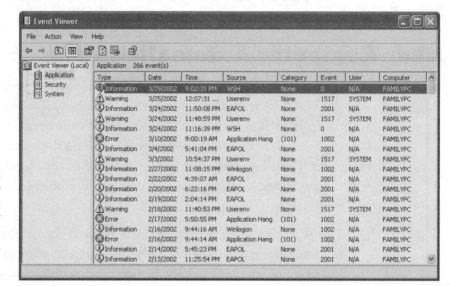

Figure 7.10

Using the Windows XP Event Viewer Console to examine event messages recorded in event logs.

If you want, you can log your own message events using VBScript. You can then use the application event log as a central log for all your scripts.

To record a message to the application event log, you need to use the WshShell object's LogEvent() method. Its syntax is

```
WshShell.LogEvent(event_type, message_text, [target])
```

Event_type is a numeric representation of the type of event being logged. There are a number of different event types that you can use, including

- ✿ **0**. Indicates a successful event.
- ✿ **1**. Indicates that an error event has occurred.
- ✿ **2**. Indicates a warning event.
- ✿ **4**. Indicates an informational event.
- ✿ **8**. Indicates a successful audit event.
- ✿ **16**. Indicates a failed audit event.

Message_text is a string containing the message text to be logged. *Target* is an optional parameter. It allows you to specify another computer where the event should be logged. By default all events are logged in the computer's local event logs. `Target` is useful in situations where you want to try to create a single, consolidated application event log so that you can go to one place and view all application events regardless of the computer where the event occurred. However, unless you are working on a network, you'll have no use for this parameter.

Let's look at a quick example. Here an event is logged that records the beginning of a script's execution.

```
Set wshObject = WScript.CreateObject("WScript.Shell")
wshObject.LogEvent 0, "Script 7.X Beginning script execution."
```

By adding this statement to the beginning of a VBScript, along with a similar statement at the end of the script, you can keep a record of the script's execution. This may prove especially beneficial if you have scripts that run under the control of the Windows Task Scheduler and want to be able to verify that your scripts are in fact running when expected.

NOTE Windows 95, 98, and Me operating systems do not support the Windows event log. If you are working with any of these operating systems your only option for creating a central log for all your scripts is to build it yourself. You already learned all the basics of file administration, including how to write to files, this afternoon and should have everything that you need to set up your own personal log files.

Figure 7.11 shows how the log event appears when viewed from the Windows XP event viewer.

NOTE You can open the Windows XP application event viewer console by clicking Start, Control Panel, Performance and Maintenance, Administrative Tools, Event Viewer, and then selecting the Application Log.

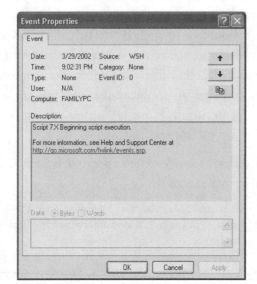

Figure 7.11

Examining your application event message.

Manipulating the Windows Registry

The utilities found on the Windows Control Panel are used to configure Windows. Each utility is actually an interface for editing the contents of the Windows registry. The *registry* is a database that stores configuration information about the operating systems, hardware, applications, and user settings. Earlier you learned how to open Control Panel utilities from within your VBScripts, making it easy to start these utilities or applets any time you want. However, to change any configuration settings you still have to manually make the changes using the applets. Now let's take a look at how to make configuration changes by working directly with the registry.

NOTE The Windows registry contains critical configuration settings. You should be very careful anytime that you work with it. Always backup the registry before making changes to it. Even a small configuration error can cause a problem or even potentially disable your computer.

The registry is made up of five top-level root keys as shown in Table 7.5. Together these root keys store all the configuration settings for a Windows computer in a tree-like hierarchy.

Data is stored in the registry in individual keys located under the various root keys using the following format.

```
Key : key_type : value
```

TABLE 7.5 TOP LEVEL REGISTRY KEYS

Key	Abbreviated Name	Contents
HKEY_LOCAL_MACHINE	HKLM	Global computer settings
HKEY_USERS	—	Information about all users of the computer
HKEY_CURRENT_CONFIG	—	Information about the computer's current configuration
HKEY_CLASSES_ROOT	HKCR	Windows file associations
HKEY_CURRENT_USER	HKCU	Information about the currently logged on user

Key represents the name of a registry key. Key_type specifies the type of data stored in the key and value is the actual information being stored. A number of different types of data can be stored in the registry. The types of data include

○ **REG_BINARY**. A binary value.

○ **REG_DWORD**. A hexadecimal DWORD value.

○ **REG_EXPAND_SZ**. A string, such as %windir%, that can be expanded.

○ **REG_MULTI_SZ**. Multiple strings.

○ **REG_SZ**. A text string.

You can manually configure the Windows registry using the Windows Regedit utility. Figure 7.12 shows this utility and its view of the Windows registry.

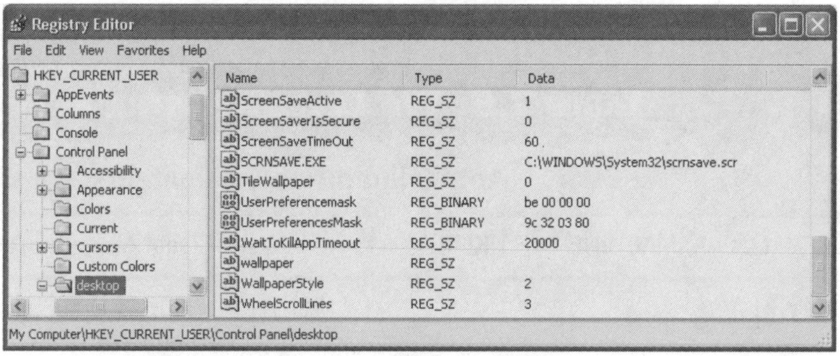

Figure 7.12

Using the Regedit utility to view and change the configuration settings stored in the Windows registry.

You can programmatically configure registry settings using three methods provided by the WshShell object. These methods and their function are outlined here.

○ **RegWrite()**. Writes or changes a registry key or value.

○ **RegRead()**. Returns a registry key or value.

○ **RegDelete()**. Removes a registry key or value.

Writing to the Registry

Let's start things off by looking at how to add or change a registry key and value using the `RegWrite()` method. To accomplish this task you need to supply the name of the key and its location within one of the registry root keys. You also have to assign a value. For example, the following VBScript statements create a new registry key named `MyKey` under the `HKEY_Current_USER` root key and assign it a value of `MyName`. The string `Jerry Ford` is then assigned to `MyName`.

```
Set wshObject = WScript.CreateObject("WScript.Shell")
wshObject.RegWrite "HKCU\MyKey\MyName", "Jerry Ford"
```

When executed these statements create the new key and value, unless they already exist, in which case the statements modify the string assigned to the value.

Reading from the Registry

Now that we have created the new key you can use REGEDIT to view it. You can also use the following script to display its value.

```
Set wshObject = WScript.CreateObject("WScript.Shell")
results = wshObject.RegRead("HKCU\MyKey\Myname")
WScript.Echo("The Value of HKCU\MyKey\Myname is: " & results)
```

In this example the `WshShell` object's `RegRead()` method is used to retrieve the string assigned to `HKCU\MyKey\Myname`.

Deleting from the Registry

Now that you've learned how to create, modify, and retrieve registry keys and values let's try to delete them using the `WshShell` object's `RegDelete()` method. After all, the key that you were just working with isn't really of any value and there is no point to leaving it in your registry.

You can delete the value `MyName` using the following example.

```
Set wshObject = WScript.CreateObject("WScript.Shell")
wshObject.RegDelete "HKCU\MyKey\MyName"
```

However, this example leaves the parent key still in place. If you want to get rid of the entire key and all its child values and subkeys you could use the following example.

```
Set wshObject = WScript.CreateObject("WScript.Shell")
wshObject.RegDelete "HKCU\MyKey\"
```

Modifying Windows Configuration Settings

You now know how to read, write, and delete registry keys and values. Let's look at a more practical example of how to programmatically work with the Windows registry. This time let's write a VBScript that can reconfigure your computer's screensaver.

```
' *********************************************
' * Script Name: Script 7.5.vbs             *
' * Author: Jerry Ford                       *
' * Address: Richmond Virginia               *
' * Created: 03/23/02                        *
' *********************************************

' **** Perform script initialization here ****

Option Explicit

On Error Resume Next

Dim wshObject, response

Set wshObject = WScript.CreateObject("WScript.Shell")

' ********* Main processing section **********

'Ask the user for permission to set up the screen saver

response = MsgBox("This VBScript will set up your default screen ➥
        saver. " & "Do you wish to continue?", 4)

Set_Screen_Saver()
```

```
' ********** Procedures go here ************

Function Set_Screen_Saver()

  'If the user clicks Yes then set up and configure our screen ➡
      saver

  If response = 6 Then

    'Enable the screen saver
    wshObject.RegWrite "HKCU\Control Panel\Desktop\ScreenSaveActive", 1

    'Enable screen saver password protection
    wshObject.RegWrite "HKCU\Control Panel\Desktop\ ➡
        ScreenSaverIsSecure", 1

    'Set the wait value to 10 minutes (e.g. 600 seconds)
    wshObject.RegWrite "HKCU\Control Panel\Desktop\ ➡
        ScreenSaveTimeOut", 600

    'Enable the 3D Pipes (OpenGL) screen saver
    wshObject.RegWrite "HKCU\Control Panel\Desktop\SCRNSAVE.EXE", ➡
        "C:\%windir%\System32\sspipes.scr"

  End If

End Function
```

The first thing that this example does is define two variables in its initialization section. One variable provides a reference to the WshShell object. The other variable stores the user's response to a question displayed using the MsgBox() pop-up dialog. This MsgBox() statement is located in the script's main processing section. If the user clicks Yes then a function named Set_Screen_Saver() is executed.

The Set_Screen_Saver() function performs 4 RegWrite() method operations. The first RegWrite() operations set the value of HKCU\Control Panel\Desktop\ScreenSaveActive equal to 1 (or true). This enables the Windows screensaver. Next HKCU\Control Panel\Desktop\ScreenSaverIsSecure is set equal to 1. This enables the password protection option. Then `HKCU\Control Panel\Desk-top\ScreenSaveTimeOut` is set equal to `600` which sets the amount of time that passes without any user activity before the screensaver kicks in. Finally, `HKCU\Control Panel\Desktop\SCRNSAVE.EXE` is assigned a value of `C:\WINNT\System32\sspipes.scr`. This statement selects the `3d Pipes (OpendGL) screen saver`.

● ●

On Windows XP you will find the Windows screensavers in C:\Windows\System32. Their file names make them difficult to recognize but you can double-click them to open them and figure out which is which.

● ●

Run this script and then right-click the Windows desktop and select Properties from the menu that appears. This opens the Display Properties dialog. Select the Screen Saver property sheet and you will see that the script has configured your screensaver as shown in Figure 7.13.

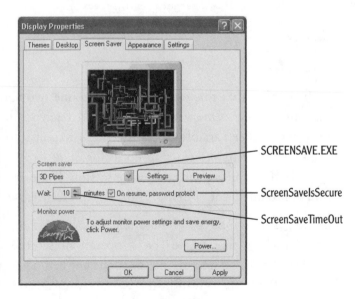

Figure 7.13

By modifying the Windows registry you can programmatically reconfigure Windows settings such as the screensaver.

Taking a Break

Okay. Time out. Let's pause and take a 15-minute break. The evening is still young and we have plenty of material left to cover. So stretch your legs a bit and build up your strength for a final push. When you return we'll tackle the Windows command line and learn how to leverage the power of Windows commands from within your VBScripts. While you are at it, you will learn how to create new user accounts, manage Windows services, create scripts that can modify the Windows Task Scheduler, and map network drives.

Working with Commands and Command-Line Utilities

You have already seen how to use the WshShell object's Run() method to start Windows applications. The Run() method is even more useful when used as a means of integrating VBScript and the WSH with the Windows command line. What this means is that you can run any Windows command or command-line utility from within your VBScripts.

Windows NT, 2000, and XP operating systems provide a number of built-in commands and utilities that allow you to perform administrative tasks. In the sections that follow I'll demonstrate how to use a number of these commands to work with network resources, manage Windows services, create user accounts, and interact with the Windows Task Scheduler.

TIP

If you have access to Windows Resource Kits, then you can also execute any of these kits' command-line utilities. For example, the Resource Kit's Dumpel command provides you with the capability to read Windows event logs.

Sending Messages over a Network

Windows commands can be difficult to work with and often go unused by many people who refuse to leave the safety and familiarity of the Windows GUI and venture out into the deeper water of command-line administration. One option is to use VBScript and the WSH to create a wrapper around a Windows command that allows the user to execute it by responding to pop-up dialogs that collect all the information needed to run the command. For example, the next VBScript that you'll see demonstrates how to give a GUI front end to the NET SEND command.

The NET SEND command allows you to send text-based messages to users and computers on a network. The NET SEND command is relatively easy compared to some other commands and therefore makes for a good example. The syntax for this command is shown here.

```
NET SEND [name | * | /DOMAIN[:name] | /USERS] message
```

Name is the name of the user or computer to which the message should be sent. To send the message to all the users in your workgroup or domain, type * instead of a name. /DOMAIN[:name] specifies a domain to which to address the message. /Users sends the message to all users currently connected to your computer and *message*, of course, is the message to be sent.

The NET SEND command is relatively easy to use. For example, you could send a message that says Hi there to the user currently logged onto a computer named citrix-366 by typing the following command at the Windows command prompt.

```
C:\>net send citrix-366 Hi there
The message was successfully sent to CITRIX-366.
```

If you find this command useful but do not want to have to open the Windows command prompt every time you want to send a message, then write a VBScript. Have the script collect the name of a user or computer and the message to be sent using the VBScript InputBox() function. Then use this data as arguments to be fed to the WshShell object's Run() method as demonstrated here.

```
' **********************************************
' * Script Name: Script 7.6.vbs                *
' * Author: Jerry Ford                          *
' * Address: Richmond Virginia                  *
' * Created: 03/17/02                           *
' **********************************************


' **** Perform script initialization here ****

Option Explicit

On Error Resume Next

Dim wshObject, destination, messageText

Set wshObject = WScript.CreateObject("WScript.Shell")

destination = InputBox("Please type the user name or " & _
   "computer name to which you wish to send a message: ")

messageText = InputBox("Please type your message: ")

' ********* Main processing section **********

' Call a function that sends the message using the NET SEND command

Send_Msg()

' *********** Procedures go here *************

' Use the NET SEND command to send a message to a user or computer

Function Send_Msg()

  wshObject.Run "Net Send " & destination & " " & messageText, 7, ➥
          False

End Function
```

As this example shows, it is fairly easy to use VBScript and the WSH to front most Windows commands and make them easier to use.

Administrating Windows Services

Windows NT, 2000, and XP are modular operating systems that provide a lot of their functionality in the form of services. These services, when enabled, perform tasks such as managing the Windows Task Scheduler, print spooler, plug and play, and UPS.

TIP

You can display the list of services installed on your computer by typing NET START at the Windows command prompt or by opening the Services console, which on Windows XP can be found by clicking Start, Control Panel, Performance and Maintenance, Administrative Tools, and then Services.

By controlling these services you can limit the things that users or their computers can do. You can even provide a small performance improvement while freeing up resources by stopping unused services. Windows services can be managed from the Windows command prompt using the following commands.

- **NET START**. Starts a service.
- **NET PAUSE**. Pauses a service without stopping it.
- **NET CONTINUE**. Resumes a paused service.
- **NET STOP**. Stops a service.

By combining these commands with the WshShell object's Run() method you can start and stop any service from within your VBScripts. For example, the following VBScript statements can be used to stop the Eventlog service.

```
Set wshObject = WScript.CreateObject("WScript.Shell")
wshObject.Run "net stop Eventlog ", 0, "True"
```

Similarly, you can start the Eventlog service as shown here.

```
Set wshObject = WScript.CreateObject("WScript.Shell")
wshObject.Run "net start Eventlog ", 0, "True"
```

Managing User Accounts

Another good example of how to combine VBScript and the WSH with Windows commands is the creation of new user accounts. Windows NT, 2000, and XP all support the creation of user and group accounts using the following commands.

○ **net user**. Creates and deletes user accounts.

○ **net group**. Manages user account and global account membership within global groups.

○ **net localgroup**. Manages user account membership within local groups.

NOTE Group accounts are used to manage collections of user accounts. By making a user account a member of a group account, the user account inherits all the security permissions assigned to the group. It's easier to manage a few groups than a large collection of individual user accounts.

For example, the following VBScript statements create a new user account named JFord on the local computer and assign it an initial password of bluebird.

```
Set wshObject = WScript.CreateObject("WScript.Shell")
return = wshObject.Run("net user JFord bluebird /add", 0)
```

By adding /domain to the NET USER command as shown in the code that follows, you can create a network account instead of a local account, assuming that you are working on a Windows network and have network administrator privileges.

```
Set wshObject = WScript.CreateObject("WScript.Shell")
return = wshObject.Run("net user JFord bluebird /add /domain", 0)
```

Let's look at a more complete example. Here we have a VBScript that creates new user accounts and adds them to the local computer's administrative group. The names of the new user accounts are listed in an external text file named c:\userlist.txt. The script opens the external file and uses a Do...While loop to process it. The NET USER and NET LOCALGROUP commands are executed on each iteration of the loop to create new accounts and add them to the administrators group.

```
' **********************************************
' * Script Name: Script 7.7.vbs               *
' * Author:  Jerry Ford                        *
' * Address: Richmond Virginia                 *
' * Created: 06/09/01                          *
' **********************************************


' **** Perform script initialization here ****

Option Explicit

On Error Resume Next

Dim fsoObject, wshObject, workingFile, newAcct, return

'Instantiate the FileSystemObject so that the script can work with
'the Windows file system

Set fsoObject = CreateObject("Scripting.FileSystemObject")

'Instantiate the WshShell object so that the script can work with the
'WshShell's Run method

Set wshObject = WScript.CreateObject("WScript.Shell")

'Specify the path to the external file where the new account names
'are stored

Set workingFile = fsoObject.OpenTextFile("c:\userlist.txt", 1, "True")

' ********* Main processing section **********

'Call the function that processes the new user accounts

Create_Accts()

' ********** Procedures go here *************
```

```
'This function performs the actual account creation and configuration

Function Create_Accts()

  'Loop through and read the file a line at a time
  Do while False = workingFile.AtEndOfStream
    newAcct = workingFile.ReadLine()
    'Create the new domain account
    return = wshObject.Run("net user " & newAcct & " newpasswd /add", 0)
    If return = 0 then
      'Add the account to the Administrators local group
      return = wshObject.Run("net localgroup Administrators /add " ➡
        & newAcct, 0)
    End If
  Loop

  'Close the file when done working with it
  workingFile.Close

End Function
```

Scripting Scheduled Script Execution

Another use of the WshShell object's Run() method is to interact with the Windows Task Scheduler using the AT command. This provides your scripts with the capability to add and remove scheduled tasks. For example, suppose you had a script that you scheduled to run once a week and that this script performed several maintenance tasks, including checking for the presence of files in several sets of folders. If the script found that files were present it could then schedule the execution of another script although it might copy the files to a network drive before deleting them later that night. On the other hand if no files were found, then no addition would be made to the Task Scheduler.

The following VBScript statements demonstrate how to programmatically schedule the execution of a VBScript that will run at 10 PM on Tuesday and Thursday as a background task.

```
Set wshObject = WScript.CreateObject("WScript.Shell")
wshObject.Run "at 22:00 /every:T,Th cmd /c Script 7.7.vbs", 0, "True"
```

As you can see, leveraging the power of AT from within your VBScripts is straightforward and provides you with the capability to automate the conditional execution of your VBScripts.

Accessing Network Resources

We've already looked at an example of how to send text messages over a network using the Windows NET SEND command. I also explained how to modify the NET USER, NET GROUP, and NET LOCALGROUP commands to create new user accounts on a network. Now let's look at the WshNetwork object and how it can be used to develop scripts that can interact with network resources.

The WshNetwork object provides a number of properties that can be used to collect information about a network. The properties of the WshNetwork object include

- **UserName**. Identifies the name assigned to the user's account.
- **ComputerName**. Retrieves the name of the user's computer.
- **UserDomain**. Retrieves the name of the domain to which the user is currently logged in.

The WshNetwork object also provides several methods that allow you to view and access shared network drives. These methods include

- **EnumNetworkDrives**. Provides access to drive mappings.
- **MapNetworkDrive**. Maps a network drive.
- **RemoveNetworkDrive**. Removes a network drive mapping.

The WshNetwork object also provides a number of methods that you can use to view network printers and work with them.

- **EnumPrinterConnection**. Provides information about network printers.
- **AddPrinterConnection**. Connects to a network printer.

⚙ **RemovePrinterConnection**. Removes a connection to a network printer.

⚙ **SetDefaultPrinter**. Sets the default printer.

As an example of how to work with the methods belonging to the Wsh-Network object let's look at the steps involved in connecting to and disconnecting from network drives. A network drive is simply a hard drive that can be accessed from over the network. By creating a connection to a network drive you establish a logical connection that makes the network drive look and act as if it were one of your computer's own drives.

NOTE

If you already have one or more mapped network drives, then your scripts will automatically be able to access these drives as if they were locally connected to your computer as long as you personally run the scripts yourself. If you use the Task Scheduler to initiate the execution of your scripts, then your drive mappings will not be available to your scripts. Therefore, you'll need to add the appropriate statements to scripts to connect and disconnect from network drives.

After you have established a connection or mapping to a network drive you can read and write to it just like any other disk drive (assuming that you have the appropriate set of security permissions). You can create a mapping to a network drive using the WshNetwork object's MapNetworkDrive() method. The syntax of this method is shown here.

```
WshNetwork.MapNetworkDrive letter, name, [persistent], [username], ➥
        [password]
```

Letter is the letter that you want to assign to the drive. *Name* is the UNC name of the shared resource. *Persistent* is an optional value of either true of false. True retains the drive mapping across user sessions. If omitted, the default value of false is used and the connection lasts only for the current login session. Finally *username* and *password* are optional parameters that specify a username and password that may be required to access the drive (for example, if the drive is protected with security permissions).

NOTE Embedding a real user name and its associated password inside a script is frowned upon as a major security breach. I'd recommend to avoid this at all costs. Perhaps you could set up your script to query you for this information each time it runs using the VBScript `InputBox()` function.

Mapping to Network Drives

Okay, let see what it takes to map to a network drive from within a VBScript. First you have to use the `WScript` object's `CreateObject()` method to instantiate an instance of the `WshNetwork` object. You then can use the `WshNetwork` object's `MapNetworkDrive()` method as follows.

```
Set wshNet = WScript.CreateObject("WScript.Network")
wshNet.MapNetworkDrive "x:", "\\OfficeSvr\C"
```

That's it, just two lines of code. It's amazing how powerful and yet simple working with VBScript can be. As you can see the network drive is named `C:` and is located on a computer named `OfficeSvr`. After executing the script you will find that a new drive will appear on the local computer with a drive letter of `x`. The drive mapping created here is temporary and will not be present the next time the user logs on.

You can tell mapped network drives apart from local hard drives by the appearance of their icons. Figure 7.14 shows the icon that was created using the previous example.

Disconnecting Mapped Drives

As easy as it is to create a drive mapping, it's even easier to disconnect one. You should disconnect any mapped drives that you no longer use. You can do this using the `WshNetwork` object's `RemoveNetworkDrive()` method. Its syntax is shown here.

```
WshNetwork.RemoveNetworkDrive letter, [kill], [persistent]
```

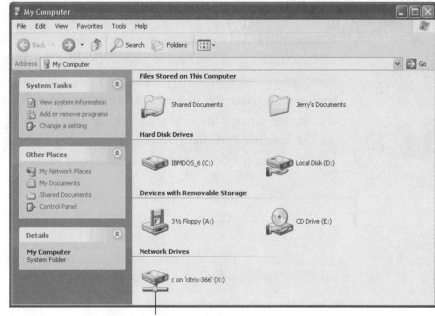

Figure 7.14

A picture of a cable connection just beneath the drive icon identifies mapped network drives.

Mapped Network Drive

Letter is the drive letter that has been assigned to the mapped drive. Kill is optional and is a value of either true or false. True disconnects the connection to the mapped drive even if it is currently in use. Persistent is another optional true or false value that allows you to disconnect persistent mappings to network drives.

As the final example in the weekend's endeavor, let's take a look at how to disconnect the mapping to the network drive that we created in the previous example.

```
Set wshNet = WScript.CreateObject("WScript.Network")
wshNet.RemoveNetworkDrive "x:"
```

Once executed, this example removes all traces of the mapped drive.

What's Next?

Congratulations! You are well on your way to adding more fun and excitement to your web pages and developing VBScripts that will help you become more productive than ever. So, what's next? I'd recommend that you keep digging deeper into VBScript. There's a lot more to learn. The best way to do this is to start writing your own scripts. Keep your eye on the Internet and make a habit of searching for new ideas and examples of VBScripts developed by others. Good luck!

VBScript
Language
Reference

VBScript is a scripting language provided by Microsoft that is supported by both Internet Explorer and the Windows Script Host. VBScript is also a member of the Visual Basic family of programming languages.

This appendix has been designed to serve as a VBScript programmer's reference. Here you will find lists and tables that identify the major programming constructs that comprise the VBScript programming language.

Topics covered in this appendix include

✪ Rules for formatting VBScripts

✪ A review of VBScript constants

✪ Rules for naming VBScript variables

✪ A list of different ways to declare variables

✪ A review of VBScript variant subtypes

✪ A review of VBScript dialogs

✪ A list of VBScript errors

✪ A review of VBScript events

✪ A review of Browser handlers

✪ A review of VBScript functions

✪ A review of VBScript keywords

✪ A review of VBScript objects and collections

✪ A review of VBScript methods

✪ A review of VBScript properties

✪ A review of VBScript operators

✪ A review of VBScript reserved words

✪ A review of VBScript special characters

✪ A review of VBScript statements

VBScript Formatting Rules

Like any programming language, VBScript has certain rules that must be followed when you are writing scripts. The following list provides a review of some basic VBScript formatting rules that you should keep in mind.

- ✿ VBScript is case insensitive in regard to variable, constant, subroutine, and procedure names.

- ✿ The Option Explicit statement can be used to enforce case sensitivity.

- ✿ Blank spaces are ignored, allowing you to indent VBScript statements and provide an organizational structure for your VBScripts.

- ✿ By default, a VBScript statement must reside on a single line.

- ✿ Multiple VBScript statements can be placed on a single line by using the colon character (:) to mark the end of each preceding VBScript statement.

- ✿ VBScript statements can be spread over multiple lines by adding the _ character to the end of the line being continued.

VBScript Constants

A constant is a value, such as PI, that does not change. VBScript allows you to create your own constants. In addition, VBScript provides a number of collections of constants. VBScript constants provide you with access to values without requiring you to know them.

VBScript Color Constants

Table A.1 provides a list of constants that define a collection of known colors.

VBScript Date and Time Constants

Table A.2 provides a list of constants that define the days of the week and other date-related values.

TABLE A.1 VBSCRIPT COLOR CONSTANTS

Constant	Description
vbBlack	Black
vbBlue	Blue
vbCyan	Cyan
vbGreen	Green
vbMagenta	Magenta
vbRed	Red
vbWhite	White
vbYellow	Yellow

TABLE A.2 VBSCRIPT DATE AND TIME CONSTANTS

Constant	Value	Description
vbSunday	1	Sunday
vbMonday	2	Monday
vbTuesday	3	Tuesday
vbWednesday	4	Wednesday
vbThursday	5	Thursday
vbFriday	6	Friday
vbSaturday	7	Saturday

TABLE A.2 CONTINUED		
Constant	**Value**	**Description**
vbFirstFourDays	2	First full week with a minimum of 4 days in the new year
vbFirstFullWeek	3	First full week of the year
vbFirstJan1	1	Week which includes January 1
vbUseSystemDayOfWeek	0	Day of week as specified by the operating system

VBScript Date and Time Format Constants

Table A.3 provides a list of constants that define the date and time formats.

The VBScript Error Constant

Table A.4 provides a constant that defines the value assigned to a VBScript error.

TABLE A.3 VBSCRIPT DATE AND TIME FORMAT CONSTANTS		
Constant	**Value**	**Description**
vbGeneralDate	0	Display date and time
vbLongDate	1	Display date in long format
vbShortDate	2	Display date in short format
vbLongTime	3	Display time in long format
vbShortTime	4	Display time in short format

TABLE A.4 VBSCRIPT ERROR CONSTANT		
Constant	**Value**	**Description**
vbObjectError	-2147221504	Value assigned to VBScript errors.

VBScript MsgBox Button Constants

Table A.5 provides a list of constants that define the buttons that can appear on a pop-up dialog displayed using the VBScript MsgBox() function.

VBScript MsgBox Icon Constants

Table A.6 provides a list of constants that define the icons that can appear on a dialog created using the VBScript MsgBox() function.

TABLE A.5 VBSCRIPT MSGBOX BUTTON CONSTANTS		
Constant	**Value**	**Description**
vbOKOnly	0	Display OK button
vbOKCancel	1	Display OK and Cancel buttons
vbAbortRetryIgnore	2	Display Abort, Retry, and Ignore buttons
vbYesNoCancel	3	Display Yes, No, and Cancel buttons
vbYesNo	4	Display Yes and No buttons
vbRetryCancel	5	Display Retry and Cancel buttons

TABLE A.6 VBSCRIPT MSGBOX ICON CONSTANTS

Constant	Value	Description
vbCritical	16	Display critical icon
vbQuestion	32	Display question icon
vbExclamation	48	Display exclamation mark icon
vbInformation	64	Display information icon

VBScript MsgBox Button Default Constants

Table A.7 provides a list of constants that can be used to define the default button on a pop-up dialog displayed using the VBScript Msg-Box() function.

VBScript MsgBox Modal Setting Constants

Table A.8 provides a list of constants that can be used to define the modality of a pop-up dialog displayed using the VBScript MsgBox() function.

TABLE A.7 VBSCRIPT MSGBOX BUTTON DEFAULT CONSTANTS

Constant	Value	Description
vbDefaultButton1	0	Makes the first button the default
vbDefaultButton2	256	Makes the second button the default
vbDefaultButton3	512	Makes the third button the default
vbDefaultButton4	768	Makes the fourth button the default

TABLE A.8 VBSCRIPT MSGBOX MODAL SETTING CONSTANTS

Constant	Value	Description
vbApplicationModal	0	User must respond before the script can continue
vbSystemModal	4096	User must respond before the script can continue. Also the pop-up dialog remains displayed on top of other active applications

VBScript MsgBox Return Value Constants

Table A.9 provides a list of constants that can be used to define the values that can be returned when a user clicks a button on a pop-up dialog displayed using the VBScript MsgBox() function.

TABLE A.9 VBSCRIPT MSGBOX RETURN VALUE CONSTANTS

Constant	Value	Description
vbOK	1	User clicked the OK button
vbCancel	2	User clicked the Cancel button
vbAbort	3	User clicked the Abort button
vbRetry	4	User clicked the Retry button
vbIgnore	5	User clicked the Ignore button
vbYes	6	User clicked the Yes button
vbNo	7	User clicked the No button

VBScript Script Constants

Table A.10 provides a list of constants that can be used to define string related constants.

TABLE A.10 VBScript String Constants

Constant	Value	Description
vbCr	Chr(13)	Carriage return
vbCrLf	Chr(13) and Chr(10)	Carriage return and line feed
vbFormFeed	Chr(12)	Form feed
vbLf	Chr(10)	Line feed
vbNewLine	Chr(13) and Chr(10)	Newline character
vbNullChar	Chr(0)	0
vbNullString	String with no value	An empty string
vbTab	Chr(9)	Horizontal tab
vbVerticalTab	Chr(11)	Vertical tab

VBScript Tristate Constants

Table A.11 provides a list of constants that equate to a value of true or false or that specify a value defined by the operating system.

VBScript VarType Constants

Table A.12 provides a list of constants that represent an integer that indicates the type of data stored in a variant.

TABLE A.11 VBScript Tristate Constants

Constant	Value	Description
vbUseDefault	-2	Get default from the operating system
vbTrue	-1	True
vbFalse	0	False

TABLE A.12 VBScript VarType

Constant	Value	Description
vbEmpty	0	Uninitialized value
vbNull	1	Empty / no data
vbInteger	2	Integer
vbLong	3	Long
vbSingle	4	Single
vbDouble	5	Double
vbCurrency	6	Currency
vbDate	7	Date
vbString	8	String
vbObject	9	Object
vbError	10	Error
vbBoolean	11	Boolean

TABLE A.12 CONTINUED		
Constant	**Value**	**Description**
vbVariant	12	Variant
vbDataObject	13	Data access object
vbDecimal	14	Decimal
vbByte	17	Byte
vbArray	8192	Array

VBScript Variables

VBScript allows for the temporary storage of values using variables. Variables allow scripts to retain values and reference them throughout a script. VBScript has specific rules that must be followed when declaring and working with variables. VBScript supports a single type of variable called a variant. However, VBScript also provides the capability to further classify the type of data stored in a variant using subtypes.

VBScript Variable Naming Rules

VBScript imposes some strict rules on the names of VBScript variables. VBScript variable names:

- ◆ Must be unique within their scope
- ◆ Must be less than 255 characters long
- ◆ Must begin with an alphabetic character
- ◆ Cannot contain spaces
- ◆ Can only consist of alphabetic and numeric characters and the _ character
- ◆ Cannot consist of VBScript reserved words

Declaring VBScript Variables

VBScript provides a number of different statements that can be used to declare variables, arrays, and constants. Table A.13 provides a list of these statements.

TABLE A.13 VBSCRIPT VARIABLE DECLARATION	
Statement	**Description**
Const	Defines a VBScript constant
Dim	Defines a VBScript variable or array
Private	Defines a VBScript variable that is only available within the script that declares it
Public	Defines a VBScript variable that is global in scope throughout a script and which can be accessed from other scripts
ReDim	Defines a dynamic array

VBScript Data Types

VBScript only supports one type of variable known as a variant. However, VBScript does allow you to classify variants into subtypes. Table A.14 lists the variant subtypes supported by VBScript.

TABLE A.14 VBSCRIPT VARIANT SUBTYPES	
Subtype	**Description**
Boolean	A value of True or False.
Byte	An integer whose value is between 0 - 255.

TABLE A.14 CONTINUED	
Subtype	**Description**
Currency	A currency value between -922,337,203,685,477.5808 and 922,337,203,685,477.5807.
Date	A number representing a date between January 1, 100 and December 31, 9999.
Double	A floating-point number whose range is between -1.79769313486232E308 and -4.94065645841247E-324 or 4.94065645841247E-324 and 1.79769313486232E308.
Empty	An uninitialized variant.
Error	An error number.
Integer	An integer whose value is between -32,768 and 32,767.
Long	An integer value whose range is between -2,147,483,648 and 2,147,483,647.
Null	A variant to a null value.
Single	A floating-point number whose range is between -3.402823E38 and -1.401298E-45 or 1.401298E-45 and 3.402823E38.
String	A string up to two billion characters long.

VBScript Pop-Up Dialogs

VBScript supports two functions that provide the capability to display graphical pop-up dialogs and directly interact with the user. Table A.15 describes these functions and their capabilities.

TABLE A.15 VBSCRIPT DIALOGS	
Function	**Description**
MsgBox	Displays pop-up dialogs that can be used to display messages and provide the user with a list of options from which to select
InputBox	Displays a pop-up dialog that can be used to collect a text response

VBScript Errors

Like any programming language, errors sometimes occur during the execution of VBScripts. VBScript errors are classified according to two categories, runtime and syntax. By default, Internet Explorer suppresses the display of error messages to hide them from the end user.

VBScript Runtime Errors

A VBScript runtime error is an error that occurs while a script is executing. Runtime errors occur when the VBScripts attempt to do something that they are not permitted to do such as trying to open a file that does not exist. Table A.16 lists VBScript's runtime error messages.

TABLE A.16 VBSCRIPT RUNTIME ERRORS	
Error	**Description**
5	Invalid procedure call or argument Overflow Out of Memory
6	Overflow
7	Out of Memory
9	Subscript out of range

TABLE A.16 CONTINUED

Error	Description
10	This array is fixed or temporarily locked
11	Division by zero
13	Type mismatch
14	Out of string space
17	Can't perform requested operation
28	Out of stack space
35	Sub or function not defined
48	Error in loading DLL
51	Internal error
91	Object variable not set
92	For loop not initialized
94	Invalid use of Null
424	Object required
429	ActiveX component can't create object
430	Class doesn't support Automation
432	File name or class name not found during Automation operation
438	Object doesn't support this property or method
445	Object doesn't support this action
447	Object doesn't support current locale setting
448	Named argument not found

Error	Description
TABLE A.16 CONTINUED	
449	Argument not optional
450	Wrong number of arguments or invalid property assignment
451	Object not a collection
458	Variable uses an Automation type not supported in VBScript
462	The remote server machine does not exist or is unavailable
481	Invalid picture
500	Variable is undefined
502	Object not safe for scripting
503	Object not safe for initializing
504	Object not safe for creating
505	Invalid or unqualified reference
506	Class not defined
507	An exception occurred
5008	Illegal assignment
5017	Syntax error in regular expression
5018	Unexpected quantifier
5019	Expected] in regular expression
5020	Expected) in regular expression
5021	Invalid range in character set

VBScript Syntax Errors

A VBScript syntax error is a error that occurs when a VBScript begins loading but before it actually begins executing. Syntax errors occur when you fail to follow the rules for formatting VBScript statements. For example, a VBScript syntax error will occur if you fail to provide a closing quotation mark or parenthesis when required in a VBScript statement. Table A.17 lists VBScript's syntax error messages.

TABLE A.17 VBSCRIPT SYNTAX ERRORS	
Error	**Description**
1001	Out of Memory
1002	Syntax error
1005	Expected ' ('
1006	Expected ') '
1010	Expected identifier
1011	Expected '='
1012	Expected 'If'
1013	Expected 'To'
1013	Invalid number
1014	Expected 'End'
1014	Invalid character
1015	Expected 'Function'
1015	Unterminated string constant

TABLE A.17 CONTINUED	
Error	**Description**
1016	Expected 'Sub'
1017	Expected 'Then'
1018	Expected 'Wend'
1019	Expected 'Loop'
1020	Expected 'Next'
1021	Expected 'Case'
1022	Expected 'Select'
1023	Expected expression
1024	Expected statement
1025	Expected end of statement
1026	Expected integer constant
1027	Expected 'While' or 'Until'
1028	Expected 'While', 'Until', or end of statement
1029	Expected 'With'
1030	Identifier too long
1037	Invalid use of 'Me' keyword
1038	'loop' without 'do'
1039	Invalid 'exit' statement

TABLE A.17 CONTINUED

Error	Description
1040	Invalid 'for' loop control variable
1041	Name redefined
1042	Must be first statement on the line
1044	Cannot use parentheses when calling a Sub
1045	Expected literal constant
1046	Expected 'In'
1047	Expected 'Class'
1048	Must be defined inside a class
1049	Expected Let or Set or Get in property declaration
1050	Expected 'Property'
1051	Number of arguments must be consistent across properties specification
1052	Cannot have multiple default property/method in a class
1053	Class initialize or terminate do not have arguments
1054	Property Set or Let must have at least one argument
1055	Unexpected Next
1057	'Default' specification must also specify 'Public'
1058	'Default' specification can only be on Property Get

VBScript Events

VBScript provides two events that execute when an instance of an associated class is either initialized or terminated. These events are defined in Table A.18.

TABLE A.18 VBSCRIPT EVENTS	
Event	**Description**
Initialize	Executes when an instance of an associated class is initialized.
Terminate	Executes when an instance of an associated class is terminated.

Browser Event Handlers

Internet Explorer provides a number of events that you can program your VBScripts to react to. Table A.19 provides a list of browser events and the event handlers that respond to them.

TABLE A.19 DOCUMENT OBJECT MODEL PROPERTIES		
Property	**Event**	**Description**
Abort	onAbort	Executes when the visitor aborts an image while it is loading
Blur	onBlur	Executes when the currently selected object loses focus
Change	onChange	Executes when the visitor changes an object
Click	onClick	Executes when the visitor clicks an object
DblClick	onDblClick	Executes when the visitor double clicks an object

TABLE A.19 CONTINUED

Property	Event	Description
DragDrop	onDragDrop	Executes when the visitor drags and drops an object onto a frame or window
Error	onError	Executes when an error occurs on the HTML page
Focus	onFocus	Executes when a visitor selects an object
KeyDown	onKeyDown	Executes when a visitor presses down on a key
KeyPress	onKeyPress	Executes when a visitor presses and releases a key
KeyUp	onKeyUp	Executes when a visitor releases a key
Load	onLoad	Executes when a HTML page or image finishes loading
MouseDown	onMouseDown	Executes when a visitor presses a mouse button
MouseMove	onMouseMove	Executes when a visitor moves the pointer
MouseOut	onMouseOut	Executes when a visitor moves the pointer off an object
MouseOver	onMouseOver	Executes when a visitor moves the pointer over an object
MouseUp	onMouseUp	Executes when a visitor releases a mouse button
MouseWheel	onMouseWheel	Executes when a mouse wheel is rotated
Move	onMove	Executes when a visitor moves a frame or window
Reset	onReset	Executes when a visitor clicks on a reset button
Resize	onResize	Executes when a visitor resizes a frame or window

Property	Event	Description
TABLE A.19 CONTINUED		
Select	onSelect	Executes when a visitor selects the contents of a form text field
Submit	onSubmit	Executes when a visitor clicks on a submit button
Unload	onUnload	Executes when a visitor closes the browser window or frame or loads a different URL

VBScript Functions

One of the strengths of VBScript is its collection of functions. By referencing VBScript functions in your scripts you can save yourself the time and effort of having to write your own procedures to accomplish the tasks performed by VBScript's built-in functions. Table A.20 provides a list of VBScript functions.

Function	Description
TABLE A.20 VBSCRIPT FUNCTIONS	
Abs	Returns a number's absolute value
Array	Returns an array based on the supplied argument list
Asc	Returns the ANSI code of the first letter in the supplied argument
Atn	Inverse trigonometric function that returns the arctangent of the argument
CBool	Converts an expression to a Boolean value and returns the result

TABLE A.20 CONTINUED	

Function	Description
CByte	Converts an expression to a variant subtype of Byte and returns the result
CCur	Converts an expression to a variant subtype of Currency and returns the result
Cdate	Converts an expression to a variant subtype of Date and returns the result.
CDbl	Converts an expression to a variant subtype of double and returns the result
Chr	Returns a character based on the supplied ANSI code
Cint	Converts an expression to a variant subtype of Integer and returns the result
CLng	Converts an expression to a variant subtype of Long and returns the result
Cos	Trigonometric function that returns the cosine of the argument
CreateObject	Creates an Automation object and returns a reference to it
CSng	Converts an expression to a variant subtype of Single and returns the result
Date	Returns the current date
DateAdd	Adds an additional time interval to the current date and returns the result
DateDiff	Compares two dates and returns the number of intervals between them
DatePart	Returns a portion of the specified date

	TABLE A.20 CONTINUED
Function	**Description**
DateSerial	Returns a Variant (subtype Date) based on the supplied year, month, and day
DateValue	Converts a string expression into a variant of type Date and returns the result
Day	Converts an expression representing a date into a number between 1 and 31 and returns the result
Eval	Returns the results of an evaluated expression
Exp	Returns the value of an argument raised to a power
Filter	Returns an array based on a filtered set of elements using supplied filter criteria
FormatCurrency	Returns an expression that has been formatted as a currency value
FormatDateTime	Returns an expression that has been formatted as a date or time value
FormatNumber	Returns an expression that has been formatted as a numeric value
FormatPercent	Returns an expression that has been formatted as a percentage (including the accompanying %)
GetLocale	Returns the locale ID
GetObject	Returns a reference for an Automation object
GetRef	Returns a reference for a procedure
Hex	Returns a hexadecimal string that represents a number

TABLE A.20 CONTINUED

Function	Description
Hour	Returns a whole number representing an hour in a day (0–23)
InputBox	Returns user input from a dialog box
InStr	Returns the starting location of the first occurrence of a substring within a string
InStrRev	Returns the ending location of the first occurrence of a substring within a string
Int	Returns the integer portion from the supplied number.
IsArray	Returns a value of True or False depending on whether a variable is an array
IsDate	Returns a value of True or False depending on whether an expression is properly formatted for data conversion
IsEmpty	Returns a value of True or False depending on whether a variable is initialized
IsNull	Returns a value of True or False depending on whether an expression is set to Null
IsNumeric	Returns a value of True or False depending on whether an expression evaluates to a number
IsObject	Returns a value of True or False depending on whether an expression has a valid reference for an Automation object
Join	Returns a string that has been created by concatenating the contents of an array
Lbound	Returns the smallest possible subscript for the specified array dimension

TABLE A.20 CONTINUED	
Function	**Description**
Lcase	Returns a lowercase string
Left	Returns characters from the left side of a string
Len	Returns a number or string's character length
LoadPicture	Returns a picture object
Log	Returns the natural log of the specified argument
LTrim	Trims any leading blank spaces from a string and returns the result
Mid	Returns a number of characters from a string based on the supplied start and length arguments
Minute	Returns a number representing a minute within an hour in range of 0–59
Month	Returns a number representing a month within a year in the range of 1–12
MonthName	Returns a string containing the name of the specified month
MsgBox	Returns a value specifying the button users click in a dialog box
Now	Returns the current date and time
Oct	Returns a string containing an octal number representation
Replace	Returns a string after replacing occurrences of one substring with another substring
RGB	Returns a number that represents an RGB color

TABLE A.20 CONTINUED

Function	Description
Right	Returns characters from the right side of a string
Rnd	Returns a randomly generated number
Round	Returns a number after rounding it by a specified number of decimal positions
RTrim	Trims any trailing blank spaces from a string and returns the result
ScriptEngine	Returns a string identifying the current scripting language
ScriptEngineBuildVersion	Returns the scripting engine's build number
ScriptEngineMajorVersion	Returns the scripting engine's major version number
ScriptEngineMinorVersion	Returns the scripting engine's minor version number
Second	Returns a number representing a second within a minute in range of 0–59
Sgn	Returns the sign of the specified argument
Sin	Trigonometric function that returns the sine of the argument
Space	Returns a string consisting of a number of blank spaces
Split	Organizes a string into an array
Sqr	Returns a number's square root
StrComp	Returns a value that specifies the results of a string comparison
String	Returns a character string made up of a repeated sequence of characters

TABLE A.20 CONTINUED

Function	Description
Tan	Trigonometric function that returns the tangent of the argument
Time	Returns a Variant of subtype Date that has been set equal to the system's current time
Timer	Returns a value representing the number of seconds that have passed since midnight
TimeSerial	Returns a Variant of subtype Date that has been set equal to containing the specified hour, minute, and second
TimeValue	Returns a Variant of subtype Date that has been set using the specified time
Trims	Returns a string after removing any leading or trailing spaces
TypeName	Returns a string that specifies the Variant subtype information regarding the specified variable
Ubound	Returns the largest subscript for the specified array dimension
Ucase	Returns an uppercase string
VarType	Returns a string that specifies the Variant subtype information regarding the specified variable
Weekday	Returns a whole number in the form of 1–7, which represents a given day in a week
WeekdayName	Returns a string identifying a particular day in the week
Year	Returns a number specifying the year

Keywords

In VBScript, keywords are used to indicate a range of unique or uncommon values. These values can be used when comparing the value of variables in expressions. The VBScript keywords are outlined in Table A.21.

TABLE A.21 VBSCRIPT KEYWORDS	
Keyword	**Description**
Empty	Indicates a uninitialized variable
False	Indicates a value of zero
Nothing	Removes the association of a object variable from a object
Null	Indicates that a variable does not have a valid value
True	Indicates a value of –1

Objects and Collections

VBScript provides access to a collection of built-in objects. These objects are listed in Table A.22.

VBScript Object Methods

A VBScript method is a pre-defined procedure associated with specific VBScript objects. Methods are designed to control associated objects and their data. Table A.23 defines the methods belonging to VBScript objects.

TABLE A.22 VBSCRIPT OBJECTS

Object	Description
Class	Provides access to the events Properties: N/A Methods: N/A Events: Initialize, Terminate
Err	Provides details about runtime errors Properties: Description, HelpContext, HelpFile, Number, Source Methods: Clear, Raise Events: N/A
Match	Accesses the read-only properties of a regular expression match Properties: FirstIndex, Length, Value Methods: N/A Event: N/A
Matches Collection	A collection of regular expression Match objects Properties: N/A Methods: N/A Events: N/A
RegExp	Supports regular expressions Properties: Global, IgnoreCase, Pattern Methods: Execute, Replace, Test. Events: N/A
SubMatches Collection	Accesses read-only values of regular expression submatch strings Properties: N/A Methods: N/A Event: N/A

TABLE A.23 VBSCRIPT OBJECT METHODS

Method	Description
Clear	Clears an Err object's property settings
Execute	Performs a regular expression search against a string
Raise	Simulates a runtime error
Replace	Replaces text in a regular expression search
Test	Performs a regular expression search against a string

VBScript Object Properties

A VBScript property is an attribute associated with a VBScript object. Properties contain stored values that represent a specific characteristic of the object. By manipulating an object's properties, VBScripts affect the object itself. Table A.24 defines the properties belonging to VBScript objects.

TABLE A.24 VBSCRIPT OBJECT PROPERTIES

Property	Description
Description	Retrieves an error message
FirstIndex	Returns the first position of a specified substring in a string
Global	Changes or retrieves a Boolean value
HelpContext	Retrieves the context ID of Help file topic
HelpFile	Returns the path to a Help file

	TABLE A.24 CONTINUED	
Property	**Description**	
IgnoreCase	Retrieves a Boolean value that indicates whether a pattern search is case-sensitive	
Length	Returns the length of a search string match	
Number	Returns the error number for the specified error	
Pattern	Retrieves the regular expression pattern in a search operation	
Source	Retrieves the name of the object that generates an error	
Value	Returns the value of a search string match	

VBScript Operators

VBScript operators allow you to perform mathematical calculations, the results of which can then be assigned to VBScript variables or be used by VBScript when performing conditional tests.

Arithmetic Operators

Arithmetic operators provide the ability to manipulate mathematical values. Table A.25 lists the arithmetic operators supported by VBScript.

Comparison Operators

VBScript comparison operators are used to test the values of expressions, variables, and constants against each other. Comparison operators are used in conjunction with If...Then...Else and Select Case statements to determine the logical flow within VBScripts. Table A.26 lists the comparison operators supported by VBScript.

TABLE A.25 VBSCRIPT ARITHMETIC OPERATORS

Operator	Description
+	Add
-	Subtract
*	Multiply
/	Divide
\	Integer division
Mod	Modulus
-x	Reverses the sign of x
^	Exponentiation

TABLE A.26 VBSCRIPT COMPARISON OPERATORS

Operator	Description
=	Equal
<>	Not equal
>	Greater than
<	Less than
>=	Greater than or equal to
<=	Less than or equal to

Order of Precedence

VBScript imposes a strict order of precedence in expressions involving more than one operator. Table A.27 defines the order in which VBScript evaluates mathematical operators.

Operators	Description
TABLE A.27 VBSCRIPT ORDER OF PRECEDENCE	
Operators	Description
\	Escape
0, (?:), (?=), []	Parentheses and brackets
*, +, ?, {n}, {n,}, {n,m}	Quantifiers
^, $, \metacharacter	Anchors and sequences
|	Alternation

Note: Operators listed at the beginning of the table are evaluated before those that appear later in the table and operators listed on the same line are evaluated in the order presented (from left to right).

Reserved Words

Table A.28 provides a list of words that are reserved by VBScript. These words cannot be used in your VBScripts as constants, variables or as other types of identifiers. These words comprise key elements of the VBScript language or have been set aside for future use. You can only use the words in your scripts if you use them as they are intended.

TABLE A.28 VBSCRIPT RESERVED WORDS

And	EndIf	LSet	RSet
As	Enum	Me	Select
Boolean	Eqv	Mod	Set
ByRef	Event	New	Shared
Byte	Exit	Next	Single
ByVal	False	Not	Static
Call	For	Nothing	Stop
Case	Function	Null	Sub
Class	Get	On	Then
Const	GoTo	Option	To
Currency	If	Optional	True
Debug	Imp	Or	Type
Dim	Implements	ParamArray	TypeOf
Do	In	Preserve	Until
Double	Integer	Private	Variant
Each	Is	Public	Wend
Else	Let	RaiseEvent	While
ElseIf	Like	ReDim	With
Empty	Long	Rem	Xor
End	Loop	Resume	

VBScript Special Characters

VBScript has a number of special characters that you must be aware of when writing scripts. To include these characters in VBScripts they must be escaped using the \ character. Table A.29 lists all the VBScript special characters.

	TABLE A.29 VBSCRIPT SPECIAL CHARACTERS
Character	**Description**
$	Matches the position at the end of a string
( )	Identifies the start and ending of a subexpression
*	Matches a subexpression for zero or more occurrences
+	Matches a subexpression for one or more occurrences
.	Matches a single character
[	Identifies the start of a bracketed expression
?	Matches a subexpression for zero or one occurrence
\	Identifies the character that follows as a special character
^	Matches the position starting at the beginning of a string
{	Identifies the start of a quantifier expression
|	Specifies a choice condition

VBScript Statements

Table A.30 lists the programming statements that make up the VBScript programming language.

TABLE A.30 VBSCRIPT STATEMENTS	
Statement	**Description**
Call	Redirects flow control in the script to a procedure
Class	Defines a class name
Const	Defines a constant
Dim	Defines a VBScript variable
Do...Loop	Repeats a group of statements as long as a condition is True or until the condition becomes True
Erase	Reinitializes the elements in an array.
Execute	Runs the specified statement
ExecuteGlobal	Runs the specified statement in a script's global namespace
Exit	Terminates a loop, sub, or function
For Each...Next	Iteratively processes the contents of an array or collection
For...Next	Repeats a loop a specified number of times
Function	Defines a function name and its arguments
If...Then...Else	Performs the execution of one or more statements based on the value of the tested expression
On Error	Turns on error handling

	TABLE A.30 CONTINUED
Statement	**Description**
Option Explicit	Explicitly declares all variables in your script
Private	Defines a private variable
Property Get	Defines a property name and its arguments and returns its value
Property Let	Defines a property procedure's name and arguments
Property Set	Defines a property procedure's name and arguments
Public	Defines a public variable
Randomize	Initializes the random-number generator
ReDim	Defines or redefines dynamic-array variables
Rem	Used to place comments in scripts
Select Case	Defines a collection of tests and executes only one based on the value of an expression
Set	Assigns object references to variables
Sub	Defines a Sub name and its arguments
While...Wend	Performs the execution of one or more statements as long as the specified condition remains True
With	Associates a series of statements that are to be executed for a specified object

APPENDIX B

What's on the Web Site

This book has an accompanying web site where you will find supporting materials for the book. To visit it, open your Internet browser and type http://www.premierpressbooks.com/downloads.asp in the URL field and press Enter as shown in Figure B.1.

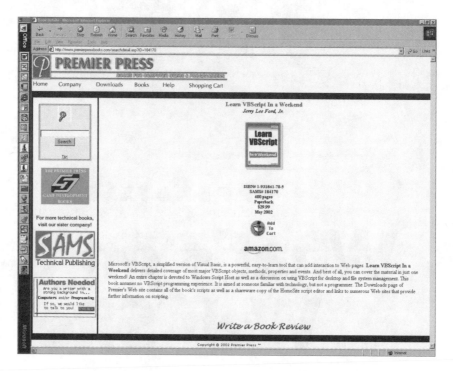

Figure B.1

The companion web site for **Learn VBScript in a Weekend**.

Some of the things that you'll find on the web site include

⬡ A links page that provides a list of links to VBScript-related web sites where you will find tons of VBScript documentation and sample VBScripts.

⬡ A download page where you will be able to download sample VBScripts from the book. You'll find the sample scripts organized by chapter. You'll also be able to download all of them as one zip file.

⬡ A page with information about the Macromedia HomeSite editor and a link to **http://www.macromedia.com/software/homesite/** where you can download a 30-day trial copy of HomeSite 5.0.

GLOSSARY

.js. A file extension used by JScripts.

.vbs. A file extension used by VBScripts.

.wsf. A file extension used by Windows Script files.

.wsh. A file extension used by Windows Script Host files.

<?job ?>. An WSH XML tag that specifies whether error handling or debugging is enabled within Windows Script files.

<?XML ?>. An WSH XML tag that specifies the XML level used in a Windows Script file.

<comment>. An WSH XML tag that allows you to place comments within your Windows Script files.

<job>. An WSH XML tag that defines job names within Windows Script files.

<object>. An WSH XML tag that sets up an object reference within a Windows Script file.

<package>. An WSH XML tag that is used to add more than one job to a Windows Script file.

<reference>. An WSH XML tag establishes a reference to external libraries.

<resource>. An WSH XML tag that defines a constant that can be referenced by the scripts within a Windows Script file.

<script>. An WSH XML tag that is used to identify scripts within Windows Script files.

A

Abort. A browser event that occurs when a user aborts the loading of the HTML page or an image. This event triggers the onAbort event handler.

ActiveX. ActiveX is a set of dynamic resources that any Windows-based application can use. Microsoft uses ActiveX technology to allow Windows components to be embedded into web pages.

Alert method. A method belonging to the document object that can be used to display graphical alerts and await the user's response.

Argument. Data passed to a script or to a procedure as input.

Array. An indexed list of values stored in memory that can be accessed as a unit.

ASP (Active Server Pages). A technology provided by Internet Information Server (IIS) to deliver dynamic HTML content.

At. A Windows command that allows you to view, add, or delete scheduled tasks, including scheduled VBScripts and Windows Script Files.

B

Binary code. The collection of 0s and 1s that make up the instructions that computers understand and process.

Blur. A browser event that occurs when the user causes an object to loose focus. This event triggers the onBlur event handler.

Boolean. A variable that stores a true or false value.

Browser. A software application that displays HTML pages.

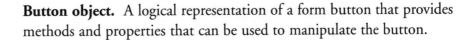

Button object. A logical representation of a form button that provides methods and properties that can be used to manipulate the button.

C

Change. A browser event that occurs when a user changes an object, such as the value stored in a form's text field. This event triggers the onChange event handler.

Checkbox object. A logical representation of a form checkbox that provides methods and properties that can be used to manipulate the checkbox and interrogate its value.

Click. A browser event that occurs when a user clicks on a mouse button while the pointer is positioned over an object such as a link or image. This event triggers the onClick event handler.

Collection. An array that provides references to a collection of objects on an HTML page. For example, the forms array contains a list of forms that exist on a HTML page.

Cookie. A small amount of data which a web site can store on your computer when you visit the web site. This data usually contains information collected about you or your activity on the web site and can be retrieved the next time you visit.

Comments. Statements that can be added to scripts to document their function and their construction and which are ignored during scripts execution.

Compiling. The process of converting a program into a format that can be executed by the computer.

Concatenation. A programming technique in which two strings are combined into a single string.

Confirm method. A method belonging to the document object that can be used to display graphical text messages and wait for the user to respond by clicking OK or Cancel.

Constant. A static value that does not change during the execution of a script.

Core Object Model. A component of the Windows Script Host that provides access to Windows resources via the properties and methods of the objects that make up the model.

CScript. A WSH script execution host that supports the execution of scripts that run in the background or that interact with the user via the Windows command prompt.

D

DblClick. A browser event that occurs when the user double-clicks a mouse button while the pointer is positioned over an object. This event triggers the onDblClick event handler.

Debug. The process of testing scripts during their development and correcting any errors that may occur.

Dictionary. A VBScript runtime object that stores data key item pairs.

Dim. A VBScript statement that is used to define VBScript variables.

Document object. An object that provides access to a Windows resource via its properties and methods.

DOM (Document Object Model). Within the context of an Internet browser, an object model provides access to every element on a HTML page.

Do...While. A VBScript statement that is used to create a loop that executes as long as a specified condition is true.

Do...Until. A VBScript statement that is used to create a loop that executes until a specified condition becomes true.

Drive. A VBScript runtime object that provides a script with access to a disk drives.

Drives. A VBScript runtime collection that provides access to information about all the drives on the computer where a script is executed.

E

Element. An individual entry in an array that may be referenced by its assigned name or by its indexed position within the array.

Error. A browser event that occurs when the browser detects an error. This event triggers the onError event handler.

Event. An action, such as a mouse click, that occurs within Internet browsers and that triggers event handlers.

Event handler. A trap that executes when an event occurs, allowing you to programmatically respond to browser events.

Execution host. A program, such as a web browser or the WSH, which interprets and executes scripts.

Expression. A programming statement that evaluates the value of variables.

F

File. A VBScript runtime object that provides access to individual files on the Windows file system.

Files Collection. A VBScript runtime collection that provides access to all the files stored in a folder.

FileSystemObject. The primary runtime object in the VBScript runtime library. This object exposes file system resources, including files and folders.

Focus. A browser event that occurs when the user selects an object, such as a form text field. This event triggers the onFocus event handler.

Folder. A VBScript runtime object that provides access to individual folders on the Windows operating system.

Folders Collection. A VBScript runtime collection that provides access to all the folders stored within a specified folder.

For Each...Next. A VBScript programming statement that is used to iterate through all the properties belonging to a specified object.

For...Next. A VBScript programming statement that creates a loop that executes a specified number of times.

Form object. An object that provides access to the elements located on the form which it represents.

Frame object. An object that provides the ability to manipulate the HTML frame with which it is associated.

Function. A collection of statements that have been grouped to perform a specific action and which are referenced as a unit and can return a result to the calling statement. Functions can be called from any location within a VBScript and can be called as many times as necessary.

G

Global variable. A script variable that has been established outside a procedure and which can be referenced from any point within the script.

GUI (Graphical User Interface). A point-and-click graphical interface that allows users to interact with the operating system without having to work from the command prompt.

H

Hidden object. A text-based form element that is not visible on a HTML FORM, but that can be assigned text data.

History object. A browser object that provides access to a list of URLs that the have been visited during the current browser session.

HomeSite. A multipurpose editor created by Macromedia which supports HTML and scripts development and can be used to develop both HTML pages and VBScripts.

Hypertext Markup Language (HTML). A data format built that describes the layout of a document using plain text.

I

IDE (Integrated Development Environment). An advanced script or program development environment that provides tools that assist in the development and testing of scripts and programs.

If. A VBScript statement that performs a conditional test to determine if a value equated to true or false and is used to provide an alternative logical execution path based on the results of the comparison.

IIS (Internet Information Server). A Microsoft web server application that supports the development and administration of web sites.

Internet Explorer. A Microsoft Internet browser that provides support for VBScript and JScript.

Interpreted language. A programming language used to develop scripts that are stored as plain text and which must later be interpreted at the time of their execution.

J

JavaScript. A Internet scripting language developed by Netscape that is supported by both the Netscape and Internet Explorer browsers.

JScript. Microsoft's implementation of Netscape's JavaScript scripting language. The Windows Script Host also supports JScript.

K

KeyDown. A browser event that occurs when the user depresses a keyboard key. This event triggers the onKeyDown event handler.

KeyPress. A browser event that occurs when the user presses and releases a keyboard key. This event triggers the onKeyPress event handler.

KeyUp. A browser event that occurs when the user releases a keyboard key. This event triggers the onKeyUp event handler.

L

Load. A browser event that occurs immediately after the browser loads a web page. This event triggers the onLoad event handler.

Local variable. A script variable that has been established inside a procedure and which cannot be referenced from any other point within the script.

Location object. A browser object whose properties provide access to browser navigation information.

Loop. A series of programming statements that are set up to execute repeatedly.

M

Macros. Small scripts that are developed to automate application functionality using VBA and the host application.

Method. A predefined function that is provided by an object.

MouseDown. A browser event that occurs when the user depresses a mouse button while the pointer is positioned over an object. This event triggers the object's onMouseDown event handler.

MouseMove. A browser event that occurs when the user moves the mouse. This event triggers the object's onMouseMove event handler.

MouseOut. A browser event that occurs when the user moves the pointer off an object. This event triggers the object's onMouseOut event handler.

MouseOver. A browser event that occurs when the user moves the pointer over an object. This event triggers the object's onMouseOver event handler.

MouseUp. A browser event that occurs when the user releases a mouse button while the pointer is positioned over an object. This event triggers the object's onMouseUp event handler.

MsgBox. A built-in VBScript function that is used to display graphical pop-up dialogs and collect a user response.

Multidimensional array. An indexed list that consists of more than two dimensions.

N

Navigator object. A browser object that provides access to information that identifies the version and type of the browser that has loaded the HTML page.

O

Object. A programming construct that provides predefined properties and methods than can be used to gather information about or manipulate the resource being represented.

onAbort. An event handler triggered by the Abort event. This event executes when the user aborts the loading of a web page or image.

onBlur. An event handler triggered by the Blur event. This event executes when an object loses focus.

onChange. An event handler triggered by the Change event. This event executes when the user makes a change to an object such as the contents of a form text field.

onClick. An event handler triggered by the Click event. This event occurs when a user clicks the mouse while the pointer is positioned over an object.

onDblClick. An event handler triggered by the DblClick event. This event occurs when a user double-clicks the mouse while the pointer is positioned over an object.

onError. An event handler triggered by the Error event. This event occurs whenever an error is detected within a script.

onFocus. An event handler triggered by the Focus event. This event occurs when the user selects an object, such as a form's text field.

onKeyDown. An event handler triggered by the KeyDown event. This event occurs when a user presses down on a keyboard key.

onKeyPress. An event handler triggered by the KeyPress event. This event occurs when a user presses a keyboard key.

onKeyUp. An event handler triggered by the KeyUp event. This event is triggered when a keyboard key that has been pressed by the user is released.

onLoad. An event handler triggered by the Load event. This event occurs when a HTML page has completed loading.

onMouseDown. An event handler triggered by the MouseDown event. This event occurs when the user depresses a mouse button while the point is positioned over an object.

onMouseMove. An event handler triggered by the MouseMove event. This event occurs whenever the user moves the mouse.

onMouseOut. An event handler triggered by the MouseOut event. This event occurs when the user moves the pointer off an object.

onMouseUp. An event handler triggered by the MouseUp event. This event occurs when the user releases a mouse button and the pointer is positioned over an object.

onMouseOver. An event handler triggered by the MouseOver event. This event occurs when the user positions the pointer over an object.

onReset. An event handler triggered by the Reset event. This event occurs when the user clicks a form's reset button.

onResize. An event handler triggered by the Resize event. This event occurs whenever the user changes height or width of a browser window.

onSelect. An event handler triggered by the Select event. This event occurs when the user selects an object such as a link or image.

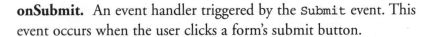

onSubmit. An event handler triggered by the Submit event. This event occurs when the user clicks a form's submit button.

onUnload. An event handler triggered by the UnLoad event. This event occurs when the browser is closed or a new HTML is loaded.

Option object. A logical representation of a form's OPTION tag, which provides methods and properties that can be used to check or uncheck the option and test its status.

P

Parameter. An argument passed to a command, utility, script, or application that is then processed as input.

Password object. A logical representation of a form password field that provides methods and properties that can be used to retrieve any text typed into the field.

Perl (Practical Extraction and Reporting Language). A scripting language first used on Unix operating systems, which has since been ported over to Windows.

PerlScript. A version of Perl compatible with the WSH.

Procedure. A collection of statements in the form of a function or subroutine that is called and executed as a unit.

Program. A collection of programming statements that makes up a script or application.

Prompt. A mechanism that is used to request information or instructions from the user.

Prompt method. A method belonging to the document object that can be used to display a pop-up dialog that asks the user to provide a typed response.

Property. An attribute associated with an object that controls or describes a particular feature or aspect of the object.

Python. A scripting language made popular by the Linux operating system and later ported over to Windows.

Q

Quick Launch bar. A Windows feature that provides single-click access to any Windows resource that is added to it.

R

Radio object. A logical representation of a form radio button that provides methods and properties that can be used to manipulate the radio button and interrogate its value.

ReDim. A VBScript statement used to create and resize dynamic arrays.

Registry. A Windows database where configuration information, including software, hardware, system, user, and application settings, is stored.

Rem. A VBScript comments statement that allows descriptive comments to be added within scripts without affecting script execution.

Reserved Words. A collection of words that have been set aside for current or future use in a programming language that cannot be used as variable and procedure names within scripts.

Reset. A browser event that occurs when the user clicks a form's reset button. This event triggers the onReset event handler.

Reset Object. A logical representation of a form reset button, which is used to clear the contents of a form and restore its default values, that provides methods and properties that can be used to manipulate the button.

Resize. A browser event that occurs when the user changes the dimensions of a browser window. This event triggers the onResize event handler.

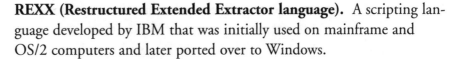

REXX (Restructured Extended Extractor language). A scripting language developed by IBM that was initially used on mainframe and OS/2 computers and later ported over to Windows.

Rollover. A graphical effect, used to enhance the appearance of web pages, in which two images are swapped every time the pointer moves on and then off an object.

Runtime error. An error that occurs during the execution of a script usually because the script attempted to do something that is against the rules, such as referencing a function that does not exist within the script.

S

Scheduled Task Folder. A special Windows folder that provides access to scheduled tasks.

Scheduled Task Wizard. A wizard that guides you through the process of setting up new scheduled tasks.

Scope. A term that refers to the accessibility of a variable throughout a script.

Script. A group of statements embedded inside a web page or saved as a plain text file, which are interpreted and executed by an execution host such as the Windows Script Host or a web browser.

Scripting engine. A host independent script interpreter that allows a script written in a particular scripting language to execute under the control of the Windows Script Host.

Select. A browser event that occurs when the user selects an object such as a form text field. This event triggers the onSelect event handler.

Select Case. A VBScript statement that is used to compare a value against a series of expressions or values where the first matching value is used to trigger the execution of a particular statement or group of statements.

Select object. A logical representation of a drop-down list created by a HTML SELECT tag that provides methods and properties that can be used to manipulate the drop-down list and interrogate its value.

Statement. A line of code within a script.

Status Bar. An area at the bottom of a browser where text messages are displayed.

String. An group of text characters referenced as a unit.

Submit. A browser event that occurs when the user clicks a form's submit button. This event sends the form's contents to a web server or emails the contents. This event triggers the onSubmit event handler.

Submit object. A logical representation of a form's submit button that provides methods and properties that can be used to manipulate the button.

Subroutine. A type of VBScript procedure that executes a collection of statements but which does not return a result to its calling statement.

Syntax Error. An error that occurs when loading a web page or VBScript that contains one or more statements that are incorrectly formatted.

T

Text object. A representation of a form's text field that provides methods and properties that can be used to manipulate the value typed in the text field.

Textarea object. A representation of a form's textarea field that provides methods and properties that can be used to manipulate the value typed in the textarea field.

TextStream. A VBScript runtime object that provides sequential file access.

UnLoad. A browser event that occurs when the user closes the browser or loads a different web page. This event triggers the onUnLoad event handler.

U

URL (Universal Resource Locator). An address used to identify a document within a web site.

V

Validation. The process of verifying that data entered on a form conforms to required specifications.

Variable. A programming construct that provides for the storage and retrieval of data in memory that can be referenced based on its assigned name.

Variant. The only type of variable supported by VBScript. Variants can be used to store a number of different types of data.

VBScript. A scripting language created by Microsoft as an alternative to JavaScript. VBScript represents a subset of the Visual Basic programming language. Both the Windows Script Host and Internet Explorer support it.

W

While...Wend. A VBScript programming statement that sets up a loop that will execute as long as a condition remains true.

Window object. An object representing a browser window or frame that provides methods that can be used to control the window or frame.

Windows Shell scripting. A scripting language built into Windows NT, 2000, and XP that is substantially more limited than the WSH.

WScript. The root object in the WSH core object model that provides access to script arguments and allows for the creation of new objects.

WScript is also a WSH script execution that provides the capability to incorporate graphical pop-up dialogs into scripts.

WSF (Windows Script File). A file that allows two different types of scripts to be combined into a single job that has a `.wsf` file extension.

WSH (Windows Script Host). A Microsoft scripting technology that supports the execution of different scripting languages on Windows operating system and which provides direct access to Windows resources using object models.

WshArguments. A WSH object that provides access to command line arguments.

WshEnvironment. A WSH object that can be used to access environment variables.

WshNetwork. A WSH object that can be used to access network resources.

WshShell. A WSH object that can be used to access environment variables and the Windows registry.

WshShortcut. A WSH object that can be used to programmatically create shortcuts.

WshSpecialFolders. A WSH object that provides programmatic access to Windows folders.

WshUrlShortcut. A WSH object that can be used to programmatically create URL shortcuts.

WSH.ocx. The ActiveX control that provides the core object model for the Windows Script Host.

X

XML (Extensible Markup Language). XML is a data format model for plain text files. WSH implements a subset of XML tags that support the development of Windows Script files.

INDEX

Looking for something to do this weekend?

Want to create your own Web page? Organize your finances? Upgrade your PC? It's time to put your weekends to work for you with the Premier Press In a Weekend® series. Each book in the series is a practical, hands-on guide focused on helping you master the skills you need to achieve your goals. While you have the time, let our In a Weekend series show you how to make the most of it.

Create Macromedia Flash Movies In a Weekend
0-7615-2866-0 • U.S. $29.99
Can. $44.95 • U.K. £21.99

Tune Up Your PC In a Weekend, 2nd Ed.
1-941841-03-9 • U.S. $19.99
Can. $29.95 • U.K. £14.99

Create Microsoft PowerPoint 2002 Presentations In a Weekend
0-7615-3397-4 • U.S. $24.99
Can. $37.95 • U.K. £18.99

Learn JavaScript In a Weekend, 3rd Ed.
0-7615-3332-X • U.S. $24.99
Can. $37.95 • U.K. £18.99

OTHER HOT TOPICS

Build Your Home Theater In a Weekend
0-7615-2744-3 • U.S. $24.99
Can. $37.95 • U.K. £18.99

Create FrontPage 2002 Web Pages In a Weekend
0-7615-3447-4 • U.S. $24.99
Can. $37.95 • U.K. £18.99

Increase Your Web Traffic In a Weekend, 3rd Ed.
0-7615-2313-8 • U.S. $24.99
Can. $37.95 • U.K. £18.99

Create Your First Web Page In a Weekend, 3rd Ed.
0-7615-2482-7 • U.S. $24.99
Can. $37.95 • U.K. £18.99

Learn HTML In a Weekend, Rev. Ed.
0-7615-1800-2 • U.S. $24.99
Can. $37.95 • U.K. £18.99

Learn Microsoft Windows Me In a Weekend
0-7615-3297-8 • U.S. $19.99
Can. $29.95 • U.K. £14.99

Electrify Your Web Site In a Weekend
0-7615-2505-X • U.S. $24.99
Can. $37.95 • U.K. £18.99

Jumpstart Your Online Job Search In a Weekend
0-7615-2452-5 • U.S. $24.99
Can. $37.95 • U.K. £18.99

Learn Digital Photography In a Weekend
0-7615-1532-1 • U.S. $24.99
Can. $37.95 • U.K. £18.99

Set Up Your Home Office In a Weekend
0-7615-3054-1 • U.S. $24.99
Can. $37.95 • U.K. £18.99

DO IT In a Weekend

Premier Press
www.premierpressbooks.com

Call today to order!
1.800.428.7267

The **Premier Press** *fast&easy* series

Fast Facts, Easy Access

Offering extraordinary value at a bargain price, the *fast & easy* series is dedicated to one idea: To help readers accomplish tasks as quickly and easily as possible. The unique visual teaching method combines concise tutorials and hundreds of screen shots to dramatically increase learning speed and retention of the material. With the Premier Press *fast & easy* series, you simply look and learn.

**The Official Family Tree Maker®
Version 9 Fast & Easy®**
1-931841-02-0
U.S. $18.99 ▪ Can. $28.95 ▪U.K. £13.99

**Microsoft® Windows®
Millennium Edition Fast & Easy®**
0-7615-2739-7
U.S. $18.99 ▪ Can. $28.95 ▪ U.K. £13.99

**Paint Shop Pro™ 7
Fast & Easy®**
0-7615-3241-2
U.S. $18.99 ▪ Can. $28.95 ▪ U.K. £13.99

**Quicken® 2001
Fast & Easy®**
0-7615-2908-X
U.S. $18.99 ▪ Can. $28.95 ▪ U.K. £13.99

**Microsoft® Works Suite 2001
Fast & Easy®**
0-7615-3371-0
U.S. $24.99 ▪ Can. $37.95 ▪ U.K. £18.99

**Microsoft® Access 2002
Fast & Easy®**
0-7615-3395-8
U.S. $18.99 ▪ Can. $28.95 ▪ U.K. £13.99

**Microsoft® Excel 2002
Fast & Easy®**
0-7615-3398-2
U.S. $18.99 ▪ Can. $28.95 ▪ U.K. £13.99

**Microsoft® FrontPage® 2002
Fast & Easy®**
0-7615-3390-7
U.S. $18.99 ▪ Can. $28.95 ▪ U.K. £13.99

**Microsoft® Office XP
Fast & Easy®**
0-7615-3388-5
U.S. $18.99 ▪ Can. $28.95 ▪ U.K. £13.99

**Microsoft® Outlook 2002
Fast & Easy®**
0-7615-3422-9
U.S. $18.99 ▪ Can. $28.95 ▪ U.K. £13.99

**Microsoft® PowerPoint® 2002
Fast & Easy®**
0-7615-3396-6
U.S. $18.99 ▪ Can. $28.95 ▪ U.K. £13.99

**Microsoft® Word 2002
Fast & Easy®**
0-7615-3393-1
U.S. $18.99 ▪ Can. $28.95 ▪ U.K. £13.99

Premier Press
www.premierpressbooks.com

Call now to order
(800)428-7267

Fast & Easy is a registered trademark of Premier Press. All other product and company names are trademarks of their respective companies.

fast&easy web development

Less Time. Less Effort. More Development.

Don't spend your time leafing through lengthy manuals looking for the information you need. Spend it doing what you do best— Web development. Premier Press's *fast & easy* web development series leads the way with step-by-step instructions and real screen shots to help you grasp concepts and master skills quickly and easily.

Adobe® LiveMotion™
Fast & Easy®
Web Development
0-7615-3254-4 ▪ CD Included
$29.99 U.S. ▪ $44.95 Can. ▪ £21.99 U.K.

ASP 3 Fast & Easy®
Web Development
0-7615-2854-7 ▪ CD Included
$24.99 U.S. ▪ $37.95 Can. ▪ £18.99 U.K.

CGI Fast & Easy®
Web Development
0-7615-2938-1 ▪ CD Included
$24.99 U.S. ▪ $37.95 Can. ▪ £18.99 U.K.

ColdFusion® Fast & Easy®
Web Development
0-7615-3016-9 ▪ CD Included
$24.99 U.S. ▪ $37.95 Can. ▪ £18.99 U.K.

Macromedia®
Director® 8 and Lingo™
Fast & Easy®
Web Development
0-7615-3049-5 ▪ CD Included
$24.99 U.S. ▪ $37.95 Can. ▪ £18.99 U.K.

Macromedia®
Dreamweaver® 4
Fast & Easy®
Web Development
0-7615-3518-7 ▪ CD Included
$29.99 U.S. ▪ $44.95 Can. ▪ £21.99 U.K.

Macromedia®
Dreamweaver® UltraDev™ 4
Fast & Easy®
Web Development
0-7615-3517-9 ▪ CD Included
$29.99 U.S. ▪ $44.95 Can. ▪ £21.99 U.K.

Macromedia®
Fireworks® 4 Fast & Easy®
Web Development
0-7615-3519-5 ▪ CD Included
$29.99 U.S. ▪ $44.95 Can. ▪ £21.99 U.K.

Macromedia®
Flash™ 5 Fast & Easy®
Web Development
0-7615-2930-6 ▪ CD Included
$24.99 U.S. ▪ $37.95 Can. ▪ £18.99 U.K.

HomeSite™ 4.5 Fast & Easy®
Web Development
0-7615-3182-3 ▪ CD Included
$29.99 U.S. ▪ $44.95 Can. ▪ £21.99 U.K.

Java™ 2 Fast & Easy®
Web Development
0-7615-3056-8 ▪ CD Included
$24.99 U.S. ▪ $37.95 Can. ▪ £18.99 U.K.

JavaServer Pages™
Fast & Easy®
Web Development
0-7615-3428-8 ▪ CD Included
$29.99 U.S. ▪ $44.95 Can. ▪ £21.99 U.K.

PHP Fast & Easy®
Web Development
0-7615-3055-x ▪ CD Included
$24.99 U.S. ▪ $37.95 Can. ▪ £18.99 U.K.

XHTML Fast & Easy®
Web Development
0-7615-2785-0 ▪ CD Included
$24.99 U.S. ▪ $37.95 Can. ▪ £18.99 U.K.

Premier
Press™
Premier Press, Inc.
www.premierpressbooks.com

Call now to order!
1.800.428.7267

for the absolute beginner

PREMIER PRESS Series

AYDT01LEARNDPROGRAMMING

the fun way
to learn programming

Let's face it.

C++, JavaScript, and **Java** can be a little intimidating. That's why Premier Press has developed our newest series, for the absolute beginner—a fun, non-intimidating introduction to the world of programming.

Each book in this series teaches a specific programming language using simple game programming as a teaching aid. If you are new to program-ming, want to learn, and want to have fun, then Premier Press's for the absolute beginner series is just what you've been waiting for!

**ASP Programming
for the Absolute Beginner**

ISBN 1-931841-01-2
U.S. $29.99, Can. $44.95, U.K. £21.99

**C++ Programming
for the Absolute Beginner**

ISBN 1-931841-43-8
U.S. $29.99, Can. $44.95, U.K. £21.99

**Java™ Programming
for the Absolute Beginner**

ISBN 0-7615-3522-5
U.S. $29.99, Can. $44.95, U.K. £21.99

**JavaScript™ Programming
for the Absolute Beginner**

ISBN 0-7615-3410-5
U.S. $29.99, Can. $44.95, U.K. £21.99

**Palm™ Programming
for the Absolute Beginner**

ISBN 0-7615-3524-1
U.S. $29.99, Can. $44.95, U.K. £21.99

**Visual Basic® Programming
for the Absolute Beginner**

ISBN 0-7615-3553-5
U.S. $29.99, Can. $44.95, U.K. £21.99

Premier Press
www.premierpressbooks.com

**Call now to order
(800)428-7267**